# WHEN HEALTH CARE EMPLOYEES STRIKE

## A Guide for Planning and Action

**Norman Metzger**
Vice-President for Labor Relations

**Joseph M. Ferentino**
Director of Labor Relations

**Kenneth F. Kruger**
Employee Relations Manager

The Mount Sinai Medical Center
New York, New York

AN ASPEN PUBLICATION®
Aspen Systems Corporation
Rockville, Maryland
Royal Tunbridge Wells
1984

Library of Congress Cataloging in Publication Data

Metzger, Norman, 1924 —
When health care employees strike.

"An Aspen publication."
Includes bibliographical references and index.
1. Strikes and lockouts — Hospitals — United States. 2. Collective labor agreements — Hospitals — United States. I. Ferentino, Joseph M. II. Kruger, Kenneth F. III. Title. [DNLM: 1. Strikes, Employee. 2. Health services — Manpower. WX 159.8 M596w]
KF3452.H6M47   1984   344.73′01892   84-2870
ISBN: 0-89443-588-4 347. 3041892

Publisher: John R. Marozsan
Associate Publisher: Jack W. Knowles, Jr.
Editor-in-Chief: Michael Brown
Executive Managing Editor: Margot G. Raphael
Managing Editor: M. Eileen Higgins
Editorial Services: Jane Coyle
Printing and Manufacturing: Denise Hass

Copyright © 1984 by Aspen Systems Corporation

This book is not intended to offer legal advice, which should be obtained from an attorney.

All rights reserved. This book, or parts thereof, may not be reproduced in any form or by any means, electronic or mechanical, including photocopy, recording, or any information storage and retrieval system now known or to be invented, without written permission from the publisher, except in the case of brief quotations embodied in critical articles or reviews. For information, address Aspen Systems Corporation, 1600 Research Boulevard, Rockville, Maryland 20850.

Library of Congress Catalog Card Number: 84-2870
ISBN: 0-89443-588-4

*Printed in the United States of America*

1  2  3  4  5

*To Irene Wehr,*
who shepherded the authors
from germination to publication

# Table of Contents

Acknowledgments ........................................................ vii

Introduction ............................................................. ix

PART I—    HEALTH CARE STRIKES: LEGAL AND MORAL
           IMPLICATIONS ............................................... 1

Chapter 1— The Impact of Labor Legislation on the Health Care
           Industry ..................................................... 3

           P.L. 93-360 Impact on Health Facilities ............... 3
           The 1974 Health Care Amendments to the NLRA ... 18
           Guidelines for Serving Section 8(g) Notices .......... 19

Chapter 2— Types of Strikes: Their Causes and Characteristics .... 23

           Economic Strikes ........................................ 23
           Unfair Labor Practice Strikes ........................ 24
           Sympathy Strikes ........................................ 25
           Jurisdictional Strikes ................................. 27
           Recognition Strikes .................................... 27
           Illegal Strikes .......................................... 28
           Strikes in Violation of No-Strike Clauses ............. 28

Chapter 3— Strike-Related Actions: Union and Management ....... 33

           Major Elements of Strikes in Progress ............... 39
           Appendix 3-A ........................................... 53
           Appendix 3-B ........................................... 59
           Appendix 3-C ........................................... 63

### Chapter 4— Nursing Strikes: A Breed Apart .......................... 89

A Series of Conflicts .................................... 91
Early Objectives and Changing Directions ............ 93
A Breed Apart ............................................ 98
The Bargaining Process ................................ 99
Strike Impact ........................................... 102
Appendix 4-A ........................................... 104
Appendix 4-B ........................................... 115

### Chapter 5— The Future: Proposals for Change ...................... 141

The Effect of Strikes .................................. 142
Health Care Strikes: Are They Defensible? ........... 143
Alternatives to the Strike ............................. 144
Proposal for the Future ............................... 150
Appendix 5-A ........................................... 158
Appendix 5-B ........................................... 163

**Addendum 1**—A Guide to Basic Law and Procedures under the National Labor Relations Act ........................ 173

**Addendum 2**—Federal Mediation and Conciliation Service Offices .... 245

### PART II— STRIKE MANUAL ..................................... 259

About the Manual ...................................... 261
Employee Strike Contingency Plan .................... 261
Strike Plan Administration and Committees .......... 264
Personnel Policies ..................................... 266
Financial Division Operations ......................... 269
Personnel/Manpower Planning ........................ 274
Supplies and Services ................................. 283
Engineering and Plant Operations .................... 293
Staff Accommodations ................................. 299
Security ................................................ 300
Medical Services ...................................... 302
Ancillary Services ..................................... 318
Hints for Post-Strike House Rebuilding .............. 331
American Hospital Association Guidelines .......... 332

**Index** ................................................................. 337

# Acknowledgments

Within three short years the authors faced a threatened strike of nurses (which, fortunately, did not materialize), a week-long illegal work stoppage by service and maintenance employees (which was finally enjoined), and a strike lasting less than an hour of some 40,000 employees in voluntary hospitals throughout New York City. The preparation for that short strike was as distracting and potentially dangerous as the actuality. Patients and their families had to be warned. In some cases, admission had to be curtailed. These experiences were the seeds of this book.

Growth from seed to flowering plant is a torturous nurturing process, and only with enormous assistance were we able to produce what we consider an important study of a critical challenge to our industry. Special recognition is in order for Irene Wehr, who labored diligently to organize, transcribe, and edit what, at times, were disconnected and undefined drafts. She deciphered the scribblings of anxious authors, received the necessary permissions for reprints and citations, and kept us all on track. Norman Metzger wants to recognize specifically the enormous contribution Irene Wehr has made to his last five books. In addition, Claudia McAlman was extremely supportive and helpful in transcribing original drafts, which, at times, sorely needed refinement. We extend special gratitude to Nicholas Fialo, who gathered, categorized, and reviewed research material used in our study. Finally, we received cooperation, advice, and material from Richard Whelan, Saul Kramer, Ronald Del Mauro, Robert Troy, Carol Nicol, Sylvia Barker, Gail Weissman, E. Dorsey Smith, Herbert Bienstock, Paul Yager, Kenneth Kowalski, Mary Ann DeCristofaro, Frederick Kramarow, and Martin Shields. Without their assistance this book could not have been published.

# Introduction

The strike is among the most highly publicized and the least studied social phenomena of our time . . . [It] is the mechanism which produces that increment of pressure necessary to force agreement where differences are persistent and do not yield to persuasion or argument around the bargaining table. . . . The alternate to such a system might result in the demise of the collective bargaining system as we know it; some form of coercion exercised by a supreme authority whether a government board, an industrial relations court, compulsory arbitrations, or some other of the many proposals which have been advanced from time to time, would supplant the voluntarism implicit in the American collective bargaining experience. Thus, the strike, or threat of strike, is the ultimate device whereby the competing interests of antagonistic parties are expediently resolved, leading to modus operandi which permits both sides to accommodate their differences and live with one another.[1]

In an earlier book,[2] authors Metzger and Pointer stated that a prime concern of health administrators in whose institutions unions begin organizational drives is the possibility of strikes. Strikes and strike threats are indeed essential parts of the total industrial collective bargaining process. Many administrators believe that recognizing a union is a direct invitation to strikes. Of course, the statistics do not confirm this theory. Nevertheless, the law does not compel parties to agree to the terms of a labor contract; rather, it only mandates that they bargain "in good faith." Unions do strike to support their positions and management will "take a strike" in an effort to resist union demands.

In any industry strikes put economic pressure on both parties: The workers lose wages, while the employers lose revenue. The key to a successful strike from a union's viewpoint is to inflict inordinate discomfort, expense, and pressure on the employer so as to effect a compromise or move toward the union's position. Hospital and nursing home strikes differ from those in other industries in that the resulting discomfort—and the word "discomfort" may be an understatement—is thrust upon patients, not employers. Certainly hospital strikes also inconvenience the public, but the greatest threat is to public health and safety. Metzger and Pointer suggested in their book that the real losers in such strikes are the patients, their families, and prospective patients (the public). The patients will be underserved; they may be moved from a struck hospital or nursing home; they may be discharged earlier than they should be. Their families will be subjected to anxiety over the limited care available and may well be forced to administer home care. Prospective patients will be troubled by the limited beds available; operations will be delayed and outpatient care discontinued.[3]

A strike at a health care facility is the most severe form of labor-management dispute. Strikes usually produce mass picketing, and sometimes violence. Such activities disrupt patient care services, and result in lost revenue and bad publicity.[4]

The authors, who have been exposed over many years to strikes, walkouts, withdrawals of service, and, unfortunately, violence on the picket line and in employee protest, have structured this book to present the reader with an overall view of strikes in the health care industry. Chapter One contains a review of the National Labor Relations Act, with a specific discourse on health care strike notice periods and remedies. The role of the Federal Mediation and Conciliation Service and boards of inquiry is discussed in relation to strike deterrence. Chapter Two defines types of strikes, from economic to unfair labor practice strikes, from sympathy strikes to violation of no-strike clauses. Chapter Three examines the strike itself, with specific emphasis on union actions and management actions. Chapter Four develops the critical difference between a strike of nurses and a strike of nonnursing personnel. Chapter Five looks at the future, and makes proposals for change. A separate part of the book contains a strike manual that is applicable, with appropriate adaptation, to most health care facilities.

No threat to the viability of health care services in the community is more serious than a strike of health care workers, and, in many ways, health care facilities are more vulnerable to strikes than manufacturing facilities. Unlike nonhealth care facilities, which can stock inventory, hospitals and nursing homes cannot maintain a store of patient care.

Therefore, health care facilities should plan for the worst and hope for the best.

More and more people are questioning the propriety of health care facility strikes. Patients' lives often hang in the balance. The authors believe that present remedies for impasse resolutions are ineffective. One of the areas they explore in the following pages is the viability of an approach to health care collective bargaining that minimizes the possibility of strikes, while not undercutting the collective bargaining process itself.

---

**NOTES**

1. Bernard Karsh, *Diary of a Strike* (Urbana, Ill.: University of Illinois Press, 1958), *passim*.

2. Norman Metzger and Dennis D. Pointer, *Labor Management Relations in the Health Services Industry: Theory and Practice* (Washington, D.C.: Science and Health Publications, Inc., 1972).

3. *Id.*, pp. 220-221.

4. Paul Monroe Heylman, "Developing a Strike Contingency Plan," *Health Care Labor Law*, edited by Ira Michael Shepard, J.D. and A. Doudera, J.D. (Washington, D.C.: AUPHA Press, 1981), p. 137.

# Part I
# Health Care Strikes: Legal and Moral Implications

# Chapter 1

# The Impact of Labor Legislation on the Health Care Industry

On July 26, 1974, in his last official act as President of the United States, Richard M. Nixon signed Public Law 93-360. Since that time labor relations in the health care industry has been subject to a complex body of statutory, administrative, and case law. All nongovernmental health care facilities (hospitals, clinics, health maintenance organizations, nursing homes, and homes for the aged) are now covered by the federal labor law, the National Labor Relations Act (NLRA or the Act).

In 1974, health care facility administrators, who had had little experience with or exposure to the NLRA prior to enactment of the law, were required for the first time to operate under its complex provisions. Pointer and Metzger stated that labor law was a topic that most administrators have had little acquaintance with during their formal training and specialized course work had not prepared them to deal effectively with labor law.[1] Unfortunately, not much has changed since then. Most educational programs in health care administration deal sparingly, if at all, with labor law.

To understand the subject of strikes in health care institutions, it is essential to be familiar with the provisions of the Act. The major provisions of P.L. 93-360, which extended coverage of the NLRA to the health care industry, were directed toward the special nature of that industry.

## P.L. 93-360 IMPACT ON HEALTH FACILITIES

### Coverage

The NLRA covers any privately operated health care institution, defined as "any hospital, convalescent hospital, health maintenance organization, health clinic, nursing home, extended care facility or other institutions devoted to the care of the sick, infirm or aged person." A hospital is covered if it has a total annual business volume of $250,000 or more; the minimum for a nursing home is $100,000. The $100,000 minimum also applies to visiting nurse associations and related associations. For all other types of private health care institutions the minimum is $250,000. Section 2 of the Act still excludes public hospitals.

**Contract Notice**

A party to a health care facility collective bargaining agreement wishing to modify or terminate the existing agreement must serve written notice prior to modification or termination. That notice must be served 90 days before the contract expires. The Federal Mediation and Conciliation Service (FMCS) must be notified at least 60 days prior to contract modification or termination. When a health care facility negotiates for the first time with a union for a particular bargaining unit, the FMCS must receive 30 days' notice. Figures 1-1 and 1-2 depict two charts developed by the FMCS to reflect the notice requirements for health care institutions. Figure 1-1 is related to initial contract negotiations, and Figure 1-2 is related to contract renewal negotiations.

**Mediation**

A special provision for the health care industry requires mandatory mediation between the parties by the FMCS. Congress designed this legislation in this way to minimize work stoppages in the private health care sector through the use of special notice and mediation procedures and through the use of boards of inquiry. FMCS is an independent agency of the federal government, established to promote labor-management peace. A stated policy of the FMCS is to attempt to prevent or minimize work stoppages in the health care industry through the use of mediation and fact-finding boards of inquiry.

After receipt of the 60-day notice of either party, the FMCS has 30 days to decide whether to appoint a board of inquiry. Under Title Two—Conciliation of Labor Disputes in Industries Affecting Commerce, National Emergencies—a provision covering labor disputes in the health care industry has been added.

> Section 213 (a). If, in the opinion of the Director of the Federal Mediation and Conciliation Service a threatened or actual strike or lockout affecting a health care institution will, if permitted to occur or to continue, substantially interrupt the delivery of health care in the locality concerned, the Director may further assist in

**Figure 1-1** Notice Requirements for Health Care Institutions—Initial Contract Negotiations

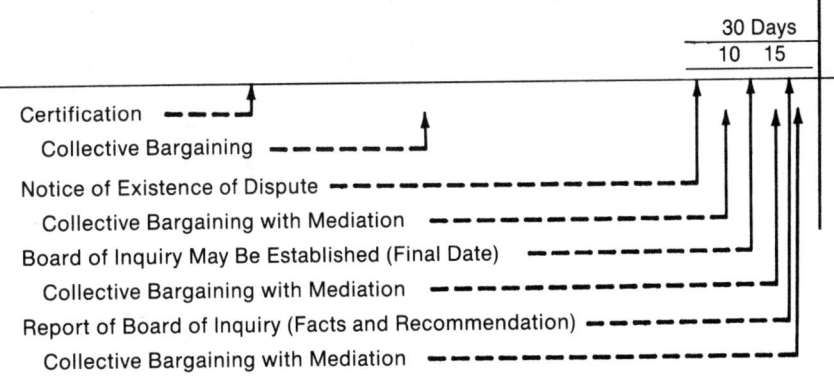

**Figure 1-2** Notice Requirements for Health Care Institutions—Contract Renewal Negotiations

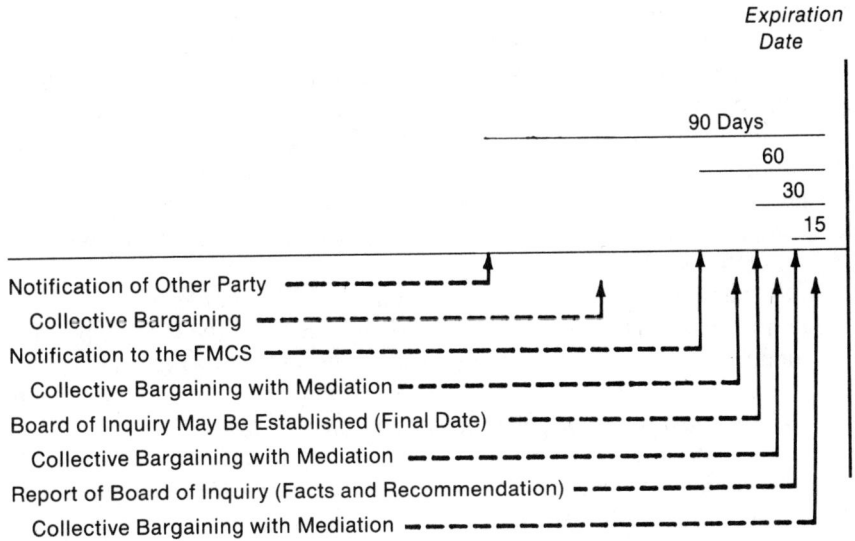

> the resolution of the impasse by establishing within thirty days after the notice to the Federal Mediation and Conciliation Service . . . an impartial Board of Inquiry to investigate the issues involved in a dispute and to make a written report thereon to the parties within fifteen (15) days after the establishment of such a Board. The written report shall contain the findings of fact, together with the Board's recommendation for settling the dispute, with the objective of achieving a prompt, peaceful and just settlement of the dispute.

In addition, this new provision states that

> after the establishment of a board . . . and for fifteen days after any such board has issued its report, no change in the status quo in effect prior to the expiration of the contract in the case of negotiations for a contract renewal, or in effect prior to the time of the impasse in the case of an initial bargaining negotiation, except by agreement, shall be made by the parties to the controversy.[2]

The board of inquiry (BOI) has 15 days to investigate the issues and make a written report of its findings of fact and its recommendations for settling the dispute. The board's recommendations are not binding on the parties. For 15 days after the issuance of a board report, a continued effort ensues to further negotiations and mediation, based on the BOI recommendations. No strike or lockout can legally take place until this 30-day period ends. A board of inquiry can be composed of one or more individuals. Members of such boards are not FMCS mediators, but rather private arbitrators or other qualified neutrals who are selected from the FMCS official roster maintained in the FMCS Office of Arbitration Services. Tables 1-1 through 1-7 provide examples of the numbers and types of boards of inquiry and fact finders the FMCS has appointed in typical years following passage of P.L. 93-360.

In 1979, the FMCS published regulations in the *Federal Register*.[3] These regulations established that the FMCS would defer to the party's private fact finding and interest arbitration procedures so long as they satisfy the responsibilities of the FMCS and are consistent with the Act. These private procedures must meet the following conditions:

1. They must be invoked automatically at a specified time (e.g., at contract expiration).

2. They must provide a fixed and determinate method for selecting the impartial fact finder(s).
3. They must provide that no strike or lockout take place and no change in conditions of employment (except by mutual agreement) be made prior to or during the fact finding and for at least seven days after the procedure is completed.
4. They must provide that the fact finder(s) will make a written report to the parties, containing the findings of fact and recommendations for settling the dispute; a copy of this report must be forwarded to the FMCS (the agency is empowered to pay for the services of those boards of inquiry and fact finders appointed by the FMCS, but it cannot and does not pay for a fact finder appointed under the party's own agreement).

The FMCS will defer to the party's private *interest arbitration procedure* and will decline to appoint a board of inquiry or fact finder(s) if both sides have agreed in writing to their interest arbitration procedure and if the procedure provides that:

1. No strike or lockout can occur, and no changes in conditions of employment (except by mutual agreement) can be implemented during the contract negotiations covered by the interest arbitration procedure and during any subsequent interest arbitration proceedings.
2. The award of the arbitrator(s) will be final and binding on both sides.
3. There will be either a fixed and determinate method for selecting the impartial interest arbitrator(s), or the arbitrator(s) will make a written award.[4]

**Table 1-1** Appointment by Federal Mediation and Conciliation Service

| Calendar Year | Boards of Inquiry | Fact-Finding Boards |
| --- | --- | --- |
| 1978 | 15 | 12 |
| 1979 | 9 | 10 |
| 1980 | 12 | 13 |
| 1981 | 15 | 10 |
| 1982 (to date) | 0 | 5 |

*Source:* Jewell L. Myers, Associate Director for Arbitration Services, Federal Mediation and Conciliation Service, Washington, D.C.

The typical mediation attempt includes obtaining basic information necessary to make a personal evaluation of the situation. The mediator assembles such facts as the nature of the facility; number of beds and percentage occupied; a breakdown of a bargaining unit; identification of other bargaining units and other unions in that institution; prior bargaining experience, if any; special or unique services (this becomes an important identification preceding the decision to establish a board of inquiry); and other health care institutions in the locality, including the number of beds and special services provided by such facilities. The mediator comments on the status of negotiations and makes a recommendation regarding the appointment of a board. The FMCS regional director reviews the mediator's report and makes a recommendation to the FMCS director and to the health care coordinator in the agency's national office as to whether to appoint a board of inquiry.[5]

In many cases contract talks are slow and may not have moved to a point where the appointment of a board would be helpful. Fully aware of this possibility, the FMCS provides for the use of a joint stipulation agreement between the parties. By this agreement the parties authorize the FMCS director to appoint a fact finder at a later date, possibly when a union serves a ten-day strike notice. Such a fact finder normally operates under the same time limits and procedures as a board of inquiry does, unless the parties and the FMCS agree to others.

The legislative history contained in the committee report accompanying the health care amendments clearly indicated the intent of Congress in enacting special emergency dispute provisions for the health care industry:

> The Conferees intend that the appointment of a board of inquiry shall not operate to interrupt mediation by the FMCS, which is made mandatory under other provisions of this legislation, and that the service will pursue these parallel procedures to bring a fair, prompt, and just settlement of any dispute. The Conferees further intend that the board of inquiry, in formulating its recommendations for settlement of a dispute, shall take into account all those factors normally considered by similar tribunals in formulating recommendations for the settlement of labor disputes. The committee, in adding special mediation and conciliation procedures, including the board of inquiry, for the health care industry, recognizes the need for continuity of health services during

### Table 1-2  Federal Mediation and Conciliation Service Report

Board of Inquiry and Fact-Finding Reports
by Stipulation

August 25, 1974—December 31, 1976

Number and Types of Board by State

| State | Board of Inquiry | Stipulation Fact-Finding Boards | Total Boards |
|---|---|---|---|
| New York | 31 | 7 | 38 |
| Pennsylvania | 10 | 6 | 16 |
| California | 9 | 6 | 15 |
| Massachusetts | 7 | 3 | 10 |
| New Jersey | 9 | 0 | 9 |
| Connecticut | 4 | 2 | 6 |
| Alabama | 5 | 0 | 5 |
| Maryland | 3 | 0 | 3 |
| Missouri | 2 | 1 | 3 |
| Virginia | 2 | 0 | 2 |
| Tennessee | 2 | 0 | 2 |
| Montana | 1 | 1 | 2 |
| Washington, D.C. | 1 | 0 | 1 |
| North Carolina | 1 | 0 | 1 |
| Florida | 1 | 0 | 1 |
| Louisiana | 0 | 1 | 1 |
| Kentucky | 1 | 0 | 1 |
| Illinois | 1 | 0 | 1 |
| Indiana | 0 | 1 | 1 |
| Arizona | 0 | 1 | 1 |
| Hawaii | 1 | 0 | 1 |
| Totals | 91 | 29 | 120 |

*Source:* Jewell L. Myers, Associate Director for Arbitration Services, Federal Mediation and Conciliation Service, Washington, D.C.

### Table 1-3  Federal Mediation and Conciliation Service Report

Number of Boards of Inquiry and
Fact-Finding Boards by Union
August 25, 1974–December 31, 1976

| Month | Dist. 1199 | Service Employees International Union | State Nurses | Other | Total Boards |
|---|---|---|---|---|---|
| *1974* | | | | | |
| September | 0 | 0 | 0 | 0 | 0 |
| October | 15 | 2 | 1 | 1 | 19 |
| November | 0 | 1 | 0 | 1 | 2 |
| December | 2 | 0 | 0 | 2 | 4 |
| *1975* | | | | | |
| January | 3 | 1 | 1 | 1 | 6 |
| February | 1 | 0 | 0 | 0 | 1 |
| March | 1 | 1 | 0 | 1 | 3 |
| April | 1 | 2 | 0 | 1 | 4 |
| May | 0 | 2 | 1 | 0 | 3 |
| June | 6 | 1 | 2 | 3 | 12 |
| July | 1 | 0 | 0 | 0 | 1 |
| August | 0 | 2 | 1 | 0 | 3 |
| September | 2 | 0 | 1 | 0 | 3 |
| October | 3 | 0 | 1 | 0 | 4 |
| November | 0 | 1 | 1 | 1 | 3 |
| December | 2 | 1 | 5 | 0 | 8 |
| *1976* | | | | | |
| January | 2 | 0 | 0 | 1 | 3 |
| February | 2 | 0 | 2 | 2 | 6 |
| March | 1 | 1 | 1 | 2 | 5 |
| April | 0 | 0 | 0 | 1 | 1 |
| May | 2 | 1 | 0 | 0 | 3 |
| June | 0 | 1 | 0 | 1 | 2 |
| July | 0 | 1 | 2 | 2 | 5 |
| August | 3 | 0 | 0 | 2 | 5 |
| September | 3 | 0 | 2 | 0 | 5 |
| October | 4 | 1 | 1 | 0 | 6 |
| November | 1 | 0 | 0 | 1 | 2 |
| December | 0 | 0 | 1 | 0 | 1 |
| Totals | 55 | 19 | 23 | 23 | 120 |

*Source:* Jewell L. Myers, Associate Director for Arbitration Services, Federal Mediation and Conciliation Service, Washington, D.C.

**Table 1-4** Federal Mediation and Conciliation Service Report

Number of Boards of Inquiry and Fact-Finding*
Boards by Type of Institutions
August 25, 1974–December 31, 1976

| Month | Hospitals | Nursing Homes | Other | Total Boards |
|---|---|---|---|---|
| *1974* | | | | |
| September | 0 | 0 | 0 | 0 |
| October | 9 | 7 | 3 | 19 |
| November | 1 | 1 | 0 | 2 |
| December | 2 | 1 | 1 | 4 |
| *1975* | | | | |
| January | 4 | 0 | 2 | 6 |
| February | 1 | 0 | 0 | 1 |
| March | 2 | 0 | 1 | 3 |
| April | 3 | 1 | 0 | 4 |
| May | 1 | 2 | 0 | 3 |
| June | 12 | 0 | 0 | 12 |
| July | 0 | 1 | 0 | 1 |
| August | 3 | 0 | 0 | 3 |
| September | 3 | 0 | 0 | 3 |
| October | 1 | 3 | 0 | 4 |
| November | 2 | 0 | 1 | 3 |
| December | 7 | 0 | 1 | 8 |
| *1976* | | | | |
| January | 3 | 0 | 0 | 3 |
| February | 4 | 1 | 1 | 6 |
| March | 4 | 0 | 1 | 5 |
| April | 0 | 1 | 0 | 1 |
| May | 1 | 0 | 2 | 3 |
| June | 1 | 1 | 0 | 2 |
| July | 4 | 0 | 1 | 5 |
| August | 5 | 0 | 0 | 5 |
| September | 5 | 0 | 0 | 5 |
| October | 5 | 1 | 0 | 6 |
| November | 1 | 1 | 0 | 2 |
| December | 0 | 0 | 1 | 1 |
| Totals | 84 | 21 | 15 | 120 |

*By stipulation.

*Source:* Jewell L. Myers, Associate Director for Arbitration Services, Federal Mediation and Conciliation Service, Washington, D.C.

**Table 1-5** Federal Mediation and Conciliation Service Report

Board of Inquiry and Fact-Finding Reports*
August 25, 1974–December 31, 1976
Union by State

| State | Dist. 1199 | Service Employees International Union | State Nurses | Other | Total Boards |
|---|---|---|---|---|---|
| New York | 20 | 6 | 8 | 4 | 38 |
| Pennsylvania | 11 | 0 | 5 | 0 | 16 |
| California | 0 | 5 | 4 | 6 | 15 |
| Massachusetts | 3 | 4 | 1 | 2 | 10 |
| New Jersey | 8 | 0 | 1 | 0 | 9 |
| Connecticut | 6 | 0 | 0 | 0 | 6 |
| Alabama | 0 | 0 | 0 | 5 | 5 |
| Maryland | 3 | 0 | 0 | 0 | 3 |
| Missouri | 0 | 1 | 0 | 2 | 3 |
| Virginia | 2 | 0 | 0 | 0 | 2 |
| Tennessee | 0 | 1 | 0 | 1 | 2 |
| Montana | 0 | 0 | 2 | 0 | 2 |
| Washington, D.C. | 0 | 1 | 0 | 0 | 1 |
| North Carolina | 0 | 0 | 1 | 0 | 1 |
| Florida | 0 | 0 | 0 | 1 | 1 |
| Louisiana | 0 | 0 | 0 | 1 | 1 |
| Kentucky | 1 | 0 | 0 | 0 | 1 |
| Illinois | 0 | 0 | 0 | 1 | 1 |
| Indiana | 1 | 0 | 0 | 0 | 1 |
| Arizona | 0 | 0 | 0 | 1 | 1 |
| Hawaii | 0 | 0 | 1 | 0 | 1 |
| Totals | 55 | 18 | 23 | 24 | 120 |

*By stipulation.

*Source:* Jewell L. Myers, Associate Director for Arbitration Services, Federal Mediation and Conciliation Service, Washington, D.C.

---

labor-management disputes and that the labor organizations representing health care workers have publicly pledged their best efforts to persuade their affiliates voluntarily to avoid work stoppages through acceptance of arbitration in the event of an impasse in negotiations. Under these new procedures, it is anticipated that, in the event of such an impasse, the findings of fact and

**Table 1-6** Federal Mediation and Conciliation Service Report

Board of Inquiry and Fact-Finding Reports*
August 25, 1974–December 31, 1976
Type of Institution by State

| State | Hospitals | Nursing Homes | Other | Total Boards |
|---|---|---|---|---|
| New York | 22 | 10 | 6 | 38 |
| Pennsylvania | 15 | 1 | 0 | 16 |
| California | 9 | 0 | 6 | 15 |
| Massachusetts | 8 | 2 | 0 | 10 |
| New Jersey | 8 | 1 | 0 | 9 |
| Connecticut | 4 | 2 | 0 | 6 |
| Alabama | 2 | 3 | 0 | 5 |
| Maryland | 2 | 1 | 0 | 3 |
| Missouri | 3 | 0 | 0 | 3 |
| Virginia | 2 | 0 | 0 | 2 |
| Tennessee | 1 | 0 | 1 | 2 |
| Montana | 1 | 0 | 1 | 2 |
| Washington, D.C. | 1 | 0 | 0 | 1 |
| North Carolina | 1 | 0 | 0 | 1 |
| Florida | 1 | 0 | 0 | 1 |
| Louisiana | 0 | 0 | 1 | 1 |
| Kentucky | 1 | 0 | 0 | 1 |
| Illinois | 1 | 0 | 0 | 1 |
| Indiana | 0 | 1 | 0 | 1 |
| Arizona | 1 | 0 | 0 | 1 |
| Hawaii | 1 | 0 | 0 | 1 |
| Totals | 84 | 21 | 15 | 120 |

*By stipulation.

*Source:* Jewell L. Myers, Associate Director for Arbitration Services, Federal Mediation and Conciliation Service, Washington, D.C.

---

recommendations of the board of inquiry would provide the framework of the arbitrator's decision.

In its published documents the FMCS describes the preparation for board investigations and fact finding and the mediator's role during a board of inquiry's tenure:

> Fact-finding proceedings, formal or informal, are generally conducted in a manner similar to arbitration hearings. The short time

**Table 1-7** Federal Mediation and Conciliation Service Report

Board of Inquiry and Fact-Finding Reports*
August 25, 1974–December 31, 1978
Type of Negotiation by State

| State | Initial | Renewal | Reopener | Total Boards |
|---|---|---|---|---|
| New York | 15 | 21 | 2 | 38 |
| Pennsylvania | 2 | 13 | 1 | 16 |
| California | 1 | 13 | 1 | 15 |
| Massachusetts | 1 | 8 | 1 | 10 |
| New Jersey | 2 | 7 | 0 | 9 |
| Connecticut | 0 | 6 | 0 | 6 |
| Alabama | 4 | 1 | 0 | 5 |
| Maryland | 0 | 2 | 1 | 3 |
| Missouri | 1 | 2 | 0 | 3 |
| Virginia | 0 | 2 | 0 | 2 |
| Tennessee | 1 | 0 | 1 | 2 |
| Montana | 1 | 1 | 0 | 2 |
| Washington, D.C. | 1 | 0 | 0 | 1 |
| North Carolina | 1 | 0 | 0 | 1 |
| Florida | 1 | 0 | 0 | 1 |
| Louisiana | 1 | 0 | 0 | 1 |
| Kentucky | 1 | 0 | 0 | 1 |
| Illinois | 1 | 0 | 0 | 1 |
| Indiana | 1 | 0 | 0 | 1 |
| Arizona | 0 | 1 | 0 | 1 |
| Hawaii | 0 | 0 | 1 | 1 |
| Totals | 35 | 77 | 8 | 120 |

*By stipulation.

*Source:* Jewell L. Myers, Associate Director for Arbitration Services, Federal Mediation and Conciliation Service, Washington, D.C.

---

span involved in these matters makes it imperative that the parties come to the hearing fully prepared to provide the BOI with all the information it needs to understand the issues and formulate its recommendations.

Such information includes: (1) written proposals and counter proposals; (2) written stipulations on all matters agreed on during direct negotiations and mediated negotiations; (3) copies of proposed contract language and copies of previous contracts between the parties; (4) copies of arbitration decisions if related to the current dispute issues; (5) all pertinent economic data, such as changes in cost of living, comparison of wages, hours and conditions of employment in the industry and in comparable areas, and such other information as is normally taken into consideration in the determination of wages, hours and conditions of employment through voluntary collective bargaining, arbitration, or otherwise between the parties or in the industry; and (6) other information the BOI determines necessary.

The parties should also insure that all required witnesses are readily available should the BOI [Board of Inquiry] determine to take testimony. In preparing for the proceedings, both parties may seek technical assistance from the assigned mediator.

Depending on the circumstances of the particular dispute, the mediator may continue with his assistance concurrent with the BOI period or mediation may be suspended during this period.

In many instances, the mediator may attend board of inquiry proceedings as an observer; however, he will not participate in the proceedings in any official capacity. It is FMCS policy to maintain the neutrality of the mediator, especially as he may be required to continue mediation efforts after the BOI ceases to function.

If the parties do not accept the Board's recommendations, the mediator will normally use the time until the expiration of the contract to reinitiate mediation efforts.[6]

**Strike Notice**

A new section added to the act prohibits a labor organization from striking or picketing a health care facility without at least ten days' notice. Congress' intent when adding section 8(g) was to provide the health care institution with advance notice so as to ensure the continuity of patient care or, at the very least, lessen the impact of the intended work stoppage on such continuity. The act further states that any employees who engage in a strike within any notice period specified in the act, or who engage in any strike within the appropriate period specified in section 8(g) will lose their status as employees of the employer engaged in the particular labor dispute. Interpretation in several National Labor Relations Board (NLRB) decisions relating to activities triggering section 8(g) notice has been quite strict. The Board looks to the legislative history of the amendments when attempting to interpret where picketing that does not result in a work stoppage is proscribed by the section.[7] It noted Senator Taft's statement that "hospitals are not factories. . . . Hospitals are for human beings and actions pursuant to this legislation must take this into account." It further noted that the committee report on the 1974 amendment stated that picketing of a health care institution would in itself constitute an unusual circumstance, justifying the application of a period of less than 30 days, whereas such "unusual circumstances" in the industrial sector normally consist of violation or intimidation. The Board held that Congress intended to cover such picketing regardless of its actual impact.[8]

The section 8(g) notice requirement was intended as one of the critical compromises of the normal industrial policy of broadly permitting strikes—a compromise for the health care industry, which recognized that such notice period was in the best interest of the patients of such facilities and the public at large. The Board has consistently protected the hospital's and, of course, the patient's rights to such notice.[9]

The Board has construed section 8(g) strictly and literally, without looking to the impact of the activity involved, and it has found that picketing that does not result in work stoppage requires such notice.[10] It has also found that notice must be given by unions engaged in sympathy picketing or strike.[11] The Board has ruled that notice is not required where unorganized employees are involved. It stated that the notice requirements of section 8(g) are for unions, not employees, and that the failure of employees to give such notice leaves their activity protected.[12] The Board also does not require an 8(g) notice for a threat to strike.[13] The impact of a union's conduct does not limit the Board's finding violations of 8(g).[14] It does not matter whether the object of the picketing is representational or appropriate for resolution by the FMCS. Such activity will be construed as requiring an 8(g) notice.[15] Although the board initially found that picketing which solely involved construction work at a hospital was covered by the notice provisions,[16] the courts subsequently found that the requirements were meant only to apply to health care employees, not to employees already covered by the act.[17]

In *Montefiore Hospital and Medical Center v. NLRB*,[18] the U.S. Court of Appeals for the Second Circuit concurred with the holdings of other circuits that the statutory requirements of section 8(g) for a labor organization to provide a hospital with ten days' notice of its intention to engage in a strike, picketing, or other concerted refusal to work does not apply to actions by individual employees. In this decision the court nevertheless made it clear that not every work stoppage without proper notice is permissible under the act. If such action endangers the care of patients, the court stated that it would rule that such action is unprotected and that the employees may be disciplined. The court gave the example of an emergency room personnel walkout, leaving people in need of immediate treatment. The court made it clear that each case should be viewed on its own facts and decided as to whether the employees' action places patient care in jeopardy. In this case the court also clarified what a hospital may do to protect itself against precipitous actions by employees. The court stated that when a hospital is given notice of a union's intention to strike, "the hospital would be well advised to inquire of the rest of its employees whether they plan to stay out in sympathy. An employee who strikes after promising to show up may well forfeit protection under the Act." Within the context of this court's directive, it would be permissible for a hospital to inquire whether the employee intends to work in the event of a strike or picket, but it would be unlawful to attach any condition of employment to the employee's response. The court added that it might be lawful for a hospital to enter into "a contractual agreement not to strike without notice" with employees. Apparently, however, this ruling would be limited to physicians, registered nurses, and other professionals who serve in vital patient care capacities.

**The Ally Doctrine**

The Ally Doctrine is a legal doctrine developed from Board case law. It defines the rights of third parties who provide assistance to an employer involved in a labor dispute.[19] The doctrine affects a secondary employer, who during the course of a labor dispute performs work that would have been performed by striking employees of the primary employer. In doing such work the secondary employer loses neutral status and, therefore, is subject to the labor organization involved in the dispute, thus extending its economic activity to the secondary employer. As the reports of both houses of Congress in the deliberations regarding the amendments state:

> It is the sense of the committee that where such secondary institutions *accept the patients of a primary employer,* or otherwise provide life sustaining services to the primary employer, by *providing the primary employer with an employee or employees who possess critical skills such as EKG Technician,* such conduct shall not be sufficient to cause the secondary employer to lose its neutral status. . . .[20] (Emphasis added.)

In effect, Congress intended to permit a neutral hospital to accept the patients of a primary employer and thereby not lose its status as a neutral.

Such a neutral hospital would, however, lose its status if it supplied *noncritical* personnel to a hospital experiencing a strike or if it not only accepted patients from such a hospital, but also greatly expanded its noncritical staff in the process. Gradually the Board's exception to the Ally Doctrine for the health care industry has become dependent on the *urgency* of the medical needs of the patients who were transferred from the primary hospital to the neutral hospital.

## THE 1974 HEALTH CARE AMENDMENTS TO THE NLRA

The 1947 Taft-Hartley Act excluded from the definition of "employer" private, not-for-profit hospitals and health care institutions. The NLRB asserted jurisdiction over proprietary hospitals and nursing homes, but it was not until the 1974 amendments that Congress, through P.L. 93-360, brought the private, not-for-profit health industry within the jurisdiction of federal labor law. The 1974 amendments enacted the following changes:

1. The exemption contained in section 2(2) of the federal statute that excluded not-for-profit hospitals from the definition of "employer" was removed.
2. A new section 2(14) was added to define the term "health care institution." It included any "hospital, convalescent hospital, health maintenance organization, health clinic, nursing home, extended care facility or other institutions devoted to the care of sick, infirm or aged persons." This definition is essential in the determination of which employees would thereafter fall under the special health care provisions and within the scope of the act.
3. A new series of special notices applicable to the health care industry and unions representing employees in that industry were enacted. The section 8(d) notice period for notices of disputes, which by law must be given by one party to the other, was extended from the normal 60 days prior to contract expiration to 90 days, and notices filed with the FMCS from the normal 30 days to 60 days. In the case of initial contract disputes notice must be given 30 days prior to any strike notice.
4. A new subsection 8(g) was added to the act. It requires that a union representing employees in a health care institution must give ten days' written notice to the employer and to the FMCS of its intent to engage in a strike, picketing, or other concerted refusal to work.
5. Broader sanctions under section 8(d) of the act provide that employees represented by labor organizations who do not comply with the

requirements of the 90- and 60-day dispute notices or with section 8(g), Strike Notices, would lose their protected status under the act.
6. Mandatory mediation of disputes in the health care industry were provided under section 8(d). The FMCS must mediate health care disputes, and the parties involved in such disputes are compelled to participate in that mediation process. It is an unfair labor practice for a party to fail to participate in such mediation.
7. Section 213, the second special dispute resolution provision, provides that in disputes that threaten substantial interruptions of delivery of health care in a community, the director of FMCS may appoint a special board of inquiry to investigate the issues in the dispute and to issue publicly a written report on the dispute.
8. A new section 19 provides for an alternate to the payment of union dues by persons with religious convictions against making such payments. It allows contribution to designated 501(C)(3) charities in lieu of dues.

## GUIDELINES FOR SERVING SECTION 8(g) NOTICES

In an interpretation by the Office of the General Counsel of the NLRB, the following guidelines have been established regarding section 8(g) notices:

1. The notice should be served on someone designated to receive such notice, or through whom the institution will actually be notified.
2. The notice should be personally delivered or sent by mail or telegram.
3. The 10-day period begins upon receipt by the employer and the FMCS of the notice.
4. The notice should specify the dates and times of the strike and picketing, if both are being considered.
5. The notice should indicate which units will be involved in the planned action.

As with section 8(d) notices, workers engaged in a work stoppage in violation of the 10-day strike notice lose their status as employees. The board will probably interpret violations of the section 8(g) notice requirement as a separate and distinct unfair labor practice.

In considering the 1974 amendments to the NLRA, the congressional committee included the ten-day section 8(g) strike and picket notice to provide health care institutions with sufficient advance notice of a strike. The committee realized, however, that it would be unreasonable to expect a labor organization to commence job action at the precise time specified in a notice provided to the employer. On the other hand, if a labor organization failed to act within a reasonable period after the time specified in the notice, such action would not be in accordance with the intent of the provision. Therefore, the committee report of the amendments provided that:

> . . . it would be unreasonable, in the committee's judgment, if a strike or picketing commenced more than 72 hours after the time specified in the notice. In addition, since the purpose of the notice was to give a health care institution advance notice of the actual commencement of a strike or picketing, if a labor organization does not strike at the time specified in the notice, at least 12 hours notice should be given on the actual time for commencement of the action.

Thus, absent unusual circumstances, a union would violate section 8(g) if it struck a facility more than 72 hours after the designated notice time, unless the parties agreed to a new time or the union gave a new ten-day notice. Additionally, if the union does not start the job action at the designated time as provided in the initial ten-day notice, it would be required to provide the health care facility at least 12 hours' notice prior to actual commencement of the action. The 12-hour warning must fall totally within the 72-hour notice period.

The committee reports note that ". . . repeatedly serving ten-day notices upon the employer is to be construed as constituting evidence of a refusal to bargain in good faith by the labor organization," i.e., a violation of section 8(b)(3). What constitutes ". . . repeatedly serving notice" will have to be defined and interpreted by the NLRB in individual cases. In a memorandum, the Board's General Counsel provided the following guidelines to regional offices regarding the handling of intermittent strikes or picketing stituations:

1. Where the facts and circumstances of the labor organization strike or picketing hiatus support the reasonable conclusion that the activity has not indefinitely ceased and that it is reasonable to assume that it will commence again, no new notice will be required if the activity recommences within 72 hours of the start of the hiatus; but 12 hours notice to the institution will be required if the activity is to recommence more than 72 hours from the start of the hiatus;
2. Where the facts and circumstances of the hiatus support the reasonable conclusion that the activity has ceased indefinitely

and that it will not be resumed in the near future, 12 hours notice to the institution will be required if the activity is to resume within 72 hours of the start of the hiatus, but a new 10-day notice meeting all of the requirements of Section 8(g) will be required if the activity is to resume more than 72 hours from the start of the hiatus.

Exceptions to the requirements that labor organizations provide section 8(g) notices are indicated in two situations. First, if the employer has committed serious or flagrant unfair labor practices, notice would not be required before the initiation of the job action. Second, the employer is not allowed to use the 10-day notice period to "undermine the bargaining relationship that would otherwise exist." The facility would be free to receive supplies, but it would not be "free to stock up on the ordinary supplies for an unduly extended period," or to "bring in large numbers of supervisory help, nurses, staff and other personnel from other facilities for replacement purposes." The committee reports held that employer violation of the above principles would release the union from its obligation not to engage in a job action during the section 8(g) notice period.

---

**NOTES**

1. Dennis D. Pointer and Norman Metzger, *The National Labor Relations Act, A Guidebook for Health Care Facility Administrators* (New York: Spectrum Publications, Inc., 1975), pp.1–2.
2. Nancy Connolly Fibish, "The Board of Inquiry: A New Dimension in Private Sector Health Care Collective Bargaining," *Handbook of Health Care Human Resources Management* (Rockville, Md.: Aspen Systems Corp., 1981), *passim*.
3. "Rules and Regulations," *Federal Register*, Volume 44, No. 141, Friday, July 20, 1979, pp. 42,683–42,684.
4. Fibish, *supra, passim.*
5. *Ibid.*
6. $R_x$ *for Labor Peace, FMCS: Its Role in the Health Care Industry* (Washington, D.C.: United States Government Printing Office, 1979), Publication #0–303–728, pp. 10, 12.
7. Donald A. Zimmerman, "Trends in National Labor Relations Board Health Care Industry Decisions," *Health Care Labor Law*, eds. Ira Michael Shepard and A. Edward Doudera (Washington, D.C.: AUPHA Press, 1981), pp. 13–16.
8. 232 NLRB 443 (1977).
9. *Local Union #200, General Service Employees Union and Eden Park Management, Inc., d/b/a Eden Park Nursing Home and Health Rehabilitation Facility, Poughkeepsie, New York*, 263 NLRB #16. The Board, in a three-to-two decision, held that the union violated the notice provisions by participating in a sympathy strike; it joined a picket line set up by another union at a nursing home without first giving the required ten days' notice to the facility and the FMCS. The Board determined that the purpose of the union's picketing was

"to lend support and assistance to, as well as generate publicity for the Local 144 employees." It therefore determined that the union's action was a sympathy strike. The union's position was that it was not the certified collective bargaining representative of any employee at the nursing home and hence had no bargaining rights under the Act. It reasoned in defense of its action, that it was not obligated to give notice in those circumstances. It said its action was an "informal" showing of support for another union and that the notice requirements under section 8(g) were not intended to cover such limited and informal action. The Board in its majority decision found that "irrespective of its character, objectives, or the type of economic pressure it generates, any strike, work stoppage, or picketing, including sympathy picketing at a health care institution violates Section 8(g) if the ten-day notice requirements of that Section have not been fulfilled." The Board's reasoning is most important to health care facilities in this case. It flowed from the majority interpretation that the notice provisions were intended to give health care institutions sufficient time to make appropriate arrangements for continuing patient care during a labor dispute. It therefore reasoned that the necessity for complying with the notice requirement is not eliminated by the fact that the picketing labor organization does not represent the facility's employees. To find otherwise, the Board stated, would be to ignore the potential for unexpected disruption in health care service resulting from the addition of a second labor organization to the picketing activity.

10. *District 1199, National Union of Hospital and Health Care Employees (United Hospitals of Newark)*, 232 NLRB 443 (1977), enfd. No. 77-2472 (3d Cir. Aug. 11, 1978).

11. *District 1199, National Union of Hospital and Health Care Employees (RWDSU) (First Health Care Corporation d/b/a Parkway Pavilion Health Care)*, 22 NLRB 212 (1976), enf. den. No. 76-407 (2d Cir., Nov. 23, 1976).

12. *Walker Methodist Residence*, 227 NLRB 1630 (1977); *East Chicago Rehabilitation Center, Inc.*, 252 NLRB No. 135 (1982) (Union had no prior notice of employees' walkout); *Barry S. Solof, M.D., a Professional Corporation, d/b/a The Victoria Medical Group and the West Jefferson Medical Group*, 264 NLRB No. 19 (1982).

13. *Greater Pennsylvania Avenue Nursing Center, Inc.*, 227 NLRB 132 (1976).

14. *District 1199, National Union of Hospital and Health Care Employees, Retail, Wholesale and Department Store Union, AFL-CIO (South Nassau Communities Hospital)*, 256 NLRB (1981).

15. *St. Joseph's Hospital Corporation*, 260 NLRB No. 89 (1982).

16. *United Association of Journeymen and Apprentices of the Plumbing and Pipefitting Industry of the United States and Canada, Local 630, AFL-CIO (Lein-Steenberg)*, 219 NLRB 837 (1975), enf. den. 567 F.2d 1006 (D.C. Cir. 1977).

17. *Laborers' International Union of North America, AFL-CIO, Local Union No. 1057 (Mercey Hospital of Laredo) v. NLRB*, 567 F.2d 1006 (D.C. Cir. 1977); *NLRB v. International Brotherhood of Electrical Workers, Local Union No. 388 (Hoffman Company)*, 548 F.2d 704 (7th Cir. 1977), cert. den. 434 U.S. 837 (1977).

18. *Montefiore Hospital and Medical Center v. NLRB*, CA 2 Nos. 79-4156 and 79-4184, April 28, 1980.

19. G. Roger King and William J. Emanuel, "Legal Developments Under the Health Care Amendments," *Handbook of Health Care Human Resources Management* (Rockville, Md.: Aspen Systems Corp., 1981), p. 580.

20. S. Rep. No. 93-766, 93d Cong. 2d Sess. 5 (1974); H.R. Rep. No. 93-1051, 93d Cong., 2d Sess. 7 (1974).

# Chapter 2
# Types of Strikes: Their Causes and Characteristics

All strikes are basically the same in that they are all concerted refusals of employees to continue work unless or until their employers comply with their demands.

The Taft-Hartley Act, passed in 1947 and amended in 1974, had a two-sided impact on strikes. Certain types of strikes became unlawful, while employees involved in other types of strikes were extended protection. The degree of protection depends on the type of strike. The various types include economic, unfair labor practice, sympathy, jurisdictional, recognition, and "illegal" strikes.

## ECONOMIC STRIKES

Economic strikes are usually conducted by the employees of a particular business who hope to compel their employer to accept their demands by withdrawing their services. Economic strikes generally occur after a breakdown in the collective bargaining process, either for the development or for the modification of a contract. The Taft-Hartley Act established specific procedures that should be followed before a party engages in a strike in these situations.

According to the 1947 Act, in situations where a contract is being modified or terminated, the other party must be notified in writing 60 days prior to the modification or termination date; the Federal Mediation and Conciliation Service (FMCS) must be notified 30 days prior to this date. The 1974 amendments extended these time periods for health care institutions from 60 to 90 days for notification of the other party and from 30 to 60 days for notification to the FMCS.

The act also requires a 30-day notice to the FMCS with regard to initial contract negotiations in health care institutions, but does not require this for other industries. A ten-day notice of intent to strike must be given to health care institutions to allow them time to make arrangements for continuing patient care at their own institutions or to find other available health care providers. If a strike occurs during any of the above "cooling-off" periods, the strikers forfeit their status as "employees" as defined by the act and can be subject to discharge or discipline by the employer.[1]

During economic strikes, employers may permanently replace strikers in order to continue business. After the strike, however, the employer must offer vacant positions, if they exist, to the strikers when they apply for reinstatement. If the striker finds equivalent employment elsewhere, the employer is no longer obligated to reinstate the striker when a vacancy occurs.[2] An employer does not have to reinstate a striker who is guilty of misconduct during a strike, even if the employee was not replaced during the strike.[3]

## UNFAIR LABOR PRACTICE STRIKES

A strike that is either caused or prolonged by the unfair labor practice of an employer is an unfair labor practice strike. Unfair labor practice strikes are afforded the highest level of protection by the National Labor Relations Board (NLRB).

Unfair labor practice strikers are entitled to unconditional reinstatement to their jobs, even if replacements must be terminated. Back pay is usually awarded from the time the strikers offer an unconditional request for reinstatement.[4]

Notification for unfair labor practice strikes is required only in the health care field. In situations involving health care institutions, unions must serve a ten-day strike notice when planning to protest an unfair labor practice, except where the unfair labor practice is flagrant or serious.[5]

In the 1961 case of *Arlan's Department Stores, Inc.* a serious unfair labor practice was defined as "destructive of the foundation on which collective bargaining must rest."[6] In the case of *District 1199E, National Union of Hospital and Health Care Employees (CHC Corporation)*, the NLRB ruled that a ten-day notice was unnecessary. In this case, a 5-to-15 minute walkout took place at a nursing home after it was learned that the administrator was hiding to avoid meeting with the employees' union representative about a grievance. The administrator had previously canceled numerous meetings on the same grievance. The nursing home subsequently filed an unfair labor practice charge against the union for failure to give a ten-day notice to strike.[7] The Board determined that the nursing home had shown blatant disregard for the bargaining process, eliminating the need for a prior notice of the union's protest. The fact that no patient was harmed by the short work stoppage was also an important factor in the Board's decision.[8]

**SYMPATHY STRIKES**

The sympathy strike is fundamentally a strike by the workers of one employer or craft in support of the workers of another. A sympathy strike can also involve the refusal of one union to cross the picket line of another. Labor organizations that wish to engage in sympathy picketing must, however, provide a ten-day notice to health care institutions.

In 1953 the Supreme Court ruled in *NLRB v. Rockaway News Supply Company*[9] that an individual member's right to honor a picket line could be waived by a union through a general no-strike clause in a collective bargaining agreement. In this case, however, the bargaining history of the parties was important because the employer had rejected a union proposal that would allow its members to honor picket lines.[10]

In *Montana-Dakota Utilities v. NLRB*[11] and *News Union of Baltimore v. NLRB*[12] the Board maintained its position that a general no-strike clause prohibited sympathy strikes, based either on the bargaining history or on interpretation as such by the parties involved.[13]

The NLRB later abandoned its *News Union of Baltimore* position. In 1975 the Seventh Circuit took a different position in *Gary Hobart Water Corp. v. NLRB*,[14] indicating that unless there was clear and unmistakable language to the contrary, a no-strike clause does not waive an employee's right to respect picket lines. The court did, however, review the bargaining history to support its conclusion.[15]

In 1976, the Supreme Court held in *Buffalo Forge Co. v. United Steelworkers*[16] that an injunction against a sympathy strike was prohibited by the Norris-LaGuardia Act even though the collective bargaining agreement contained a no-strike pledge. If the employer went to arbitration and the arbitrator ruled that the strike was a breach of contract and ordered it to cease, then the employer could enjoin the sympathy strike.[17]

In a sympathy strike situation, therefore, a union might commit two wrongs: first, declining to arbitrate the issue of whether the sympathy strike itself is in violation of the no-strike clause of the collective bargaining agreement; and second, the sympathy strike being ruled a violation of the no-strike clause.[18]

If a sympathy strike is found to be in violation of the collective bargaining agreement, the employer is entitled to damages under section 301 of the Taft-Hartley Act.

Sympathy strikes that do not involve a picket line, but rather are attempts by one or more unions to aid another in return for the future help of that union, are usually unlawful. The courts have ruled that sympathy strikes, where no appreciable or observable economic interest exists, are an "unlawful infliction of damage, aimless and unjustifiable because of the absence of any direct economic advantages to the workers participating in it."[19] General strikes against all the industries of a given community or of workers in related industries have almost always been ruled illegal.

An example of a no-strike clause that prohibits sympathy strikes is found in the July 1, 1980 to June 30, 1983 collective bargaining agreement between The Mount Sinai Medical Center and Local Union #3, International Brotherhood of Electrical Workers:

Article XXIII

No Strike or Lockout

1. No Employee shall engage in any strike, sit-down, sit-in, slow-down, cessation or stoppage or interruption of work, boycott, or other interference with the operations of the Hospital.
2. The Union, its officers, agents, representatives and members, shall not in any way, directly or indirectly, authorize, assist, encourage, participate in or sanction any strike, sit-down, sit-in, slow-down, cessation or stoppage or interruption of work, boycott, or other interference with the operations of the Hospital, or ratify, condone or lend support to any such conduct or action.
3. In addition to any other liability, remedy or right provided by applicable law or statute, should a strike, sit-down, sit-in, slow-down, cessation or stoppage or interruption of work, boycott, or other interference with the operations of the Hospital occur, the Union, within twenty-four (24) hours of a request by the Hospital, shall:
    a) Publicly disavow such action by the Employees.
    b) Advise the Hospital in writing that such action by Employees has not been sanctioned by the Union.
    c) Notify Employees of its disapproval of such action and instruct such Employees to cease such action and return to work immediately.
    d) Post notices at Union Bulletin Boards advising that it disapproves such action, and instructing Employees to return to work immediately.
4. This prohibition against strikes, work stoppages or work interruptions shall include a prohibition against such activity which

is directed in sympathy with other Employees or with other unions at Mount Sinai Medical Center and at other institutions.

## JURISDICTIONAL STRIKES

A jurisdictional strike is a work stoppage resulting from a dispute between two or more unions over the assignment of work. If an employer assigns the work in dispute to a particular union, the other will strike.[20] Section 8(b)(4)c of the Taft-Hartley Act made it an unfair labor practice for a union to strike or cause concerted refusal to perform a service or to handle goods with the purpose of:

> ... forcing or requiring any employer to assign particular work to employees in a particular labor organization or in a particular trade, craft, or class rather than to employees in another labor organization or in another trade, craft or class, unless such employer is failing to conform to an order or certification of the Board determining the bargaining representative for employees performing such work. ...

In jurisdictional disputes, if one union threatens a strike, either the employer or a competing union may file an unfair labor practice charge with the regional director of the NLRB. "The regional director will then issue a complaint and immediately seek a federal district court injunction against the strike."[21] The standard used to determine if an injunction will be issued is "whether the regional director has a reasonable cause to believe that a violation has occurred."[22]

## RECOGNITION STRIKES

Strikes or work stoppages for the purpose of forcing an employer to bargain with a particular labor organization are recognition strikes. For the most part labor organizations are prohibited under section 8(b)(7) of the National Labor Relations Act from picketing or threatening to picket an employer for recognition purposes under the following conditions:[23]

> (a) the employer has lawfully recognized any other labor organization under the provisions of the Act;
> (b) a valid election has been conducted within the last twelve months; or

(c) a representational petition has not been filed within a reasonable period, not to exceed thirty days from the commencement of such picketing.

When health care institutions are involved, the congressional committee reports encourage the NLRB to consider this an unusual circumstance and limit this 30-day period allowed for recognitional picketing at health care facilities.[24]

When a valid charge has been filed with the NLRB concerning a recognition strike or picketing, the Board must seek an injunction under the act against the strike or picketing, unless a valid charge of employer domination of a union has been filed.

**ILLEGAL STRIKES**

Several types of strikes are illegal. Determination of the illegality of a strike is usually based upon the Taft-Hartley Act as amended, and in other cases by the collective bargaining agreement. Some examples of illegal strikes are:

- a sit-down strike where employees remain in the institutions and prevent work from going on.
- a strike which is violent in nature.
- a wildcat strike—one which is not authorized by the union.
- strikes in defiance of existing certification.
- jurisdictional strikes.
- secondary strikes and boycotts.
- a strike to induce the violation of a valid statute.
- a strike to obtain a featherbedding arrangement.[25]

Strikes involving issues that are applicable to the grievance and arbitration procedure of a collective bargaining agreement can also be held to be illegal.

**STRIKES IN VIOLATION OF NO-STRIKE CLAUSES**

Most collective bargaining agreements have some type of no-strike clause. For a union to agree to a no-strike clause, usually management must also agree to an arbitration clause. Exhibit 2-1 has examples of no-strike and arbitration clauses taken from the 1980–82 Collective Bargaining Agreement between the League of Voluntary Hospitals and Homes of

New York and District 1199, National Union of Hospital and Health Care Employees, RWDSU/AFL-CIO.

The United States Arbitration Act supplies significant support for arbitration. First enacted on February 12, 1925 and then amended on July 30, 1947, September 3, 1954 and July 31, 1970, the U.S. Arbitration Act makes arbitration agreements specifically enforceable with regard to contracts involving interstate or international commerce. The law, however, excludes "contracts of employment"; whether this excludes collective bargaining agreements or pertains only to individual contracts of employment has been subject to dispute with the courts issuing conflicting decisions.[26]

The 1957 Supreme Court decision in *Textile Workers v. Lincoln Mills*[27] is among the most important case law in this area. In that case the high court ruled that future dispute clauses in collective bargaining agreements could be enforced in federal courts under section 301 of the Taft-Hartley Act, thus establishing the jurisdiction of federal courts in labor matters. The federal courts could, therefore, invoke a remedy for the failure of the party to honor its agreement to arbitrate. This decision also paved the way for injunctions to be imposed in labor disputes where agreements exist to arbitrate grievance disputes.[28]

In *Charles Dowd Box Co. v. Courtney*[29] and *Local 174, Teamsters v. Lucas Flour Co.*[30] the Supreme Court left open the possibility of State court jurisdiction in the enforcement of collective bargaining agreements as long as they adhered to federal law as indicated by the *Lincoln Mills* decision.[31]

An important decision that seems to conflict with the Norris-LaGuardia Act of 1932, which specifically limits the power of federal courts to issue either temporary or permanent injunctions in nonviolent labor disputes, resulted from *Boys Markets, Inc. v. Retail Clerks Local 770*.[32] The 1970 decision set forth three tests for a strike injunction:

1. The strike must concern a grievance the parties are contractually bound to arbitrate;
2. The employer, as well as the union, must be ordered to arbitrate; and
3. Traditional equity principles must be satisfied.[33]

The first of the three principles left a basic question unanswered: What about the situation where the strike itself is potentially in violation of the collective bargaining agreement: This question was exactly the issue in *Buffalo Forge Co. v. United Steelworkers*.[34] This 1976 case involved a sympathy strike over an issue that was not arbitrable. In its decision, the court held that the possibility of the sympathy strike under the terms of

**Exhibit 2-1** Examples of No-Strike and Arbitration Clauses

NO STRIKE OR LOCK OUT

1. No Employee shall engage in any strike, sit-down, sit-in, slow-down, cessation or stoppage or interruption of work, boycott, or other interference with the operations of the Employer.
2. The Union, its officers, agents, representatives and members, shall not in any way, directly or indirectly, authorize, assist, encourage, participate in or sanction any strike, sit-down, sit-in, slow-down, cessation or stoppage or interruption of work, boycott, or other interference with the operations of the Employer, or ratify, condone or lend support to any such conduct or action.
3. In addition to any other liability, remedy or right provided by applicable law or statute, should a strike, sit-down, sit-in, slow-down, cessation or stoppage or interruption of work, boycott, or other interference with the operations of the Employer occur, the Union, within twenty-four (24) hours of a request by the Employer, shall:
 (a) Publicly disavow such action by the Employees.
 (b) Advise the Employer in writing that such action by Employees has not been called or sanctioned by the Union.
 (c) Notify Employees of its disapproval of such action and instruct such Employees to cease such action and return to work immediately.
 (d) Post notice at Union Bulletin Boards advising that it disapproves such action, and instructing Employees to return to work immediately.
4. The Employer agrees that it will not lock out Employees during the term of this Agreement.

ARBITRATION

1. A grievance, as defined in Article XXXI, which has not been resolved thereunder may, within fifteen (15) working days after completion of Step 3 of the grievance procedure, be referred for arbitration by the Employer or the Union to an arbitrator selected in accordance with the procedures of the American Arbitration Association. The arbitration shall be conducted under the Voluntary Labor Arbitration Rules then prevailing of the American Arbitration Association.
2. The fees and expenses of the American Arbitration Association and the arbitrator shall be borne equally by the parties.
3. The award of an arbitrator hereunder shall be final, conclusive and binding upon the Employer, the Union and the Employees.
4. The Arbitrator shall have jurisdiction only over disputes arising out of grievances, as defined in Section 1 of Article XXXI, and he/she shall have no power to add to, subtract from, or modify in any way any of the terms of this Agreement.
5. A grievance contesting a discharge may, within fifteen (15) working days after completion of Step 3 of the grievance procedure, be referred for arbitration to an arbitrator appointed by the American Arbitration Association from the Panel of twenty-six (26) arbitrators listed in Schedule B annexed hereto. Said arbitrators shall serve on the Panel for the period of one (1) year or until the termination date of this Agreement, whichever is sooner, and shall have jurisdiction only over grievances contesting discharges. The Association shall appoint said arbitrators from the Panel in a discharge case. If an arbitrator so appointed is unable to hold a hearing in a particular case for any reason within one (1) month from the date of his/her appointment the Association shall appoint the arbitrator next in rotation, and so on. Should none of the arbitrators on the Panel be

**Exhibit 2-1  continued**

available within such one (1) month period, then the Association shall promptly (a) so notify both parties and (b) proceed to process the case pursuant to Section 1 of this Article XXXII, unless the parties consent to a later hearing date before the arbitrator so appointed. The fees of the arbitrators shall be borne equally by the parties. In the event of a vacancy in the Panel, the parties shall expedite the selection of an arbitrator to fill the vacancy or vacancies. If, at the expiration of the term of the Panel of Arbitrators the parties are unable to reach agreement as to arbitrators to serve thereafter, the parties shall select such arbitrators by each submitting a list of fifty-two (52) names and in turn striking such names until twenty-six (26) names remain.

Source: Reprinted from *1980–82 Collective Bargaining Agreement between the League of Voluntary Hospitals and Homes of New York and District 1199, the National Union of Hospital and Health Care Employees, RWDSU/AFL-CIO.*

the collective bargaining agreement must itself be decided by arbitration before an injunction could be appropriately issued.[35]

In *Cedar Coal Co. v. UMW Local 1759*,[36] a case where the grievance causing the primary strike was arbitrable and a sympathy strike also took place to force the employer to give in on an arbitrable issue, the Supreme Court ruled in 1978 that an injunction may be issued against the primary strike as well as the sympathy strike.[37]

---

**NOTES**

1. Howard J. Anderson, sr. ed., *Primer of Labor Relations,* 2d ed. (Washington, D.C.: Bureau of National Affairs, Inc., 1975), p. 70.
2. Dennis D. Pointer and Norman Metzger, *The National Labor Relations Act: A Guidebook for Health Care Facility Administrators* (New York: Spectrum Publications, Inc., 1975), p. 138.
3. *Id.,* p. 138.
4. *Op Cit,* Anderson, p. 67.
5. Kenneth C. McGuiness, *How to Take a Case Before the National Labor Relations Board,* 4th ed. (Washington, D.C.: The Bureau of National Affairs, Inc., 1976), p. 345.
6. Douglas L. Leslie, *Labor Law* (St. Paul, Minn.: West Publishing Co., 1979), p. 97; *Arlan's Department Stores Inc.,* 133 NLRB 802 (1961).
7. *District 1199-E, National Union of Hospital and Health Care Employees (CHC) Corporation,* 229 NLRB No. 15 (1979); and G. Roger King and William J. Emmanuel, "Legal Developments Under The Health Care Amendments" in *Handbook of Health Care Human Resources Management,* Norman Metzger, ed. (Rockville, Md.: Aspen Systems Corp., 1981), p. 578.
8. *Ibid.,* King and Emanuel, p. 578.
9. 345 U.S. 71 (1953).

10. Walter B. Connolly Jr. and Michael J. Connolly, *Work Stoppages and Union Responsibility* (New York: Practicing Law Institute, 1977), pp. 212-214.
11. 455 F.2d 1088 (8th Cir. 1972).
12. 393 F.2d 673 (D.C. Cir. 1968).
13. Connolly and Connolly, *supra,* pp. 213-214.
14. *Gary Hobart Water Corp. V. NLRB*, 511 F.2d 284 (7th Cir. 1975).
15. Connolly and Connolly, *supra,* pp. 214-215.
16. *Buffalo Forge Co. v. United Steelworkers,* 428 U.S. 397, 96 S.Ct. 3141, 49 L.Ed.2d 1022 (1976).
17. Leslie, *supra,* pp. 298-299.
18. Connolly and Connolly, *supra,* p. 281.
19. Charles O. Gregory and Harold A. Katz, *Labor and the Law,* 3rd ed. (New York: W.W. Norton and Company, 1979), p. 109.
20. Leslie, *supra,* p. 176.
21. Leslie, *supra,* p. 176.
22. Leslie, *supra,* p. 177.
23. Pointer and Metzger, *supra,* p. 128.
24. *Id.,* p. 59.
25. *Id.* p. 139.
26. Dennis R. Nolan, *Labor Arbitration Law and Practice* (St. Paul, Minn.: West Publishing Co., 1979), p. 39.
27. *Textile Workers v. Lincoln Mills of Alabama,* 353 U.S. 448 (1957).
28. Maurice S. Trotta, *Arbitration of Labor Management Disputes* (New York: AMACOM, Div. of American Management Associations, 1974), p. 109.
29. *Charles Dowd Box Co. v. Courtney,* 368 U.S. 502 (1962).
30. *Local 174, Teamsters v. Lucas Flour Co.,* 369 U.S. 95 (1962).
31. Nolan, *supra,* p. 45.
32. *Boys Markets, Inc. v. Retail Clerks Local 770,* 398 U.S. 235, 90 S.Ct. 1583, 26 L.Ed.2d 199 (1970).
33. Nolan, *supra,* pp. 56-57.
34. *Buffalo Forge, supra,* note 16.
35. Nolan, *supra,* pp. 57-60.
36. *Cedar Coal Co. v. UMW Local 1759,* 560 F.2d 1153 (4th Cir. 1977), Cert. denied 434 U.S. 1047 (1978).
37. *Id.,* pp. 60-61.

# Chapter 3
# Strike-Related Actions: Union and Management

Collective bargaining is the interaction between unions and management within the limits set forth by formal rules, accepted practices, laws, and conventions.[1] The primary purpose of collective bargaining is to regulate the relations between the management of an organization and its workers. Through this process an attempt is made to establish and maintain mutually acceptable and beneficial rules and practices to guide their conduct in daily operations.[2] In most situations, labor and management will reach a mutually acceptable agreement. Occasionally, however, this agreement is reached only through a strike or, on rare occasions, a lockout. A strike at a health care facility is, of course, an extremely serious matter that can result in devastating consequences. In his book *Mediation and the Dynamics of Collective Bargaining,* William E. Simkin outlined the following reasons for strikes:

1. One (or both) of the parties is unable to or unwilling to make decisions required to reach agreement.
2. One (or both) of the parties is unable or unwilling to accept an alternative settlement procedure or a device for postponement of economic action.
3. The issues in conflict are so important to one (or both) parties that "a test of strength" is needed to change positions.[3]

Strikes have a definite effect on the positions of the bargaining parties. They increase the likelihood that initial issues will change. An example is the 1980 strike at Ashtabula Hospital in Ohio by the Ohio Nurses Association, a strike that lasted 570 days (the longest nursing strike on record). The issues upon which this strike was settled were totally different from those that initially caused the strike. Appendix 3-A provides a chronology of events in the Ashtabula strike.

Strikes can also prevent negotiators from dealing with the issues that precipitated the strike because they are preoccupied with their respective roles during a strike.[4] Emotions sometimes replace reason during a strike, and positions harden. New issues may appear, and issues thought to be resolved may reappear.[5]

The ratio of strikes to the total number of health care cases completed by the Federal Mediation and Conciliation Service (FMCS) has remained relatively stable since 1974, ranging from 4.2 to 5.5 percent of the total health care cases,[6] as shown in Table 3-1.

The Bureau of Labor Statistics lists a total of 43 major strikes occurring between June 1974 and March 1982, each involving 1,000 or more employees at health care institutions. (The strikes are enumerated here in Table 3-2).[7] The length of these strikes varied, ranging from 1 to 95 days. The average strike length was 18.8 days, but 58 percent of the strikes lasted ten days or less, with the most frequent duration being four days (see Table 3-3).[8] A 1979 study conducted by Lucretia Dewey Tanner, Harriet Goldberg Weinstein, and Alice Lynn Ahmuty and financed by the Department of Labor, found that nursing home strikes tend to last longer than hospital strikes, averaging 52 days as compared to 18 days for hospitals. One union organizer postulated that nursing home strikes last longer because the public does not exert the same pressure to resolve disputes in nursing

**Table 3-1** Health Care Industry Strike Case Report

| Fiscal Year | Total Health Care Cases* (Closed) | Total Strikes | Strike Ratio |
|---|---|---|---|
| 8/74 to 7/1/75 | 719 | 32 | 4.5 |
| 7/1/75 to 10/1/76† | 1,525 | 78 | 5.1 |
| 10/1/76 to 10/1/77 | 1,419 | 59 | 4.2 |
| 10/1/77 to 10/l/78 | 1,313 | 72 | 5.5 |
| 10/1/78 to 10/1/79 | 1,277 | 67 | 5.2 |
| 10/1/79 to 4/1/80 | 622 | 29 | 4.7 |
| Aggregate | 6,875 | 337 | 4.9 |

*These represent 6,875 out of 8,402 total health care cases in which mediators closely monitored or actively participated in the resolution of the dispute from initial contact with the parties to termination of the dispute.

†The fiscal year was changed from July 1 to October 1 in 1976, which accounts for an additional three months of caseload statistics during this transition quarter.

Source: Norman Metzger, ed., Handbook of Health Care Human Resources Management. Aspen Systems Corp. (1981).

*Strike-Related Actions* 35

**Table 3-2** Work Stoppages in the Medical and Other Health Services Industry, Involving 1,000 Workers or More, 1974–82

| Unit | Number of Workers | Dates | Issues |
|---|---|---|---|
| Hospitals (40) San Francisco Area of California | 4,000 | June 6–27, 1974 | — |
| John Hopkins Hospital and Two Others, Baltimore, Maryland | 2,500 | Dec. 2–13, 1974 | — |
| Pennsylvania State Hospitals | 1,500 | June 23, 1974 | Discharge or Suspension |
| Ohio State Hospitals | 5,400 | July 10–17, 1974 | Wages |
| Kaiser Permanente Hospitals, Los Angeles, California | 4,500 | Feb. 3–6, 1975 | — |
| League of Voluntary and Municipal Hospitals (23), New York, New York | 3,000 | Mar. 17–20, 1975 | Hours of Work and Work Assignments |
| League of Voluntary Hospitals and Homes, New York, New York | 40,000 | July 7–16, 1976 | Wages |
| University of Cincinnati Hospitals (2) | 1,900 | July 14–23, 1976 | Wages |
| Seattle Area Hospital Council | 1,400 | July 13–Sept. 17, 1976 | Wages |
| Albert Einstein College of Medicine, Bronx, New York | 1,600 | Oct. 6, 1976 | Wages |
| Cook County and Oak Forest Hospitals, Chicago and Oak Forest, Illinois | 1,500 | Nov. 3–Dec. 10, 1976 | Sick Pay and Wages |
| Massachusetts State Public Hospitals | 8,000 | June 21–23, 1976 | Wages |
| Health and Hospitals Corp., New York, New York | 18,000 | Aug. 4–7, 1976 | Layoffs |
| Temple University Hospital, Philadelphia, Pennsylvania | 1,800 | Jan. 5–8, 1977 | Wages |
| Temple University Hospital, Philadelphia, Pennsylvania | 2,600 | July 7–12, 1977 | Wages |
| Kaiser Foundation Hospitals, Los Angeles, California | 1,300 | Aug. 11–Sept. 5, 1977 | Wages |

**Table 3-2** continued

| Unit | Number of Workers | Dates | Issues |
|---|---|---|---|
| Kaiser Hospital, Fontana, California | 1,100 | Nov. 1–Dec. 14, 1977 | Wages, Cost-of-Living, Pensions |
| Youngstown Hospital Association, Ohio | 1,300 | Nov. 14, 1977–Feb. 5, 1978 | Wages |
| Harper-Grace Hospitals, Detroit, Michigan | 1,900 | June 26–July 25, 1978 | Wages |
| Metropolitan New York Nursing Home Association | 10,000 | Apr. 4–7, 1978 | Wages and Fringes |
| Albert Einstein College of Medicine, Bronx, New York | 1,200 | Oct. 5–9, 1978 | Wages |
| New York City Health and Hospitals Corp., New York, New York | 1,000 | Jan. 17, 1979 | Protest against Potential Cutback and Closings |
| Associated Hospitals of East Bay Inc., Berkeley, Oakland, and San Leandro, California | 2,100 | Apr. 16–June 3, 1979 | Wages and Pensions |
| Ohio State Department of Mental Health & Retardation | 1,300 | June 20, 1979 | N/A |
| Thomas Jefferson University Hospital, Philadelphia, Pennsylvania | 1,100 | July 1–9, 1979 | Wages |
| Temple University Hospital, Philadelphia, Pennsylvania | 2,500 | July 3–14, 1979 | Wages |
| Cedars Sinai Medical Center, Los Angeles, California | 1,800 | July 2–13, 1979 | Wages |
| Pennsylvania State Hospitals | 1,100 | Apr. 9, 1979 | Discharge or Suspension |
| Rhode Island State Hospitals | 2,200 | Sept. 13–19, 1979 | Recognition and Economic |

## Strike-Related Actions

| | | | |
|---|---|---|---|
| Pittsburgh Municipal Hospitals, Pennsylvania | 4,500 | July 1–Sept. 15, 1979* | Wages |
| Columbia Presbyterian, Maimonides & Kingsbrook Jewish Hospitals, New York, New York | 2,100 | Feb. 1–5, 1980 | Wages, Staffing, and Mandatory Overtime |
| Cuyahoga County Hospitals (2), Cleveland, Ohio | 1,500 | Mar. 6–13, 1980 | Wages |
| Kaiser Permanente Hospitals (7) in Southern California | 2,000 | May 16–June 14, 1980 | Wages |
| Johns Hopkins & Sinai Hospitals, Baltimore, Maryland | 1,900 | Dec. 1–17, 1980 | Wages and Fringes |
| New York City Hospitals | 1,800 | Oct. 10–13, 1980 | Wages |
| Hospitals (7 Municipal, 2 Private), New York, New York | 2,000 | Mar. 17–24, 1981 | Support Staff and Equipment Shortages |
| Hospitals (6) in New Jersey | 3,000 | July 6–10, 1981 | Wages |
| New Jersey State Hospitals | 2,400 | June 22–24, 1981* | Wages and Fringes |
| Massachusetts State Hospitals | 2,000 | July 9–12, 1981 | Working Conditions |
| County Hospitals of Pennsylvania | 1,500 | July 6–30, 1981 | Wages |
| County Hospitals, Pennsylvania | 2,500 | July 8–30, 1981 | Wages |
| Hospitals (4) in San Jose, California | 1,500 | Jan. 5–Apr. 10, 1982 | Wages, Retirement Benefits, Time Off Between Shifts |
| Kaiser Foundation Hospitals and Kaiser Permanente Medical Group, Oakland, California | 1,400 | Feb. 15–Mar. 14, 1982 | Term of Contract and Medical Benefits for Retirees |

*staggered dates

*Source:* U.S. Department of Labor, Bureau of Labor Statistics.

homes as it does in instances involving hospitals; therefore, nursing home strikes that were not settled in the first few days tended to have a long duration.[9]

Numerous studies have been conducted on the propensity of strikes with respect to the effect of unemployment rates, differential movements in wages and prices, and geographic factors. The occurrences of strikes vary inversely with the unemployment rate.[10] Therefore, high rates of unemployment have seriously affected the bargaining power of unions, and their inclination toward a strike is minimal.[11]

Inflation has also been found to have an impact on the number of strikes.[12] During times of high inflation unions tend to make larger demands to increase the purchasing power of their members to "catch up" with the inflation rate, thus resulting in more strikes. Where wage increases exceed the inflation rate, historically there have been fewer strikes.[13]

With regard to geographic factors, studies have found that states in the South have less strike activity than other states.[14] This, of course, results from cultural, historical, and political factors that have hindered unionization in the South.[15] Studies have demonstrated that rural areas have a higher propensity to strike[16] due to minimal social outlets and lack of alternative employment opportunities "to mediate or neutralize work-related conflicts and grievances."[17]

The cost of a strike to a hospital involves lost patient revenues, especially in the outpatient department and the inpatient medical/surgical units.[18] Strike-related expenses include overtime costs for nonstriking employees, security expenses (if additional security is needed), additional supplies and equipment expense (especially if disposables are substituted), food costs (if provided to working employees free or at reduced rates) and, in

**Table 3-3** Duration of Health Care Strikes between June 1974 and March 1982 Involving 1,000 or More Employees

| Duration of Strike (Days) | Number of Strikes | Percentage of Total |
| --- | --- | --- |
| 1 to 10 | 25 | 58 |
| 11 to 20 | 4 | 9 |
| 21 to 30 | 7 | 16 |
| 31 to 40 | 1 | 2 |
| 41 to 50 | 2 | 5 |
| More than 50 | 4 | 9 |
| | 43 | |

*Source:* U.S. Department of Labor, Bureau of Labor Statistics.

some cases, unemployment insurance costs. Also lost are less tangible management hours to such strike-necessitated functions as contingency operational planning and, to the extent possible, patient care. Legal costs associated with strike settlement efforts can be prohibitive. Patients may also seek substitute health care facilities and may not return to the struck facility. Cost of sabotage, both overt and covert, can also be significant, as can costs of arbitrating strike-related discharge and discipline cases.

The cost of the strike to the union can also be considerable. Striking workers could be replaced, having an impact, albeit temporarily, on union dues. The struck facility might have to shut down completely, as in the case of Ashtabula General. Even if the union's members are reinstated, the union faces administrative and strike benefit costs in addition to member dissatisfaction with lost wages and fringes. The union must also consider the ramifications of an unsuccessful strike on future decertification and representation elections. A common management tactic (often used during organizing drives) is to publicize the union's strike record, and the potential effects of strikes on employees, e.g., the loss of pay and the relationship of a day of lost pay to the settlement necessary to make up for such loss.

## MAJOR ELEMENTS OF STRIKES IN PROGRESS

Discussed below, among other topics, are management and union conduct relative to strike actions, strike-related discipline, and the employee's option of resigning from the union in the event of a work stoppage.

### Preparing for the Strike

When faced with the threat of a strike, management must develop a plan that will both provide care for those patients remaining in the hospital and protect nonstriking employees.

One of management's first decisions must be to determine whether the hospital will continue to operate and, if so, at what level. This decision will be determined to a large degree by the number and classifications of striking employees. A strike by service and maintenance employees, for instance, may not require a significant reduction in patient services. However, if the technical and clerical employees join the service and maintenance workers, services reduction will accelerate. A strike of nurses poses more immediate problems to hospital administrators than does a strike of nonnurse personnel due to its obvious direct patient care impact. A strike contingency plan, such as the plan outlined in the section of this book titled "Strike Manual," is essential for health care facilities coping with a strike.

**Damage Suits for Unlawful Strikes**

In certain circumstances, employers may sue a labor organization for damages to business or property resulting from an illegal strike or boycott under section 303 of the Taft-Hartley Act, as amended. Some of the strikes considered illegal under section 8(b)(4) of the National Labor Relations Act (NLRA) are those involving "hot cargo" agreements, secondary strikes and boycotts, strikes in defiance of existing certification, jurisdictional strikes, sit-down strikes where employees remain in the institution and prevent work from being performed, violent strikes, and wildcat strikes. Section 303 of the NLRA provides the following:

(a) It shall be unlawful, for the purpose of this section only, in an industry actively affecting commerce, for any labor organization to engage in any activity or conduct defined as an unfair labor practice in section 8(b)(4) or 8(g) of the National Labor Relations Act, as amended.

(b) Whoever shall be injured in his business or property by reason of any violation of subsection (a) may sue therefore in any district court of the United States subject to the limitations and provisions of Section 301 hereof without respect to the amount in controversy, or in any other court having jurisdiction of the parties, and shall recover the damages by him sustained and the cost of the suit.

Sec. 301. (a) Suits for violation of contracts between an employer and a labor organization representing employees in an industry affecting commerce as defined in this Act, or between any such labor organizations, may be brought in any district court of the United States having jurisdiction of the parties, without respect to the amount in controversy or without regard to the citizenship of the parties.

(b) Any labor organization which represents employees in an industry affecting commerce as defined in this Act and any employer whose activities affect commerce as defined in this Act shall be bound by the acts of its agents. Any such labor organization may sue or be sued as an entity and in behalf of the employees whom it represents in the courts of the United States. Any money judgment against a labor organization in a district court of the United States shall be enforceable only against the organization as an entity and against its assets, and shall not be enforceable against any individual member or his assets.

(c) For the purposes of actions and proceedings by or against labor organizations in the district courts of the United States, district courts shall be deemed to have jurisdiction of a labor organization (1) in the district in which such organization maintains its principal offices, or (2) in any district in which its duly authorized officers or agents are engaged in representing or acting for employee members.

(d) The service of summons, subpoena or other legal process of any court in the United States upon an officer or agent of a labor organization, in his capacity as such, shall constitute service upon the labor organization.

(e) For the purposes of this section, in determining whether any person is acting as an "agent" of another person so as to make such other person responsible for his acts, the question of whether the specific acts performed were actually authorized or subsequently ratified shall not be controlling.

Under section 303 of the law, therefore, any person suffering business or property losses may sue for the damages caused by an unlawful boycott or strike. This includes customers, suppliers, and others doing business with the affected employer, as well as the employer itself. The courts, however, have declared that recovery may come only from labor organizations and not from individuals involved in unauthorized strikes.[19]

Persons suing for damages caused by unlawful strike or the coercive action can recover actual dollar-and-cents losses, plus court costs. However, they cannot collect additional amounts as penalties for malicious injury nor to curb future misconduct. Nor can attorney fees incurred during NLRB proceedings relating to a union's unlawful secondary activity be recovered in a later suit for damages, the U.S. Supreme Court has ruled.[20]

A federal appeals court ruled that, while it is true that only compensation damages can be collected under federal law, punitive damages may be collected where tactics were used in violation of state criminal law.[21] An arbitrator may also rule against a union for damages where it can be shown that the union violated a no-strike clause.

An example of such an award is *Fortex Manufacturing Co., Inc. and Local 1065, Amalgamated Clothing and Textile Workers of America*.[22] In this case a picket line was established in violation of the no-strike clause of the collective bargaining agreement, to protest the discharge of an employee. The union's contention was that it did end the strike and, therefore, the claim for damages should be dismissed. The arbitrator held, however, that the union should have taken more forceful action by disciplining the strikers as provided for in the union's constitution and bylaws. The union was held liable for damages sustained, including reasonable attorney's fees, overhead expenses not offset by production, direct expenses, and overtime costs. The arbitrator also found the union liable for the arbitrator's fee and expenses.

Another example is *Foster Grading Co.*[23] In this case, the arbitrator awarded the company, which was working on a highway project, compensatory damages for "labor costs, rental value of equipment (its own and outside rentals), and the prorated costs of traffic protection."[24]

**Union Actions during a Strike**

When calling a strike, unions follow procedures generally outlined in their constitutions. The following is an example of a strike procedure, found in the Constitution of District 1199, National Union of Hospital and Health Care Employees, RWDSU/AFL-CIO, November 29, 1973, amended December 1975, November 1977, and December 1979:

ARTICLE XV—STRIKES

Section 1—The National Union shall be informed of any decision to call or terminate a strike.

Section 2—A strike may be called by a District or a sub-division thereof only with the approval of the members involved at a meeting duly called to consider the matter. Such approval shall be voted on by secret ballot.

Section 3—Any proposal to settle or terminate a strike shall require the approval of the membership involved at a meeting duly called to consider the matter and voted on by secret ballot.

Section 4—All requests for benefits from the National Strike and Defense Fund shall be made in the first instance to the president of the National Union, who may appoint a standing committee of the National Executive Board to act upon such requests.

Based on District 1199 Constitution language, a strike can only be called or terminated with membership approval and by secret ballot.

The American Nurses Association (ANA) bargains collectively through its Economic and General Welfare Program. The program provides the necessary assistance and establishes the guidelines for the various state nurses associations. Each state association is composed of a number of local bargaining units.

Local units must make their own collective bargaining decisions, including authorization to strike.[25] Strike authorization by the New York State Nurses Association, Council of Nurse Practitioners of the Mount Sinai Hospital, requires the following:

1. A well-publicized meeting shall be held.
2. Voting shall be by open ballot.
3. Tellers shall be appointed by the chairperson prior to voting period.
4. A two-thirds (2/3rds) vote of the Council shall be required.
5. A NYSNA General Representative shall be in attendance at this meeting.

The Service Employees International Union (SEIU) represents employees working in hospitals, nursing homes, other health care facilities, and in nonhealth care industries. To call a strike, a local of SEIU must secure the approval of its International president.[26]

The Retail Clerks International Union (RCIU) represents employees primarily engaged in the distribution or provision of consumer products. Food, apparel, shoe, hardware, furniture, and variety stores, as well as health care facilities are considered potential areas for organization. RCIU strikes must be approved by two-thirds of the members involved in the strike and by RCIU's International president.[27]

*Strike Funds*

Most unions have established strike funds, which are allocated during a strike to cover strike benefits, legal fees, publicity, and other related expenses. Some unions assess each member a small amount each month to build the fund. The amount of the fund often determines the staying power of the workers and, consequently, the success or failure of the strike. District 1199 has a National Union Strike and Defense Fund, which can be utilized through a request to the president of the National Union, who may establish a standing committee of the national executive board to act on the request. The National Union allocates 10 percent of total dues, initiation fees, and assessments collected by its locals for the National Union Strike and Defense Fund. The executive board, composed of the president, the executive vice president, the secretary-treasurer, the executive secretary, and the secretary and vice presidents of the National Union can authorize collection of additional revenue to supplement the fund, if necessary.[28]

The ANA has no general strike fund. Some state associations have established their own strike-assistance funds. The ANA will, however, assist state associations in need of additional strike funds by soliciting donations nationally.[29]

Locals of the SEIU must first obtain approval from the International president before drawing money from their own strike funds. The fund is fed by a per capita tax to the membership. During an authorized strike, each local, with presidential approval, may use the equivalent of its contributions to the fund and borrow an additional equal amount.[30]

The RCIU pays no strike benefits until the strike has continued for two weeks. These benefits come from the general fund.[31]

*Strike Strategy*

For a strike to be successful the union must: ensure adequate participation by membership employed at the struck facility, establish a base of operation near the site of the strike, and develop a theme or mechanism that will muster public support. Delegates and assigned union representatives will help union leaders encourage membership participation in the strike. They usually visit the target facility prior to the strike, gathering support of the membership. Flyers are normally distributed, outlining management's position in negotiations. During the strike itself, the union usually attempts to get as many organizers or business agents as possible to the strike site, or appoints captains to distribute signs and organize picket lines in an attempt to maximize operational interruption and ineffectiveness, while affording picketers high visibility to the public and media.

The union generally will establish an operations base near the strike site, utilizing vacant storefronts or trailers. The base serves as strike headquarters, where strike efforts are coordinated and, in some cases, coffee and food are distributed to the strikers. Of paramount concern to strike coordinators are the media—the vehicles to the public. Due to the unpopularity of strikes in the health care industry, the union must carefully develop a theme that will put management on the defensive, while justifying its action to strike. The union may accuse management of trying to "bust the union," or indicate that the quality of care in the institution is poor and that the strike is an effort to improve that situation.

**Discipline for Activity during the Strike**

Violence on the picket line is not uncommon. One of the primary objectives of the picket line is to discourage ingress to the facility. In this effort confrontations with patients, vendors, police, and others can be serious. Picketing employees are often disciplined at the conclusion of the strike for their actions while on the line. Union leaders often demand amnesty for their members as a condition of strike settlement. Management should be aware when considering such amnesty that amnesty may encourage similar violent action by striking employees in future strikes.

*Union Disciplinary Action against Its Members*

Most union constitutions and bylaws provide for disciplinary action against members who violate enunciated rules or policies. Such action can be a simple reprimand, or take the form of a more serious censure, fine, suspension, or expulsion. Appendix 3-B is an example of a disciplinary procedure. It comes from the Bylaws of District 1199, National Union of Hospital and Health Care Employees.

*Employer Discipline of Striking Employees*

Illegal strikes could result in management disciplinary action up to and including discharge against all strikers or at least those responsible for strike initiation or exacerbation.[32] In other strike situations, disciplinary action might be taken against one or more striking employees for individual acts of violence. Such acts should be identified by solid evidence.[33] Employers may not discipline striking employees for merely participating in legal strikes.

In *Metropolitan Edison Company v. NLRB*,[34] the Supreme Court found that severe discipline imposed by management on union delegates for activity (or lack of it) in attempting to end a strike was unlawful under section 8(a)(3) of the NLRA. The Supreme Court did suggest, however, that an employer could negotiate into its collective bargaining agreement with the union specific actions that must be taken by union representatives during unlawful strikes.

In *Price Brothers Co.*,[35] eight employees protested their discharge, which resulted from their participation in a wildcat strike. In this case the arbitrator upheld the discharges, despite the fact that the employer merely believed the grievants to be guilty of a higher level of participation than other employees. The arbitrator ruled that the employer did not have to prove any greater degree of participation by the grievants. He reasoned that the employer acted in good faith:

> In the opinion of the arbitrator, it is not incumbent upon the Company to prove that the grievant participated in the strike to a greater degree than the other strikers before it can impose discipline upon him and not upon other strikers. The only obligation which the Company must meet is to show that it acted fairly and in good faith in arriving at its decision to discharge the grievant. The fact that its decision might be incorrect is irrelevant.
>
> When the grievant engaged in the wildcat strike, he subjected himself to the penalty of discharge. This penalty was prescribed by the Plant Rules and is a reasonable penalty for the offense involved. Likewise, the other strikers subjected themselves to the same penalty. The fact that the Company had a right to impose the penalty does not require it to do so. If it sees that it can invoke a lesser penalty or none at all, provided, however, that in making its decision as to who will be penalized it acts fairly and in good faith.

In *Avco Wyoming Division*,[36] the arbitrator upheld the company's selective discharge despite the absence of specific reference to discipline in the contract's no-strike clause, reasoning that:

> ... it would be an unconscionable denial of justice to "tinker" with the discipline assessed. ... The company is not obligated to denude its working force by wholesale discharges in order to preserve the validity of its no-strike agreement. It is not required to achieve a rigid, mechanical uniformity of treatment to a mathematical certainty, rather it is entitled to single out those more culpable and to be selective.

Some arbitrators have ruled differently, however. In *Superior Switchboard and Service Division*,[37] an arbitrator reinstated five workers who were discharged for organizing an illegal strike. He reasoned that disciplinary action was not specified in the contract's no-strike clause and, in addition, management did not warn the individuals that they could or would be discharged for their actions. In this case, management not only failed to inform the individuals of possible disciplinary action, but also "stood or sat idly by while employees around them argued about walking out, and some supervisors even actively encouraged the walkout."[38]

In *Payne & Keller, Inc.*,[39] the arbitrator reinstated an employee discharged for inciting a walkout. Here the arbitrator found that the individual making the accusations against the grievant was an unreliable witness and that there was no indication of actual job desertion.[40]

As indicated earlier, discipline may be imposed for employee misconduct during a legal strike. Examples of such misconduct are taunting strikebreakers, vandalism, and assaulting supervisors or others. The Bureau of National Affairs' *Grievance Guide* has outlined the following criteria for discipline during a legal strike based on statements made by several arbitrators:

- What is the extent of participation? In any mob situation the degree of involvement of the individual in any action is important.
- What was the nature of the violence? This has both quantitative and qualitative aspects. Participation in several incidents is more serious than in only one. Some actions are more reprehensible than others. Shouting insults and shoving are of a different order from striking a person.
- Was the violence provoked? To the extent that the violence is retaliatory and defensive, it is less culpable than if undertaken as an act of aggression.
- Was the violence premeditated or undertaken on the spur of the moment? Premeditated violence is more inexcusable.
- What will be the impact of the punishment? Discharge is more of a penalty for an old man than a young one, for a long service employee than a short-service employee.
- Was the disciplinary action discriminatory? A company is under some obligation to treat persons similarly situated in a comparable, although not necessarily identical, manner. Violence can hardly be said to be the real basis for discharge if other unjustifiable factors enter in.
- How serious was the offense in terms of injury to persons or damage to property?
- Were remedies at law available and were they involved?
- Was the conduct destructive of good employee-employer relations?
- Was the conduct destructive of good community relations?

- Will the discipline restore good relations, or is it the result of a spirit of vindictiveness?
- Was the conduct such that the employee could be reabsorbed into the workforce?[41]

Arbitrators have generally held that discipline less severe than discharge be imposed on employees for strike-related offenses committed after a strike ends. They reason that such offenses are emotionally generated.[42] An example is an offense of one union employee active in the strike against another who did not participate.

In general, the end of a strike triggers temporary feelings of bitterness, pride, and frustration. Returning strike-supporting employees might harbor feelings of ill will against management, union employees who did not support the strike, and striker replacements. Their pent-up emotions are easily transformed into acts of misconduct.[43] The case of *Chromalloy American Corp.*[44] provides an example. In this case, an employee, upon returning to work after participating in a six-month strike, harassed workers hired as striker replacements, first through name-calling, labeling them "scabs," and later through actual threats to their safety and well-being. The employee was counseled for these actions and was finally terminated when he reported to work wearing a T-shirt imprinted with an obscene caption directed toward the replacement employees. The arbitrator reduced the termination to a suspension. The prior counseling, the arbitration said, was not sufficient because the employee had not been specifically warned that he would be terminated if he continued the misconduct.[45]

**Resignation from the Union**

Union employees who work during a strike can be subject to fines and/or other disciplinary action by the union. Employees can avoid this disciplinary action by resigning their union membership. Two sections of the NLRA support the employee's right to resign. Section 8b(1)(A), 29 U.S.C. Sec. 158 (b)(1)(A), provides:

> It shall be an unfair labor practice for a labor organization or its agents (1) to restrain or coerce . . . employees in the exercise of the rights guaranteed in Section 7. Provided, that this paragraph shall not impair the right of a labor organization to prescribe its own rules with respect to the acquisition or retention of membership therein. . . .

Section 7, 29 U.S.C. Sec. 157, provides:

> Employees shall have the right to self-organization, to form, join, or assist labor organizations, to bargain collectively through representatives of their own choosing, and to engage in other concerted activities for the purpose of collective bargaining or other mutual aid or protection, and shall also have the right to refrain from any or all of such activities except to the extent that such right may be affected by an agreement requiring membership in a labor organization as a condition of employment as authorized in section 8(a)(3).

The Supreme Court ruled in *NLRB Granite State Joint Board, Textile Workers Union of America, Local 1029, AFL-CIO (International Paper Box Machine Co.)*[46] and *Booster Lodge No. 405, International Association of Machinists and Aerospace Workers, AFL-CIO (Boeing Co.) v. NLRB*[47] that any attempt by the unions in these cases to fine former members for crossing an authorized picket line violated section 8(b)(1)(A) of the Act, since the unions' constitutions and bylaws contained no provisions restricting members' rights to tender resignation.

The NLRB addressed a case in *Machinists Local 1327, International Association of Machinists and Aerospace Workers, AFL-CIO, District Lodge 115 (Dalmo Victor)*,[48] where a restriction was placed on resignation. Machinists Local 1327 had added the following amendment to its constitution:

> *Improper Conduct of a Member.* . . . Accepting employment in any capacity in an establishment where a strike or lockout exists as recognized under this Constitution, without permission. Resignation shall not relieve a member of his obligation to refrain from accepting employment at the establishment for the duration of the strike or lockout within 14 days preceding its commencement. Where observance of a primary picket line is required, resignation shall not relieve a member of his obligation to observe the primary picket line for its duration if the resignation occurs during the period that the picket line is maintained or within 14 days preceding its establishment.

The Board found that the above restriction ". . . which limits the right of a union member to resign only to nonstrike periods[,] constitutes an unreasonable restriction on a member's Section 7 right to resign." Any attempt by the union to impose and to enforce fines was, therefore, in violation of section 8(b)(1)(A).

The majority in this case found, however, that ". . . a rule which restricts a union member's right to resign for a period not to exceed 30 days after the tender of such a resignation reflects a reasonable accommodation between the right of union members to resign from the union and return to work, and the union's responsibility to protect the interests of employees who maintain their membership as well as its need to dispose of administrative matters arising from such resignations." The Board further stated that under extraordinary circumstances, more than 30 days may be found to be reasonable. Some Board members resoundingly criticized this 30-day notice of intention to resign; it may not survive an NLRB decision that would require a direct ruling on it. Appendix 3-C sets out the full text of the decision.

Any union member considering resignation from a union should first check the constitution and bylaws of that union. These documents should be available to all members. Upon making the decision to resign, the letter of resignation should be sent, return receipt requested, to the union and should clearly indicate the effective date of such resignation.

---

**NOTES**

1. Edwin F. Beal, Edward D. Wickersham, and Philip K. Kienest, *The Practice of Collective Bargaining*, 5th ed. (Homewood, Ill.: Richard D. Irwin, Inc., 1976), pp. 19–20.
2. *Id.*, p. 20.
3. William K. Simkin, *Mediation and the Dynamics of Collective Bargaining* (Washington, D.C.: The Bureau of National Affairs, Inc., 1971), p. 159.
4. *Id.*, p. 160.
5. *Id.*
6. Nancy Connolly Fibish, "The Board of Inquiry: A New Dimension in Private Sector Health Care Collective Bargaining," *Handbook of Health Care Human Resources Management*, ed. Norman Metzger (Rockville, Md.: Aspen Systems Corp., 1981), p. 756.
7. Provided by the U.S. Department of Labor, Bureau of Labor Statistics, Washington, D.C. on February 16, 1983 (their letter reference 370) at the authors' request.
8. *Id.*
9. Lucretia Dewey Tanner, Harriet Goldberg Weinstein, and Alice Lynn Ahmuty, *Impact of the 1974 Health Care Amendments to the NLRA on Collective Bargaining in the Health Care Industry*, Labor Management Service Communication (Washington, D.C.: U.S. Department of Labor), pp. 323–324.
10. Orley Ashenfelter and George Johnson, "Bargaining Theory, Trade Unions and Industrial Strike Activity," *American Economics Review*, Vol. 59 (March 1969), pp. 35–49; Michael Shaler, "Trade Unionism and Economic Analysis: The Case of Industrial Conflict," *Journal of Labor Research*, Vol. 1 (Spring 1980), pp. 133–174; and Bruce E. Kaufman,

"Bargaining Theory, Inflation and Cyclical Strike Activity in Manufacturing," *Industrial and Labor Relations Review,* Vol. 34 (April 1981), pp. 333-355; Bruce E. Kaufman, "The Determinants of Strikes in the United States, 1900-1977," *Industrial and Labor Relations Review,* Vol. 35 (July 1982).

11. Bruce E. Kaufman, "The Determinants of Strikes Over Time and Across Industries," *Journal of Labor Research,* Vol. IV (Spring 1983), p. 161.

12. Ashenfelter and Johnson (1969), Kaufman (1981, 1982); and William J. Moore and Douglas K. Pearce, "A Comparative Analysis of Strike Models during Periods of Rapid Inflation: 1966-1977," *Journal of Labor Research,* Vol. 3 (Winter 1982), pp. 39-54.

13. Kaufman, *supra,* note 11, p. 161.

14. Robert Wallace, "Factors Affecting Strike Decisions," unpublished Ph.D. dissertation (New York: New School for Social Research, 1972); and Robert N. Stern, "Intermetropolitan Patterns of Strike Frequency," *Industrial and Labor Relations Review,* Vol. 29 (January 1976), pp. 218-235.

15. Kaufman, *supra,* note 11, p. 164.

16. Clark Kerr and Abraham Siegal, "The Interindustry Propensity to Strike," *Industrial Conflict,* eds. Arthur Kornhauser, Robert Dubin and Arthur Ross (New York, N.Y.: McGraw-Hill, 1954), pp. 189-212.

17. Kaufman, *supra,* note 11, p. 165.

18. Paul E. Brody, M.D. and Joseph B. Stamm, "Strike Two: Hospitals Down But Not Out," in *Handbook of Health Care Human Resources Management,* ed. Norman Metzger, (Rockville, Md.: Aspen Systems Corp., 1981), p. 760.

19. *Williams v. Pacific Marine Corp.,* 384 F.2d 935 (9th Cir. 1967), CA 1970; *Jersey Farms Milk Service, Inc. v. Meat Cutters,* Cir. 4877 (M.D. Tenn., Jan. 16, 1969); and *Navajo Freight Lines, Inc. v. Teamsters,* Civ. C-693 (D.C. Colo., October 18, 1968).

20. *Id.,* p. 285.

21. *Id.,* p. 286.

22. 76-2 ARB 8594.

23. 52 LA 197.

24. BNA Editorial Staff, *Grievance Guide,* 6th ed. (Washington, D.C.: The Bureau of National Affairs, Inc., 1982), pp. 316-317.

25. Tanner, *et al., supra,* 94-96.

26. *Id.,* p. 73.

27. *Id.,* p. 99.

28. *District 1199—National Union of Hospital and Health Care Employees Constitution,* p. 39.

29. Tanner, *supra,* p. 94.

30. *Id.,* p. 73.

31. *Id.,* p. 99.

32. BNA Editorial Staff, *supra,* p. 111.

33. *Id.,* p. 111.

34. *Metropolitan Edison Company v. NLRB,* 663 F.2d 478, 108 LRRM 3020 (CA 3, 1981).

35. 74 LA 748.

36. 51 LA 1228.

37. 75 LA 1107.

38. BNA Editorial Staff, *supra*, pp. 114–115.
39. 70 LA 114.
40. BNA Editorial Staff, *supra*, p. 115.
41. *Id.*, p. 116.
42. BNA Editorial Staff, *supra*, p. 118.
43. *Id.*, p. 118.
44. 72 LA 8383.
45. BNA Editorial Staff, *supra*, p. 118.
46. 109 U.S. 213 (1972).
47. 412 U.S. 84 (1973).
48. 263 NLRB 141 (1982).

## Appendix 3-A

# Ashtabula General Hospital Nurse Strike Chronology

**1980**

July 21      The Ashtabula Nurses Association begins strike as about 160 nurses walk off the job. Ashtabula General Hospital (AGH) closes, except for the outpatient clinic.

July 31      First negotiation since strike began ends with no progress.

August 15      Nonunion hospital employees protest lack of unemployment benefits and urge both sides to bargain in good faith in talks today. No progress reported.

August 21      No progress reported in bargaining session.

September 3      AGH reopens 30-bed medical unit, as nurses increase pickets in response.

Nursing supervisor found guilty in tomato throwing incident that occurred August 15.

Nurses begin series of informational picketing at businesses and homes of hospital trustees.

September 9      The ANA agrees to drop its demand that its professional code of ethics be part of the contract. AGH agrees to print the code next to the contract.

September 18      Hopes for further progress in bargaining are dashed as talks end in deadlock.

October 7      No progress reported in bargaining session.

*Source: Ashtabula Star-Beacon,* Ashtabula, Ohio, February 1982.

| | |
|---|---|
| October 13 | AGH reopens two intensive-care-unit beds. |
| October 25 | Area unions support nurses at North Park rally. |
| October 30 | No progress reported in bargaining session. |
| November 14 | No progress reported in bargaining session. |
| December 15 | AGH reopens 16-bed surgical unit. |
| December 17 | No progress reported in bargaining session. |

1981

| | |
|---|---|
| January 10 | ANA supporters hike 56 miles in frigid weather from the hospital to Youngstown, home of Ohio Nurses Association's (ONA) oldest contract, to raise money for the nurses' strike fund. |
| January 12 | AGH opens ten beds in maternity unit. |
| January 15 | ANA polls membership regarding the direction it wants the strike to take. |
| January 23 | ANA announces one of its four major demands will be dropped in a bargaining session set for January 31. |
| January 24 | ANA asks that all unresolved issues pending in the six-month-old strike go to fact finding. |
| January 30 | AGH undergoes its major accreditation inspection by the Joint Commission on Accreditation. ANA criticizes the quality of patient care in statements before the Joint Commission. |
| January 31 | AGH negotiators reject ANA proposal to go to fact finding. ANA proposes to go to binding arbitration. |
| February 4 | AGH negotiators reject ANA proposal to go to binding arbitration. |
| February 11 | National Labor Relations Board (NLRB) investigator Bernard Levine files complaint against AGH alleging that the hospital committed some unfair labor practices during the seven-month-old strike. |
| February 18 | Ashtabula General Hospital Association holds annual meeting and hears reports from hospital administrator on strike status and reports from the board of trustees and |

Strike-Related Actions 55

|||
|---|---|
| | the chief of staff. Press is barred from the meeting. Four trustees are reelected to new four-year terms. |
| March 3 | AGH announces that certified letters have been mailed to all nurses in hospital bargaining unit notifying them the hospital will start hiring permanent replacements March 9 for all nurses still on strike. |
| March 6 | Hearing is set for March 11 in Ashtabula County Common Pleas Court on whether cars must stop for pickets at AGH or if pickets are to be regulated. |
| March 10 | AGH hires 16 additional nurses. |
| March 11 | After six hours of courtroom negotiations, Common Pleas Judge Joseph Mahoney issues order stipulating that ONA is to refrain from interfering with movement of vehicles entering or leaving the hospital premises, but each vehicle must stop at gate upon entrance or exit. Judge Mahoney also limited number of pickets at each hospital entrance. |
| March 15 | AGH opens full maternity unit. |
| | Negotiation session set for March 25. Both parties in strike clarify that only employees' cars must stop for pickets for a reasonable amount of time. Hospital administrator said hospital hired another nurse. ONA stated it knew of only six nurses who had been hired. |
| March 25 | No progress reported in negotiations. Hospital rejects ONA proposals for modified membership (new nurses would have to join union but could donate their dues to charity) and conditional no-strike clause. |
| March 28 | American Nurses' Association president Barbara Nichols gives striking nurses her support and speaks twice at Kent State University, Ashtabula campus. |
| April 7 | Ashtabula City Board of Health vetoes AGH license application for maternity ward. |
| April 8 | Ashtabula County Common Pleas Court Judge Ronald Vettel issues court injunction to keep the AGH maternity ward open pending city board of health approval of license. |
| April 9 | City board of health president Gerald Severino says before full courtroom at emergency health board meeting that the meeting is illegal and refuses to transact any business. |

|  |  |
|---|---|
|  | Some progress on some minor issues made in negotiations. |
| April 13 | City board of health approves AGH license application to operate the maternity ward. |
| April 24 | Ashtabula County Medical Society announces, in resolution described as the unanimous opinion of its membership, that no individual or group should for any reason be allowed to strike or close a health care facility. |
| May 6 | AGH makes final offer to striking nurses in negotiations. |
| May 9 | ANA rejects hospital's final offer by a 79-to-13 vote. ONA attorney says main reasons for rejection were hospital's position against a union shop and a strike settlement that would cause striking nurses to lose positions they previously held. |
| May 15 | AGH opens additional beds as staff increases. |
| May 15 | No new talks are scheduled between the two sides. Striking nurses plan car wash and bake sale. |
| May 18 | Ashtabula City Manager Clifford McClure calls for continuous negotiations between strikers and hospital. |
| May 22 | Emergency room opens temporarily during fire at Raser Tannery property. |
| May 28 | NLRB files complaint with five allegations that AGH violated part of National Labor Relations Act. |
| May 29 | Both sides meet to talk about why striking nurses rejected hospital's "final offer." |
| July 23 | A 24-hour examination area is established in emergency room area. Physicians can see patients in this area rather than in their offices. |
|  | Talks between AGH administrators and striking Ashtabula nurses broken off indefinitely by Federal Mediation and Conciliation Service (FMCS), "until either side has a change in its bargaining position." |
| August 5 | Hospital reopens emergency room. |
| September 10 | A public hearing on NLRB charges of unfair labor practices against AGH set for January 18. |

*Strike-Related Actions* 57

At a meeting between the two bargaining units, FMCS recommends settlement of strike. All agree contents of settlement will not be released until both sides have decided on it.

September 16  Federal mediator sets 3:00 p.m., September 18 as deadline for decision on mediation proposal. Mediator releases four points of settlement proposal.

September 18  AGH rejects mediator's proposal, while striking nurses accept it. Nurses hold mass meeting at Mt. Carmel Church for discussion of hospital's rejection.

September 21  Federal mediator says compromise recommendation is usually last step in mediation process.

September 25  FMCS ends its involvement with the strike, saying, "There's nothing more we can do."

September 27  Members of Ashtabula Interfaith Clergy offer to act as mediators. Striking nurses reject offer, saying they want outside group.

October 13  ONA accepts offer from group of Youngstown area clergy to hold a fact-finding hearing October 29 to be headed by Monsignor Patrick Breen Malone. AGH rejects the fact-finding offer.

October 15  AGH announces it will invite Monsignor Malone to moderate negotiations between hospital and striking nurses.

October 23  Both negotiating teams meet without moderator or mediator. No progress reported in negotiations.

Monsignor Malone declines to be moderator.

October 24  Ashtabula Interfaith Clergy declines to participate in the fact-finding hearing, reiterating its statement of willingness to act as a mediator in negotiations.

October 29  Fact-finding hearing is held with nurses, citizens, and Youngstown area panel of clergymen. AGH board and administrators decline to attend.

November 15  Solidarity rally at Ashtabula's North Park is held at finish of 56-mile walk. Unions from across state send representatives to rally. An estimated 200 to 250 people attend.

November 18   AGH files contempt-of-court charges against ONA stemming from actions during solidarity rally.

November 19   Striking nurses deny contempt-of-court charges.

December 9    Youngstown clergy panel releases written statement of conclusions and six recommendations for resolution of strike from fact-finding hearing.

December 17   AGH offers striking nurses their jobs in a bargaining session.

December 18   Striking nurses meet to discuss hospital proposal on returning nurses to their prestrike positions.

December 29   Striking nurses hold two meetings for discussion of latest AGH offer.

1982

January 4     Striking nurses hold two separate votes on last AGH offer, which includes a 12 percent pay raise, a 17-month contract, and the return of the nurses to their prestrike positions. Nurses reject hospital offer by undisclosed margin.

January 14    Striking nurses present final offer to AGH.

January 18    Public hearing on NLRB unfair labor practices charges against AGH canceled because of settlement offer signed by hospital.

January 26    NLRB regional director announces that ONA has filed written objections to settlement offered to the NLRB by AGH.

January 26    It is disclosed that the County Common Pleas Court hearing on contempt of court charges filed by AGH against ONA in November has been postponed at request of hospital's attorney.

February 8    Striking nurses reconsider the December 17 AGH proposal and ratify contract by an undisclosed margin. What is referred to as nation's longest nursing strike ends after 570 days.

## Appendix 3-B

# District 1199, National Union of Hospital and Health Care Employees (Bylaws)

## ARTICLE IX: Hearings and Appeals Board

Section 1

It is the objective of the District to provide a democratic and orderly procedure for its members in order to hear and determine grievances, complaints and/or charges and appeals (hereinafter called collective "complaints") brought by or against a member, Organizer, representative or Officer.

The following shall be included among the grounds for filing such complaints: disloyalty of a member to the District; incompetence of an Organizer or representative or Officer; corrupt or unethical practices; dual unionism; conduct calculated to bring the District into disrepute; violation of the District By-Laws and/or National Union Constitution; failure to enforce the collective bargaining agreement; violation of District decisions; scabbing; strike-breaking or violation of wage or work standards established by the District.

To this end, the following Hearing and Appeals Board procedures are established:

(a) In the Hospital, Guild and RN Divisions:
   1. The Delegates of each Chapter shall elect a Hearing Board of not less than three (3) and not more than seven (7) Delegates.
(b) In the Drug Division:
   1. The Delegates of each Area shall elect a Hearing Board of not less than three (3) and not more than seven (7) Delegates.
(c) Each Division Delegates Assembly shall elect five (5) of its Delegates to act as a Division Hearing and Appeals Board.

*Source:* Bylaws of District 1199, National Union of Hospital and Health Care Employees. RWDSU/AFL-CIO adopted May 1974, amended January 1975, March 1976, May 1977, and March 1978.

(d) The Division Appeals Boards, acting together, shall constitute the District Appeals Board.
(e) Each Board shall have a chairman and a secretary elected by the members of the Board.
(f) The Board's decisions shall be in writing and shall require a majority vote. A quorum necessary for a hearing or appeal shall be a majority of the members of the Board.
(g) Any other Appeals Board hereinafter mentioned shall be constituted as provided in these By-Laws.
(h) No person shall sit on any Board who is directly or indirectly involved in the subject matter of the hearing or appeal.
(i) Parties by whom complaints are made and against whom complaints are preferred must appear personally at all stages of the proceedings. They may select a member of the District to act as spokesman on their behalf in presenting their evidence and argument. Should a party fail to appear at a hearing, without having obtained a postponement of the hearing, the Board may proceed in his/her absence and render its decision.
(j) It shall be a condition of membership and the continuation of membership that a member must exhaust all remedies provided for in these By-Laws, and that he/she will not file or prosecute any action in any court, tribunal or other agency until these remedies have been exhausted.

A. Complaints Against a Member, Organizer or Representative

Section 2—Chapter or Area Hearing Board
(a) A member shall have the right to bring a complaint against another member, Organizer or representative for any of the reasons set forth in these By-Laws or the National Union Constitution. A complaint by a member against another member shall be filed with the Vice President assigned to the Chapter or Area in which the member, against whom the complaint is filed, is employed. A complaint against an Organizer or representative shall be filed with the Vice President responsible for supervision of the Organizer or representative.

A hearing shall be held on any such complaint within thirty (30) days of the receipt of the complaint by the Vice President. Notice of the hearing date, time and place shall be sent by the Vice President to the parties concerned in the complaint. It shall be the duty of such Vice President to convene the Board for the hearing.
(b) The Board shall hear the parties and their witnesses and based on all the evidence, oral and documentary, presented, shall render its

decision. The Board may dismiss the complaint, impose a reprimand, a censure and/or fine up to a maximum of $25. It may also recommend to the Division Hearing and Appeals Board a greater fine and/or suspension or expulsion.
(c) The Secretary of the Board shall maintain and preserve the records of the hearing including the Board's decision, copies of which shall be forwarded to the parties, the Vice President and the President of the District. A formal transcript of the hearing need not be made.

Section 3—Division Hearing and Appeals Board
(a) In order to appeal from a decision of the Chapter or Hearing Board, a member must make a request in writing to the Executive Vice President in charge of the Division affected not later than fifteen (15) days from the date of mailing of the decision of the Board below and forward a copy simultaneously to the President of the District. Upon receipt of a timely appeal and/or in the event of a recommendation of greater fine and/or suspension or expulsion as provided in (b) above, the Executive Vice President shall convene the Division Hearing and Appeals Board within thirty (30) days from the date of the Appeal.
(b) Notice of the date, time and place of hearing shall be sent to the parties not later than ten (10) days prior to the date of the hearing.
(c) The Secretary of the Board shall maintain and preserve all records of hearings and appeals. A formal transcript of the hearing or appeal need not be made.
(d) The Board shall render its decision within ten (10) days from the date of the conclusion of the hearing and shall forward copies of its decision to the parties, the Executive Vice President and the President of the District.
(e) The Board may sustain, modify or reverse the decision of the Chapter or Area Hearing Board, and may accept, modify or reject the recommendations, if any, of the said Board.

Section 4—District Appeals Board
(a) In order to appeal from a decision of the Division Hearing and Appeals Board, a party must make a request in writing to the President of the District not later than fifteen (15) days from the date of mailing of the decision of the Board below. Upon receipt of a timely appeal, the President shall convene the District Appeals Board within thirty (30) days from the date of the appeal. Notice of the hearing date, time and place shall be forwarded to the parties involved no later than ten (10) days prior to the date of the hearing.

(b) The appeal before the District Appeals Board shall be limited to deciding (1) whether the hearings below were held in conformity to these By-Laws, and, if so, (2) whether the decisions rendered were fair and reasonable. If the Board decides that the hearings below were improper, in either respect, it may dismiss the complaint, or in the alternative, order a new hearing. If the Board decides that the hearings below were proper and in accord with these By-Laws, it may either sustain, modify or reverse the decision or decisions made below. The decision of this Board shall be rendered within ten (10) days from the date of conclusion of the appeal and shall be forwarded to the parties and the President of the District.

Section 5—National Union Executive Board and RWDSU Convention
Any further appeals must be made in accordance with the National Union Constitution which provides for appeals to the National Union Executive Board and the RWDSU convention as follows:
(a) Within fifteen (15) days from the date of the final decision under the By-Laws procedure, the accused shall send a written request for appeal to the Executive Board of the National Union. Such request should be addressed to the Secretary-Treasurer of the National Union. The Secretary-Treasurer shall inform the President of the National Union of the request for appeal, who shall in turn see to it that the Executive Board designates a Trial Board of five (5) members and sets a date of hearing within forty-five (45) days from the date the request for appeal is received.

A notice of hearing shall be sent to parties involved at least fifteen (15) days prior to the date of hearing. The hearing shall be held and conducted as provided in the National Union Constitution.
(b) If the accused is still unsatisfied he/she may appeal from the decision of the National Union Executive Board to the Executive Board of the Convention of the Retail, Wholesale, Department Store Union (RWDSU). Such request for appeal shall be forwarded in writing by the accused to the Secretary of the RWDSU and to the President of the National Union within fifteen (15) days from the date of receipt by the accused of the decision of the National Union Executive Board. This appeal shall be held as provided for in the Constitution of the RWDSU.

Appendix 3-C

# 263 NLRB NO. 141: United States of America before the National Labor Relations Board

MACHINISTS LOCAL 1327,
INTERNATIONAL ASSOCIATION OF
MACHINISTS AND AEROSPACE WORKERS,
AFL—CIO, DISTRICT LODGE 115
(Dalmo Victor)
  and
VIOLA LAPINSKI, an Individual   Case 20—CB—3488
HILDA HALL, an Individual   Case 20—CB—3491
POLMYRA GOMES, an Individual   Case 20—CB—3629

SUPPLEMENTAL DECISION AND ORDER

On August 29, 1977, the Board issued a Decision and Order in this proceeding[1] in which it found that a constitutional provision adopted by Respondent, Machinists Local 1327, International Association of Machinists and Aerospace Workers, AFL—CIO, District Lodge 115, did not constitute a restriction on a member's right to resign from Respondent but rather constituted an unlawful attempt by Respondent to restrict the postresignation conduct of former members.[2] Accordingly, the Board con-

---

**NOTE:** This decision has been overturned by the U.S. Court of Appeals for the 9th Circuit. In February 1984 the court decided that a union may restrict the right of members to resign during a strike and may fine employees who quit the union to return to work for the struck employer.

---

[1] 231 NLRB 719.
[2] The constitutional provision provided as follows:
  *Improper Conduct of a Member* . . . Accepting employment in any capacity in an establishment where a strike or lockout exists as recognized under this Constitution, without permission. Resignation shall not relieve a member of his obligation to refrain from accepting employment at the establishment for the duration of the strike or lockout within 14 days preceding its commencement. Where observance of a primary picket line is required, resignation shall not relieve a member of his obligation to observe the primary picket line for its duration if the resignation occurs during the period that the picket line is maintained or within 14 days preceding its establishment.

cluded that Respondent had violated Section 8(b)(1)(A) of the Act by imposing fines on the Charging Parties, Viola Lapinski, Hilda Hall, and Polmyra Gomes, for resigning their membership in Respondent and returning to work during the course of a strike. It then ordered Respondent to rescind the fines levied against Lapinski, Hall, and Gomes and to refund to them, with interest, any moneys they may have paid as a result of the unlawfully imposed fines. Thereafter, Respondent filed a petition for review of the Board's Decision and Order with the United States Court of Appeals for the Ninth Circuit and the Board filed a cross-petition for enforcement of its Order.

On October 10, 1979, the court issued its opinion in this case,[3] denying enforcement of the Board's Order on the ground that Respondent's constitutional provision was, contrary to the Board's finding, a restriction on a member's right to resign and not an unlawful attempt to restrict a former member's postresignation conduct. However, noting that the Board had not had the opportunity to determine whether the provision, as construed by the court, was valid, the case was remanded by the court to the Board for further proceedings consistent with its opinion.[4]

On December 12, 1979, the Board, having determined that this and another case,[5] involving the right of a labor organization to impose restrictions on a member's right to resign, presented issues of importance in the administration of the National Labor Relations Act, as amended, scheduled oral arguments for January 16, 1980. Thereafter, on January 16, 1980, Respondent, the General Counsel, the Charging Parties, and the American Federation of Labor and Congress of Industrial Organizations[6] presented their oral arguments before the Board.

The Board, having duly considered the entire record in this case and the oral arguments presented to it, finds as follows:

Pursuant to the court's remand, we are here asked to decide whether a union can, pursuant to an internal rule prohibiting resignations during a strike or within 14 days preceding its commencement, lawfully impose a fine on members who tendered resignations and returned to work during

---

[3]608 F.2d 1219.

[4]We have accepted the remand from the Court of Appeals for the purpose of determining the validity of art. L., sec. III, as a restriction on resignation. We accept the court's determination that this provision is a restriction on resignation only as the law of the case. We otherwise adhere to our earlier determination that this clause constitutes a restriction on post-resignation conduct.

[5]*Pattern Makers' League of North America, AFL-CIO, and its Rockford and Beloit Associations (Rockford-Beloit Pattern Jobbers Association)*, Case 33-CB-1132.

[6]The American Federation of Labor and Congress of Industrial Organizations appeared as *amicus curiae* and argued orally on behalf of the Respondent's position.

the course of a strike in apparent violation of the union rule prohibiting such resignations. Respondent asserts that, under the proviso to Section 8(b)(1)(A) of the Act,[7] its constitutional provision is valid and enforceable and that, consequently, the fines imposed thereunder are lawful. The Charging Parties, on the other hand, contend that the restriction in question unreasonably interferes with their Section 7 rights and that the attempt to impose and collect fines under such a provision violates Section 8(b)(1)(A) of the Act. We agree with the Charging Parties' contention.

Initially, we note that in *NLRB v. Allis-Chalmers Manufacturing Co.*, 388 U.S. 175 (1967), the Supreme Court held that a union may, without violating the Act, impose fines on persons who, while retaining full membership rights in the union, cross an authorized picket line and return to work during a strike in contravention of a union rule proscribing such conduct. The Supreme Court found that the right to impose such fines was incidental to the contractual relationship between the union and its members.[8] Once the member lawfully resigns, however, the union's control over that former member ceases and any attempt to impose and collect a fine from that former member for engaging in conduct prohibited by a union rule violates Section 8(b)(1)(A) of the Act.[9] In both *Granite State* and *Booster Lodge, supra*, the Supreme Court found that the union's constitution and bylaws contained no provision restricting a member's right to resign and that, consequently, union attempts to fine former members for crossing an authorized picket line violate Section 8(b)(1)(A) of the Act. Because of the absence of any articulated restriction on a member's right to resign, the Supreme Court in *Granite State* and *Booster Lodge* expressly left open the question, now before us, of the extent to which a "contractual restriction on a member's right to resign may be limited by the Act."[10]

---

[7]Sec. 8(b)(1)(A) of the Act provides that it "shall be an unfair labor practice for a labor organization or its agents—(1) to restrain or coerce (A) employees in the exercise of the rights guaranteed in section 7: *Provided,* that This paragraph shall not impair the right of a labor organization to prescribe its own rules with respect to the acquisition or retention of membership therein. . . ." Sec. 7 of the Act guarantees to employees the right to organize and to engage in "other concerted activities for the purpose of collective bargaining or other mutual aid or protection," and also the right to refrain from such activities.

[8]In *Allis-Chalmers, supra*, the Supreme Court did not rely on the proviso to Sec. 8(b)(1)(A) but focused its attention instead on the legislative history of the phrase "restrain or coerce" in that section of the Act.

[9]*NLRB v. Granite State Joint Board, Textile Workers Union of America, Local 1029, AFL-CIO [International Paper Box Machine Co.]*, 409 U.S. 213 (1972); *Booster Lodge No. 405, International Association of Machinists and Aerospace Workers, AFL-CIO [Boeing Co.] v. NLRB*, 412 U.S. 84 (1973).

[10]412 U.S. at 88; 409 U.S. at 217.

Addressing this question requires us to balance two fundamental principles upon which our labor laws rest, principles that inherently conflict. The first is the right of an employee to refrain from collective activity, a right specifically codified in Section 7 of the Act. The second is the legitimate interest of a certified representative in protecting employees it represents who have joined together in collective economic activity. Reasonable rules governing the acquisition or retention of membership in the union, or resignation therefrom, are necessary to protect that interest. These concerns are fundamental to the overall scheme of the Act and are recognized in the proviso to Section 8(b)(1)(A).

Guided by the Supreme Court's interpretations in this area, we find that neither of these interests is absolute. Thus, a union may impose reasonable time restrictions on the right of members to resign from the union, to facilitate the orderly management of its affairs, including times when a strike may be imminent or is under way. But, in our judgment, the restrictions imposed by Respondent here are unreasonable in that they fail to protect sufficiently the interest of individual employees and are, therefore, impermissible, and we so find.

A union's responsible and operational effectiveness is a key component of national labor policy and enables it to better represent the majority of its members in the collective-bargaining process. A union's most powerful economic weapon—the strike, approved by a majority of its members—is a right embedded in the Act. For a union to determine effectively whether to exercise its right to strike against an employer, it must be able to know with some degree of certainty whether solidarity among its members will be maintained. Indeed, the Supreme Court in *Allis-Chalmers, supra,* recognized that a union's interest in solidarity constitutes a fundamental part of our federal labor policy. The Court there noted that:

> Integral to this federal labor policy has been the power in the chosen union to protect against erosion of its status under that policy through reasonable discipline of members who violate rules and regulations governing membership. That power is particularly vital when the members engage in strikes.[11]

A literal reading of Section 7 might appear to permit a union member employee to pick and choose among the union actions he wishes to support without fear of union-imposed sanctions for refusing to participate in collective activities of which he does not approve. It is already settled, however, that Section 7 is not nearly that sweeping. The Supreme Court's

---

[11] 388 U.S. 175, 181.

endorsement of the proposition in *Allis-Chalmers,* that a union may discipline members for crossing a picket line, lays to rest any claim to an absolute right to refrain from union activity, and supports our finding that certain limited restrictions may be imposed on the right to resign from a union.

It is therefore apparent that a union's need to reflect the continuing will of a majority of its members, especially during a strike, reflects not only a legitimate union interest, but also implements a right inherent in the statutory scheme of our labor laws. This does not mean, however, that any rule which furthers this legitimate union interest can be deemed to be valid and enforceable.

Although, as Respondent correctly points out, the proviso to Section 8(b)(1)(A) of the Act leaves it free to enact rules pertaining to the acquisition and retention of membership, the Supreme Court has found that "if the rule invades or frustrates an overriding policy of the labor laws the rule may not be enforced, even by fine or expulsion, without violating Section 8(b)(1).''[12] That overriding interest is the right of an individual employee, once having joined a union, to resign from membership, which may therefore be subject only to a reasonable time limitation.

Respondent's rule prohibiting resignations during the entire course of a strike or within 14 days preceding its commencement does indeed constitute an intrusion into an employee's Section 7 right to resign. Consequently, we must determine if that rule is a reasonable restriction or whether it impermissibly contravenes other matters of concern under the national labor policy.[13]

As noted, Section 7 of the Act specifically grants employees the right to refrain from concerted activities. This right to refrain, as the Ninth

---

[12]*Scofield, et al. v. NLRB* , 394 U.S. 423, 429 (1969).

[13]In Member Fanning's view the issue in these cases is the right of an employee to exercise his Section 7 right to refrain from collective activity by working during a strike. Union coercion of an employee in the exercise of that right is, *prima facie,* a violation of Section 8(b)(1)(A). However, an employee who has joined a labor organization, enjoys full membership in that organization, and has agreed not to engage in strikebreaking, may be disciplined by internal union sanctions for violation of that undertaking. *NLRB v. Allis-Chalmers Manufacturing Co.,* 388 U.S. 175. Once the employee lawfully resigns from the union, the union's power over him ends. *NLRB v. Granite State Joint Board,* 409 U.S. 213. The significance of membership in this context is simply as a defense to what otherwise would be a plain unfair labor practice: coercion or restraint of an employee in the exercise of a Section 7 right to work during a strike. The question is not the legality of restrictions on resignation, but rather whether or not the restrictions are effective in this context. Thus, in Member Fanning's view, it is the right to refrain from collective activity by working despite a strike—not the "right" to resign—which must be balanced against the right of the labor organization and the striking employees to wage an effective strike.

Circuit correctly points out, encompasses the right of a member to resign from a union having once joined.[14] Further, this right to resign is not forever and irrevocably lost merely because an employee chooses to become a union member.[15] On the other hand, the right to resign is not a right to abandon instantaneously the union and the fellow members who have determined to exercise collectively their protected right to strike. A union faced with resignations during a strike maintains a continuing obligation to represent all employees in the unit, and to protect the interests of those employees who maintain their membership in the union and continue to honor the strike. Thus, important statutory and policy considerations compel us to balance the right to resign against the legitimate interest of the union, and the majority of its membership, which supports the strike, in maintaining its effectiveness. We cannot, as the Charging Parties would have us do, read Section 7 in isolation from the rest of the Act.

In view of the balancing of interests required, we turn to the question of whether a union rule may permissibly differentiate between strike and nonstrike periods. The Supreme Court, in *Scofield, supra,* stated that union members must be free to leave a union to escape membership conditions that they consider onerous.[16] We find nothing in that decision or, indeed, in any of the subsequent Supreme Court decisions concerning this issue, to suggest that a member's right to leave the union and escape the rule could be limited to periods when a strike is not in progress. Rather, quite the converse appears true. In *Granite State,* the Supreme Court recognized that there may be circumstances under which a member might feel compelled to resign during a strike:

> Events occurring after the calling of a strike may have unsettling effects, leading a member who voted to strike to change his mind. The likely duration of the strike may increase the specter of hardship to his family; the ease with which the employer replaces the strikers may make the strike seem less provident.[17]

---

[14]608 F.2d 1219, 1221. See also *NLRB v. Martin A. Gleason, Inc.,* 534 F.2d 466, 476 (2d Cir. 1976). Member Fanning does not here endorse the view that there is an independent Section 7 right to resign from a labor organization: Divorced from the employment relation, membership is an internal union matter.

[15]See *Local 1384, United Automobile, Aerospace, Agricultural Implement Workers, UAW (Ex-Cell-O Corporation),* 227 NLRB 1045, 1050 (1977).

[16]See *Local Lodge No. 1994, International Association of Machinists and Aerospace Workers, AFL-CIO (O.K. Tool Company, Inc.),* 215 NLRB 651, 653 (1974).

[17]409 U.S. 213, 217.

The Court, noting that there were no restraints on a member's right to resign in that case, went on to state that "the vitality of Section 7 requires that the member be free to refrain in November from the actions he endorsed in May and that his Section 7 rights are not lost by a union's plea for solidarity or by its pressures for conformity and submission to its regime."[18]

Clearly then, the Supreme Court's remarks in *Granite State*, read in conjunction with the *Scofield* requirement that union members must be free to leave the union and escape the rule, lead inescapably to the conclusion that a member's right to resign from a union applies both to strike and nonstrike situations.[19] We hold today that a union rule which limits the right of a union member to resign only to nonstrike periods constitutes an unreasonable restriction on a member's Section 7 right to resign.

In sum, the balancing of competing interests expressed in the Act has led us to find that the right of union members to resign is not absolute. A union may place some reasonable limitation on the right to resign so long as such rules are applicable during both strike and nonstrike periods. In assessing the reasonableness of such rules, we recognize that in a strike context a union may need to reassess its bargaining strategy, to adjust its conduct at the bargaining table, and to consider whether to commence, or to continue, a strike in the face of one or more resignations based on members' unwillingness to support the strike. Moreover, there may also be administrative matters associated with the termination of membership which the union is entitled to a reasonable period to complete.

Accordingly, in order to vindicate its vital interest in assessing its strength throughout the course of a strike, and to protect those employees who have committed themselves to exercise their right to strike, we find that a union is entitled to reasonable notice of the effective date of resignations which occur immediately before or during a strike.

We realize that what may constitute a reasonable period for protecting such institutional interests under one set of circumstances may be unreasonable under another. Nonetheless, we find it salutary to set forth a general rule for the behavior of parties in this area. Having carefully considered the competing interests involved, we find that a rule which restricts a union member's right to resign for a period not to exceed 30 days after the tender of such a resignation reflects a reasonable accommodation between the right of union members to resign from the union

---

[18]*Id.* at 217–218.
[19]Indeed, the Board in *Ex-Cell-O, supra*, found unenforceable a union rule that, *inter alia*, accorded no weight to the competing considerations which might have necessitated the resignation of members during a strike.

and return to work, and the union's responsibility to protect the interests of employees who maintain their membership, as well as its need to dispose of administrative matters arising from such resignations.[20] Such a rule gives clear guidance to employees and unions alike concerning their respective responsibilities and further adds stability to the field of labor relations.[21]

As stated above, the Ninth Circuit found that the constitutional provision in question here constitutes a restriction on resignations.[22] We conclude that Respondent's constitutional provision as a restriction on resignations is unenforceable. Thus, Respondent's rule permits union members to resign only if the resignations are submitted no later than 14 days preceding the commencement of a strike. However, if a member chose not to exercise his right to resign or, for whatever reason, failed to do so prior to the 14-day period preceding the strike, the member was locked into the strike and prohibited from resigning until the strike ended. Such a rule is clearly contrary to our finding here and cannot be enforced. Consequently, Respondent's attempt to impose and to enforce fines on the Charging Parties pursuant to such a rule violates Section 8(b)(1)(A) of the Act. Accordingly, the Respondent shall be ordered to comply with the Board's Order as set forth in the underlying Decision herein.

ORDER

Pursuant to Section 10(c) of the National Labor Relations Act, as amended, the National Labor Relations Board hereby orders that the Respondent, Machinists Local 1327, International Association of Machinists and Aerospace Workers, AFL-CIO, District Lodge 115, Burlingame, California, its

---

[20]Obviously, where the member has not been apprised of the existence of such a rule prior to tendering his resignation, then the member's resignation becomes effective immediately rather than upon the expiration of the 30-day period following such tender of resignation. See *General Teamsters Local 439, International Brotherhood of Teamsters, Chauffeurs, Warehousemen & Helpers of America (Loomis Courier Service, Inc.)*, 237 NLRB 220, 223 (1978); *Ex-Cell-O Corporation*, 227 NLRB at 1048. Further, where the members have been apprised of the existence of such a rule, the running of the 30-day period before the resignation becomes effective must be triggered solely by the member's notice to the union, and not contingent on any other obligations.

[21]We realize, however, that under extraordinary circumstances, a union may need more than the 30 days found reasonable herein to dispose of the administrative matters arising from the resignations. In those cases, the Board will determine whether or not circumstances exist warranting a longer period of time.

[22]We adopt this finding as law of the case only. See fn. 4, *supra*.

officers, agents, and representatives, shall take the action set forth in the Board's Order at 231 NLRB 719, dated August 29, 1977.
Dated, Washington, D.C., September 10, 1982.

John H. Fanning, Member

Don A. Zimmerman, Member
(SEAL) NATIONAL LABOR RELATIONS BOARD


CHAIRMAN VAN DE WATER and MEMBER HUNTER, concurring:
We agree with our colleagues in the majority that Respondent violated Section 8(b)(1)(A) by its imposition of fines against employees who resigned their union membership and returned to work during the strike. We also agree that Respondent's constitutional provision is an unreasonable restriction on the members' right to resign from the Union. Unlike our colleagues, however, we would not find reasonable a 30-day limitation on the effective date of an employee's resignation from a union.[23] As set forth below, we believe the 30-day rule promulgated by the majority is an arbitrary exercise of this Board's authority that is premised upon faulty analysis and rationale. The few arguments presented in support of the rule, in our view, are contrary to fundamental principles embodied in our Act, inconsistent with the teachings of relevant Supreme Court decisions, and represent a transparent effort to achieve a legislative result rather than a reasoned legal conclusion. Contrary to our colleagues, we would find any restriction imposed upon a union member's right to resign to be unreasonable and, therefore, we would find the imposition of any fines or other discipline premised upon such restrictions to be violative of Section 8(b)(1)(A).

---

[23] Although our response to the majority is cast in terms of the majority's 30-day rule, we note with dismay that the "rule" is not so precisely contained. Thus, at fn. 21 of its Decision, the majority states that "extraordinary circumstances" may justify a restriction of longer than 30 days. Accordingly, despite the expressed desire for a "salutary" rule that provides "clear guidance," the majority has constructed a loophole tailor-made for enterprising litigators that will ensure continued litigation and uncertainty in this area.

The starting point for meaningful analysis of the issue presented here is the quartet of cases[24] decided by the Supreme Court that examine the union's authority to enforce its rules against member and nonmember employees within the confines of Section 8(b)(1) and related provisions of the Act. A rather simple framework can be constructed from these holdings: (1) If an employee is not a full union member, the union may not enforce its rules against that employee; (2) If an employee is a full union member the union can, within specified limits, enforce its reasonable rules against the employee-member; and (3) if an employee resigns from the union, the union loses its authority to enforce its rules against the employee. Simply stated, the question presented here is whether a union can lawfully enforce a rule that restricts an employee's ability to place himself into the third category. In other words, can a union rule be used to compel an employee to remain subject to union discipline for 30 days beyond the employee's expressed desire to sever ties with the union?[25]

In resolving the issue before us, we believe the majority has failed to look beyond the Court's specific holdings and examine the principles and concepts that led to the particular results, for the Court's decisions contain findings and determinations that are clearly applicable to the issue before us. Indeed, the Court has established a specific test, largely ignored by the majority, by which the lawfulness of a union's enforcement of its rules against members and nonmembers is to be tested. We believe that a proper application of these principles and the specific test prescribed by the Court effectively preclude this Board from sanctioning a rule that restricts the right of resignation.

In *Allis-Chalmers,* the Court held that a union could discipline its full members for returning to work during a strike. In the simplest terms the Court ruled that a union's reasonable enforcement of a legitimate rule against its full members does not constitute restraint and coercion within the meaning of Section 8(b)(1).[26] In so ruling, the Court articulated a bright

---

[24]*NLRB v. Allis-Chalmers Manufacturing Co.,* 388 U.S. 175 (1967); *Scofield, et al. v. NLRB,* 394 U.S. 423 (1969); *NLRB v. Granite State Joint Board, Textile Workers Union of America, Local 1029, AFL-CIO [International Paper Box Machine Co.],* 409 U.S. 213 (1972); *Booster Lodge No. 405, International Association of Machinists and Aerospace Workers, AFL-CIO [Boeing Co.] v. NLRB,* 412 U.S. 84 (1973).

[25]Concededly, the Court has not specifically passed upon the precise issue of whether a union may restrict its members' right to resign. This does not, however, give rise to what appears to be a tacit assumption by the majority, i.e., that the Board has free rein to fashion a rule that satisfies some personal sense of equity and balance. Although the actual holdings of the Court may not bind us here, the principles established in reaching those holdings cannot be ignored.

[26]In its characterization of the Court's holding, we fear the majority has confused the Court's ruling with its own desire to reach a particular result. Thus, the majority states, "The Supreme Court's endorsement of the proposition in *Allis-Chalmers,* that a union may

line distinction between "internal" and "external" union actions with the former being insulated from the proscriptions of Section 8(b)(1). The Court defined internal actions as those applying to full union members pursuant to a nonarbitrary rule aimed at achieving a legitimate union objective.[27] External actions, i.e., those proscribed by Section 8(b)(1), were defined as those aimed at interfering with an employee's employment status[28] or at interfering with the rights of nonmembers or employees outside the bargaining unit.[29] Having established this distinction, the Court found that the union's enforcement of its rules prohibiting the return to work during a strike against its full members was an internal matter and, therefore, insulated from the proscriptions of Section 8(b)(1).

Significantly, for our purposes here, the Court's establishment of a dichotomy between "internal" and "external" matters by which it sanctioned union restrictions on employee-members returning to work during a strike was not predicated upon any "balancing" of conflicting rights between unions and employees. Nor was the decision predicated upon a construction of Section 8(b)(1)(A)'s proviso which allows a union to establish rules for the acquisition or retention of membership. Instead, the Court's ruling was premised upon a detailed review of the Act's legislative history and an analysis of the Act's interrelated provisions. Accordingly, the decisive importance of whether a union action is internal or external in nature in determining whether enforcement of a union rule violates Section B(b)(1)(A) is a concept embedded in the very fabric of our Act.

The concepts established in *Allis-Chalmers* were reiterated and expanded in *Scofield* where the Court again sanctioned the enforcement of what was determined to be a legitimate union rule on the basis that it was an internal union matter.[30] In so doing, the Court reiterated that a union's authority to discipline employee-members is limited to actions that are purely inter-

---

discipline members for crossing a picket line, lays to rest any claim to an absolute right to refrain from union activity, and supports our finding that certain limited restrictions may be imposed on the right to resign from a union." In reality, as noted above, the Court held only that such union discipline of its full members is not restraint and coercion within the meaning of Sec. 8(b)(1). While this holding may well mean that a full union member does not have an absolute right to refrain, without penalty, from concerted or other union activities, it simply does not necessarily follow that nonmembers do not enjoy an absolute right to refrain or that once a member acts to sever ties with the union that his Section 7 rights are any less absolute than if he never had joined the union.

[27]388 U.S. at 195.
[28]*Ibid.*
[29]*Id.* at fn. 25 and accompanying text.
[30]The union rule at issue imposed production ceilings and provided that union members who exceeded these ceilings would be subject to fines.

nal in nature.[31] In addition, the Court, for the first time, precisely articulated the test to be utilized in evaluating the lawfulness of attempts to enforce union rules. Thus, the Court held that:

> § 8(b)(1) leaves a union free to enforce a properly adopted rule which reflects a legitimate union interest, impairs no policy Congress has embedded in the labor laws, and is reasonably enforced against union members who are free to leave the union and escape the rule.[32]

In *Granite State*,[33] the Court confronted a situation where the union sought to enforce its legitimate rule against returning to work during a strike in an external manner, i.e., against nonmembers. Applying the *Scofield* test, the Court found that such efforts violated Section 8(b)(1)(A). Because, in our view, the Court's decision in *Granite State* effectively undermines the purported bases for establishing a 30-day limit on resignations, we feel it is necessary to give that decision more than the cursory treatment provided by the majority.

In *Granite State,* the union membership, several days before the existing collective-bargaining agreement expired, authorized a strike if agreement on a new contract was not reached by a specific date. No agreement was reached, and a strike commenced. A few days into the strike the employees met and *unanimously* adopted a resolution which provided that a member who "aided or abetted the Company during the strike" would be subject to a fine of up to $2,000. Six weeks into the strike, two members resigned their union membership and returned to work. Beginning six months later, 29 members resigned and returned to work. The union imposed fines against all 31 employees.

The Board held that the fines against all 31 employees violated Section 8(b)(1)(A).[34] The Court of Appeals for the First Circuit, however, denied enforcement of the Board's Order.[35] The First Circuit reasoned that, because the employees had mutually relied upon each other's commitment to strike, all employees were bound to honor the strike under a "mutual subscription" theory. The court also advanced the theory that a union's interest in strike solidarity could be reconciled with Section 7's right to refrain by treating an employee's agreement to join a strike and impose sanctions for strikebreaking as a waiver of his or her Section 7 right.

---

[31]394 U.S. at 435–436.
[32]*Id*. U.S. at 430.
[33]409 U.S. 213 (1972).
[34]187 NLRB 636 (1970).
[35]446 F.2d 369 (1st Cir. 1971).

Responding to the *Scofield* test, the First Circuit explained that it did not read *Scofield* as requiring that a union member be "free to leave the union and escape the rule" at any time and under all circumstances. Nor did the court find a deleterious impact on federal labor policy, since the court concluded that the employee-members had waived their Section 7 rights.

In an eight-to-one decision,[36] the Supreme Court reversed the First Circuit and found that the fines imposed violated Section 8(b)(1)(A). In its decision, the Court began by reiterating the *Scofield* test and by again emphasizing the distinction between a union's internal and external actions. As for the latter concept, the Court stated:

> The *Scofield* case indicates that the power of the union over the member is certainly no greater than the union-member contract. Where a member lawfully resigns from a union and thereafter engages in conduct which the union rule proscribes, the union commits an unfair labor practice when it seeks enforcement of fines for that conduct. That is to say, when there is a lawful dissolution of a union-member relation, the union has no more control over the former member than it has over the man in the street.[37]

The court then addressed the First Circuit's contention that the employees had waived their Section 7 rights by the strike vote and the authorization of fines for strikebreaking, stating: "We give that factor little weight."[38] In this regard, and also in response to the lower court's reliance upon the union's interest in strike solidarity, the Court stated:

> Events occurring after the calling of a strike may have unsettling effects, leading a member who voted to strike to change his mind. The likely duration of the strike may increase the specter of hardship to his family; the ease with which the employer replaces the strikers may make the strike seem less provident. . . . [W]e conclude that the vitality of § 7 requires that the member be free to refrain in November from the actions he endorsed in May and that *his § 7 rights are not lost by a union's plea for solidarity or*

---

[36]Chief Justice Burger rendered a concurring opinion which provided, *inter alia*, that "where the individual employee has freely chosen to exercise his legal right to abandon the privileges of union membership, it is not for us to impose the obligations of continued membership." 409 U.S. at 218 (Chief Justice Burger, concurring.)

[37]409 U.S. at 217.

[38]*Id.*

*by its pressures for conformity and submission to its regime.* [409 U.S. at 217–218. Emphasis supplied.][39]

Finally, in *Booster Lodge*,[40] a unanimous Court[41] found that the union violated the Act by fining employees who returned to work after resigning their membership. In large part, the Court simply applied its past decisions in this area. Of significance, however, is the Court's disposal of the union's claim that its rule had been consistently interpreted to bind an employee to a strike notwithstanding his resignation. After noting that no such interpretation had been found by the Board and the court of appeals, the Court stated:

> But we are no more disposed to find an implied postresignation commitment from the strikebreaking proscription in the Union's constitution here than we were to find it from the employees' participation in the strike vote and ratification of penalties in *[Granite State]*. [412 U.S. at 89.]

From the foregoing, it is plain that there are certain fundamental principles that must be applied in evaluating a union rule restricting an employee-member's right to resign for a 30-day (or any other) time period. First, the rule must be nonarbitrary and aimed at advancing a legitimate union interest. Second, there is inherent in the very fabric of our Act a bright line distinction between internal and external union actions. So long as the union action is wholly internal in nature, it may be lawful. When its reach becomes external, it runs afoul of Section 8(b)(1)(A). Third, a union rule can survive scrutiny only if it does not impair a policy Congress has embedded in the labor laws. Fourth, union rules that have been found lawful in the past have contained the implicit safeguard which provides that the rule must be reasonably enforced against union members who are free to leave the union and escape the rule. Finally, once an employee becomes a union member, he cannot be bound forever to the rules and coercive force of the union, but must be allowed to change his mind based upon subsequent developments. We contend that, when measured against these standards, the 30-day rule espoused by our colleagues must fall.

---

[39]The oft-quoted "May to November" change-of-mind period is somewhat inaccurate inasmuch as two of the fined employees resigned within 6 weeks of the strike's commencement and the fines against them were found violative of Section 8(b)(1)(A).
[40]412 U.S. 84 (1973).
[41]Justice Blackmun, who was the lone dissenter in *Granite State*, rendered a concurring opinion.

Unfortunately, however, before proceeding to what we deem to be the appropriate analysis, we are compelled to respond to the majority on its own terms because so many of the fundamental concepts enumerated above are ignored by our colleagues. Instead of a meaningful legal analysis, the majority presents what amounts to a seemingly self-evident syllogism, which goes as follows: (1) employees have a Section 7 right to refrain from concerted activities; (2) unions have a legitimate interest in maintaining strike solidarity and protecting the interests of employees who honor a strike decision; (3) neither the employees' rights nor the union's interests are absolute; (4) if the Board selects a time period for restricting resignations, the conflicting interests will be accommodated and justice will be served. As is often the case with syllogistic arguments, the conclusion only follows if all the premises are correct. We respectfully submit that some of our colleagues' premises are fatally flawed and that purported "balancing" is little more than a preemptive striking of a compromise best left in the legislative arena.

Clearly, we agree with the first premise. The text of Section 7, by its very terms, grants employees the *right* to refrain from union and other concerted activities.[42] Nor can there be serious quarrel with the premise that unions have a legitimate *interest* in maintaining strike solidarity and protecting the interests of striking employees.

The third premise is another matter, however, since there we find a fundamental flaw in the majority's analysis. For when our colleagues adopt the proposition that neither the employee *rights* at issue nor the union *interests* being advanced are absolute, they implicitly equate the express Section 7 rights of employees with a union's institutional interest in strike

---

[42]Specifically, two related Section 7 rights are involved here—the right to resign membership in a union, and the right to return to work during a strike. *Booster Lodge, supra,* 412 U.S. at 87–88; *Granite State, supra,* 409 U.S. at 217–218; *NLRB v. Machinists Local 1327, International Association of Machinists and Aerospace Workers, AFL-CIO, District Lodge 115 [Dalmo Victor],* 608 F.2d 1219, 1221 (9th Cir. 1979); *NLRB v. International Association of Machinists and Aerospace Workers, Merritt Graham Lodge No. 1871 [General Dynamics Corp.],* 575 F.2d 54, 55 (2d Cir. 1978).

The preservation of employee freedom in this sphere is also manifested in Section 8(b)(2) and the second proviso to Section 8(a)(3). For those provisions work to insure that no employee can be compelled to become a full union member, thereby leaving an employee who so chooses free to refrain from union or other concerted activities. *NLRB v. General Motors Corp.,* 373 U.S. 734, 742 (1963): " 'Membership' as a condition of employment is whittled down to its financial core." Thus, the Board has held, with court approval, that a union violates Section 8(b)(1)(A) when it refuses to accept the resignations of employees on the ground that full membership is a condition of employment. *United Stanford Employees, Local 680, Service Employees International Union, AFL-CIO (The Leland Stanford Junior University),* 232 NLRB 326 (1977), *enfd.* 602 F.2d 980 (9th Cir. 1979).

solidarity, thereby setting the stage for their purported "balancing" of "conflicting interests." Yet, such an equation ignores the fact that it is not the mere existence of conflict between labor disputants that mandates and justifies an "accommodation" or "balancing." Instead, the substantial diminution of express statutory rights is warranted only when the statutory right collides with a corresponding *right* of relatively equal import and legal significance.[43] We contend most strongly that the express Section 7 rights of employees are surely more than mere "interests" subject to limitation because their operation somehow impinges upon the institutional desires of a union. Conversely, a union's institutional *interests,* to our knowledge, have never been elevated to the point where they stand on equal footing with, and, indeed, override and negate the fundamental protections of Section 7. Thus, under the banner of "balancing," our colleagues negate for 30 days the express employee protections afforded by one of the Act's most important provisions. One can only wonder what other rights granted by the Act will be diminished or eliminated upon the majority's discovery that they too conflict with a "legitimate interest" of a union or an employer. In short, by equating institutional "interests" with statutory "rights" and utilizing the existence of "conflict" between disputants to justify reduction of the Act's protections, we respectfully submit that our colleagues are engaging in legislating rather than interpreting our Act's intent and objectives. This they may not do.

Even granting the premise that employees' statutory rights and the union's institutional interests are subject to balancing and mutual accommodation, we suggest that the majority's rule does not give sufficient consideration to all of the relevant circumstances. Thus, it seems to us that the majority underplays the significance of the practical realities facing an employee in a strike situation that the Court enumerated in *Granite State* in support of the concept that a union member must "be free to refrain in November from actions endorsed in May."[44] Indeed, as noted in footnote 39, *supra,* this period is more accurately one of 6 weeks. For nowhere in the majority opinion is there any meaningful attempt to explain why a member would not be free to refrain from an action he agreed to 30 days earlier but is free to do after 42 days.[45] Nor does the majority appear

---

[43]There are, of course, rights of sufficient import and significance to justify the imposition of some limitations on employees' Section 7 rights. See, e.g., *NLRB v. The Babcock & Wilcox Company,* 351 U.S. 105 (1956), which strikes a balance between employees' Section 7 rights and the property rights of individuals that are grounded in Common Law and the Constitution.

[44]409 U.S. at 217–218.

[45]Indeed, apart from stating the need for a "salutary" rule that eliminates confusion, we are at a total loss in perceiving the significance of 30 days as a benchmark. Why is 10 days

to take into account the Court's concern for an employee who initially supports the strike but later undergoes a change of mind because of family hardship or the relative ease with which the employer is able to secure permanent replacements.[46] Again, if we are to balance employee rights against union interests, substantially more consideration of the dilemma faced by an employee who cannot continue to adhere to a strike without placing himself and his family in dire financial straits is surely required.[47]

Apart from the fact that the 30-day rule fails in its own "balancing" premise, it also fails to withstand scrutiny under the relevant Court decisions discussed above. Initially, in this regard, it is clear that, by promulgating a 30-day restriction on resignations, this Board is seeking to redefine the internal/external dichotomy which the Supreme Court has found to be embedded in our Act's very fabric. As discussed in detail above, the Court has consistently interpreted the Act and its underlying purposes to prohibit a union from exercising its coercive power in external matters. A primary basis for defining external versus internal matters has been the fact of the employee's union membership. Yet, by allowing a union to compel an employee to remain a member subject to the union's rules and authority for 30 days beyond an expressed desire to resign, the majority has effectively altered the internal/external distinction which Congress has so carefully embedded in the Act. And the majority has accomplished this end by creating the *fiction* of continued full membership.[48] Thus, unions will be able to expand substantially their domain of authority and to regulate

---

too short a period? Why is 31 days too long? We would hope that our colleagues have some nonarbitrary basis for the selection of this time period. For if they do not, their action is nothing more than an arbitrary act of legislative compromise.

[46]It should not be forgotten that an employer can and often does hire replacements immediately after a strike commences. While a 30-day waiting period, enforceable by substantial fines, may appear to some to be "reasonable," the real life dilemma created for an employee subjected to the rule is that his job may well be long gone by the time he is able to take any meaningful steps to retain it.

[47]When viewed in the context of the potentially severe hardships visited on employees who are precluded from refraining from a strike for 30 days, one questions the majority's willingness to adhere to the Court's admonition that, in balancing conflicting rights, any accommodation must be achieved "with as little destruction of one as is consistent with the maintenance of the other." *Babcock & Wilcox, supra* at 112. Surely a union is vested with sufficient lawful means of persuasion and peer pressure to preserve strike solidarity without requiring suspension of the Act's fundamental protections. In fact, if a union is unable to preserve strike solidarity through less restrictive means than sanctions that override the Act's protections, perhaps it should reconsider its decision to strike in the first place.

[48]It bears emphasis that this fiction of continued membership arises not out of the employees' expressed desires or the practical realities of the situation but, instead, is the creation of a union rule. Thus, a boilerplate provision in a union's constitution or bylaws that can be adopted and operate in an inflexible manner, oblivious to the circumstances facing the

conduct heretofore beyond its control merely by adopting a "rule" that establishes a facade of full membership for 30 days. In other words, by a mere convention vote, a union can transform a plainly external action into an internal one and thereby insulate itself from the intended scope and objectives of the Act.[49]

The 30-day rule also fails to pass muster under the *Scofield* test, reiterated in *Granite State* and *Booster Lodge*. Under that test, a union rule must (1) serve a legitimate union interest; (2) impair no policy Congress has embedded in the labor laws; and (3) leave members free to leave the union and escape the rule. We respectfully submit that to the extent the majority opinion even seeks to apply this test, it once again confuses the applicable concepts and distorts the appropriate analysis.

Plainly, a union's interest in maintaining strike solidarity is a legitimate one that satisfies the first part of the *Scofield* test. As for the second part of the test, however, the 30-day rule runs directly afoul of at least three policies Congress has embedded in the labor laws, i.e., the right of employees to refrain from concerted activities and the policy, discussed above, limiting the coercive authority of unions to wholly internal matters. Still a third policy negated by the 30-day rule is that embodied in Section 8(b)(2) and in the proviso to Section 8(a)(3) which together allow a union to compel core membership, but prohibit it from compelling full membership.

We can only presume that the majority seeks to negate these impositions on statutory policy by again relying on the union's interest in strike solidarity. Yet, the existence of a legitimate union interest is nothing more than a threshold issue in determining the lawfulness of a union rule. For if the mere existence of a legitimate union interest is sufficient to overcome the policies Congress has embedded in the Act, why, pray tell, has the Supreme Court consistently treated the two as separate and distinct conjunctive requirements? We submit that to utilize the legitimate union interests in strike solidarity to satisfy the initial prong of the *Scofield* test, and then revive it to negate congressional policy in addressing the second prong of the test, renders the three-part test redundant and virtually use-

---

member in a strike situation, can serve to circumscribe dramatically an employee's statutory rights and potential economic livelihood. Such "agreements" that result from union membership have accurately been termed contracts of adhesion. See *Summers, Legal Limitations on Union Discipline,* 64 Harv. L. Rev. 1049; Sould, *Some Limitations Upon Union Discipline Under the NLRA: The Radiation of Allis-Chalmers,* 1970 DUKE L.J. 1137 (1970).

[49]It seems self-evident that merely because a union adopts a rule all conduct by employees that violates that rule is not, *ipso facto,* an internal union matter. The majority seems to forget, however, that the internal/external determination turns upon the scope and impact of the rule and not on the internal source of the rule's creation.

less.[50] Indeed, in *Granite State* the Court recognized that a union advanced a legitimate interest in seeking to prohibit the return to work during a strike. But the Court then moved to the second part of its test and declared that "§ 7 rights are not lost by a union's plea for solidarity or by its pressures for conformity and submission to its regime."[51]

Regarding the final portion of the *Scofield* test, a rule restricting resignations for 30 days is not a rule reasonably enforced against union members who are free to leave the union and avoid the rule. Nor is it mere sophistry to rely on this factor in striking down a restriction on resignation. For this prong of the test represents more than a consideration to be applied only in cases that do not involve resignation rules. Indeed, it embodies an essential safeguard in protecting individuals' Section 7 rights and limiting the coercive power of unions. Nor can that safeguard be eliminated without doing violence to the Act's interrelated provisions and to the precise objectives of Congress. In short, at least part of the justification for allowing the union to enact and enforce the rule in the first place is that the member is free to leave the union and thus escape the application of that rule. To allow a union to eliminate this safeguard is simply to cede congressional authority to various private parties.

In summary, we believe the majority's 30-day restriction on resignations is premised upon sham "balancing" that represents nothing more than an arbitrary compromise over how far a union can unilaterally abrogate individual statutory rights and the congressional scheme of labor relations. The 30-day rule runs directly counter to relevant Supreme Court precedent, ignores the test prescribed for evaluating the validity of a union's rules, and generally violates a host of principles and policies embedded in our Act.

Finally, since the majority has set forth what it would hold in an appropriate case, we shall state our view. Any union rule that restricts a mem-

---

[50]Here again, a major flaw in the majority's analysis springs from the faulty premise that union interests and statutory rights are coequals that can serve to negate each other and compel that a "balance" be struck between them.

[51]409 U.S. at 218. Of course, in *Granite State* there was no union rule restricting resignation although the employees there had voted to impose sanctions on themselves for any strike-breaking activity. Thus, the only substantial difference here is a union rule adopted for the avowed purpose of restricting strikebreaking rather than an employee-adopted rule with the same objective. We fail to see how the employee rule is insufficient to negate congressional policy while a union rule with the same objective can overcome the intent of Congress. Indeed, binding an employee into forsaking his statutory rights for 30 days by invoking a union rule is yet another step removed from the employees' self-limitations found insufficient in *Granite State* and also fails to take into account the plain adhesive nature of the so-called employee/union contract. See fn. 48, *supra*.

ber's right to resign is unreasonable and any discipline taken by a union against an employee predicated on such a rule violates Section 8(b)(1)(A). In addition, for a resignation to be valid, it must be in writing and is effective upon receipt by the union.[52] Finally, we would hold that a union may not condition a resignation upon the payment of any dues or assessments. Clearly enough, the union, like an employer, is able to recoup any moneys owed it through regular legal proceedings and we find no basis for holding an employee hostage by prohibiting resignations until such fiscal matters are settled.

Dated, Washington, D.C., September 10, 1982.

John R. Van de Water, Chairman

Robert P. Hunter, Member

(SEAL) NATIONAL LABOR RELATIONS BOARD

MEMBER JENKINS, dissenting:

Contrary to my colleagues, I remain convinced[53] that Respondent's constitutional provision prohibiting resignations during a strike or within 14 days preceding its commencement is a reasonable and valid restriction on members' resignations, protected by the proviso to Section 8(b)(1)(A) of the Act. Accordingly, I would dismiss the complaint in its entirety.

This proceeding was submitted to the Board through a stipulation of facts. The complaint alleged that Respondent violated Section 8(b)(1)(A) by fining three of its members who, during the course of an officially sanctioned strike against the Employer, attempted to resign their memberships in Respondent and thereafter crossed Respondent's picket line to return to work for the Employer. The stipulated record reveals that Respondent has been the collective-bargaining representative of the Employer's employees since approximately 1949. On or about April 19, 1974, Respondent held a meeting of its members and informed them of a then newly adopted constitutional amendment which provided as follows:

---

[52] We do not view such requirements as "restrictions" on resignation. Rather, they are simply the ministerial acts necessary to ensure that a member's resignation is voluntary and has, in fact, occurred.

[53] See my previous dissent in this proceeding, reported at 231 NLRB 719, 722 (1977).

> *Improper Conduct of a Member* . . . Accepting employment in any capacity in an establishment where a strike or lockout exists as recognized under this Constitution, without permission. Resignation shall not relieve a member of his obligation to refrain from accepting employment at the establishment for the duration of the strike or lockout within 14 days preceding its commencement. Where observance of a primary picket line is required, resignation shall not relieve a member of his obligation to observe the primary picket line for its duration if the resignation occurs during the period that the picket line is maintained or within 14 days preceding its establishment.

At all times since that meeting, the individual Charging Parties, each of whom was an employee of the Employer, have been aware of the constitutional provision. On June 3, 1974, Respondent held another membership meeting for the purpose of taking a strike vote. Prior to the actual strike vote, Respondent again informed its members, including the individual Charging Parties, about the constitutional provision and warned them that anyone crossing the picket line could be fined. On the same date, following affirmative authorization of the membership through the strike vote, Respondent and its membership, including the Charging Parties, began an economic strike against the Employer and established a lawful picket line. The strike continued, and the picket line was maintained, during all times relevant herein. On February 14, 1975,[54] Charging Parties Hall and Lapinski resigned membership in the Union and, on February 18, returned to work at the struck plant. The Union received notice of these resignations on February 19. On April 16, the Union fined Hall and Lapinski $2,277.50 each for working behind the Union's picket line. The amount of the fines equaled the sum received by Hall and Lapinski from the Union as strike benefits during the period that they honored the picket line. Thereafter, on May 8, Charging Party Gomes submitted her resignation from membership. The Union received Gomes' resignation on May 10, and she returned to work at the struck plant on May 12. On August 6, the Union fined Gomes $1,125 for working behind the Union's picket line. Again, the amount of the fine equaled the sum Gomes received as strike benefits while she observed the Union's picket line.[55]

The majority accepts all of the foregoing, as they must, but despite these uncontroverted facts decides today that Respondent's actions in fining the Charging Parties for violating its duly adopted constitutional provision

---

[54]Unless otherwise noted, all dates hereinafter are in 1975.
[55]There is no allegation that the amount of the fines was unreasonable or excessive.

were contrary to Section 8(b)(1)(A) of the Act, holding that the constitutional provision quoted above is *per se* illegal. I cannot agree. Rather, I would find that Respondent was entitled to levy fines against the Charging Parties as a means of enforcing a lawful constitutional provision governing retention of membership, a subject expressly excluded from the scope of Section 8(b)(1)(A) by the proviso thereto, and within the ambit of a union's control over its internal affairs.

Any analysis of the issues presented herein must begin with an examination of the Supreme Court's decisions in *Allis-Chalmers*,[56] *Granite State*,[57] and *Booster Lodge*.[58] In *Allis-Chalmers*, the Supreme Court held that a union rule prohibiting its members from crossing an authorized picket line or returning to work during the course of a strike was a legitimate internal regulation of the conduct of its members, and that neither the rule nor its enforcement against members through imposition of court-enforceable fines was violative of Section 8(b)(1)(A) of the Act. In *Granite State* and *Booster Lodge*, the Supreme Court held that sanctions against former members who resigned their membership prior to crossing authorized picket lines were violative of Section 8(b)(1)(A) of the Act, reasoning that "when there is a lawful dissolution of a union-member relation, the union has no more control over the former member than it has over the man in the street."[59] It must be stressed, however, that in both *Granite State* and *Booster Lodge* the Court expressly limited its holding to factual situations where, as in those cases, there was no constitution or bylaw provision defining or limiting the circumstances under which a member could resign from the union.[60] Indeed, the Court specifically reserved for later consideration the question now before the Board; to wit, "the extent to which contractual restriction on a member's right to resign may be limited by the Act."[61]

In examining this issue, I am guided by the explicit terms of Sections 7 and 8(b)(1)(A) of the Act, and by the Supreme Court's interpretation of Section 8(b)(1) contained in its decision in *Scofield, et al. v. N.L.R.B.*[62] Briefly stated, Section 7 gives all employees the right to engage in union

---

[56]*NLRB v. Allis-Chalmers Manufacturing Co.*, 388 U.S. 175 (1967).
[57]*NLRB v. Granite State Joint Board, Textile Workers Union*, 409 U.S. 213 (1972).
[58]*Booster Lodge No. 405, International Association of Machinists and Aerospace Workers, AFL—CIO [Boeing Co.] v. NLRB*, 412 U.S. 84 (1973). Also, see *NLRB v. Boeing Co., et al.*, 412 U.S. 67 (1973).
[59]*Granite State, supra*, at 217.
[60]*Granite State, supra*, at 216, 217; *Booster Lodge, supra*, at 88.
[61]*Booster Lodge, supra*, at 88.
[62]394 U.S. 423.

and concerted activities, or to refrain from those activities. Section 8(b)(1)(A) provides that it shall be an unfair labor practice for any labor organization to restrain or coerce employees in the exercise of the rights guaranteed them by Section 7. Importantly, however, Congress expressly limited the breadth of Section 8(b)(1)(A) by including therein a proviso specifying that such provision "shall not impair the right of a labor organization to prescribe its own rules with respect to the acquisition or retention of membership therein . . . ." These interrelated provisions were addressed by the Supreme Court in *Scofield*. There, the Court stated that it had taken and would continue to take a dual approach to the problem of evaluating the validity of union fines under Section 8(b)(1)(A) of the Act, such that properly adopted union rules, reflecting legitimate union interests, which impair no policy Congress has imbedded in the labor laws, and which are reasonably enforced against members, are permissible under that section, whereas fines against nonmembers would violate that section. That statement reflects the Court's view, set forth in *Scofield* and in *Allis-Chalmers*, that union rules and their enforcement are an internal union matter governed by contractual considerations as embodied in the union's constitution and bylaws, which are agreed to by the members in consideration for the benefits attained by membership.

Applying the *Scofield* criteria to the constitutional provision here in issue, there can be no doubt but that the provision was properly adopted by the Union and its membership, a fact conceded by my colleagues. There also is no doubt but that the provision reflects legitimate union interests. As the Supreme Court observed in *Allis-Chalmers:* [63]

> National labor policy has been built on the premise that by pooling their economic strength and acting through a labor organization freely chosen by the majority, the employees of an appropriate unit have the most effective means of bargaining for improvements in wages, hours, and working conditions. The policy therefore extinguishes the individual employee's power to order his own relations with his employer and creates a power vested in the chosen representative to act in the interests of all employees. "Congress has seen fit to clothe the bargaining representative with powers comparable to those possessed by a legislative body both to create and restrict the rights of those whom it represents. . . ."

\* \* \* \* \*

---

[63]*Supra,* at 180–181.

Integral to this federal labor policy has been the power in the chosen union to protect against erosion of its status under that policy through reasonable discipline of members who violate rules and regulations governing membership. That power is particularly vital when the members engage in strikes. The economic strike against the employer is the ultimate weapon in labor's arsenal for achieving agreement upon its terms, and "[t]he power to fine or expel strikebearers is essential if the union is to be an effective bargaining agent. . . ."

Finally, as there is no contention that Respondent's constitutional provision or the fines levied under that policy were, in any way, other than reasonably enforced against its members, there remains for consideration only the issue of whether Respondent's constitutional provision so impairs a policy Congress has embedded in the labor laws that said provision is *per se* violative of Section 8(b)(1)(A) of the Act. I conclude that this inquiry must be answered in the negative. Obviously, the constitutional provision contains some restriction on members' rights, but where, as here, the members freely, knowingly, and expressly agree to such limitations in order to attain the additional strength such a prior commitment gives to the strike as an economic weapon, I can perceive no reason in Board law, Supreme Court precedent, or overall labor policy to declare such a prior commitment a nullity.[64] It must be stressed that the constitutional provision here in issue does not constitute a flat prohibition on all resignations, but merely restricts their effect during ongoing, lawful strikes in order to protect the Union and its members who honor their prior commitment not to engage in strikebreaking.

In effect, the provision permits the Union to enforce its contract with each member—a contract which was freely entered into by all parties—and thereby protect its other members then exercising "the ultimate weapon in labor's arsenal."[65] The member may, of course, prevail upon his fellow members to cease their concerted activity or to alter the rule but voluntarily having accepted the benefits and liabilities occasioned by union membership, including an express agreement not to resign membership during a strike and thereafter cross the union's picket line, I would not permit that

---

[64]For the reasons set forth in my previous dissent in this proceeding, cited above, I would overrule *Local Lodge No. 1994, International Association of Machinists and Aerospace Workers, AFL-CIO (O.K. Tool Company, Inc.)*, 215 NLRB 651 (1974), to the extent it is inconsistent with this opinion.

[65]*Allis-Chalmers, supra*, at 181.

member thereafter to breach his contract with the union unilaterally and thereby, in effect, "have his cake and eat it too."

In sum, I would find that the Union's constitutional amendment prohibiting members from resigning during the course of a strike was a reasonable and valid restriction on resignation, protected by the proviso to Section 8(b)(1)(A) of the Act. Accordingly, I would dismiss the complaint in its entirety.

Dated, Washington, D.C., September 10, 1982.

Howard Jenkins, Jr., Member
NATIONAL LABOR RELATIONS BOARD

# Chapter 4

# Nursing Strikes: A Breed Apart

When attempting to distinguish strikes of nurses from those of service, maintenance, technical, clerical, security, and other nonmedical employees in the health care industry, the following guideposts help:

1. Significant differences exist between these employee groups in relation to the role each plays in the overall delivery of patient care as perceived by the employees, hospital administration, the public, and, above all, the patient.
2. All the groups share common concerns for security and recognition.
3. Notwithstanding the meeting ground of needs, professional nurses have established themselves as a separate and unique bargaining unit.

The functions of all employees within a health care facility are obviously important to the facility's effective operation. Patient care is a team responsibility. Any walkout can pose administrative and patient care dilemmas. Nevertheless, some groups represent more of a threat than others. The key here, of course, is the extent to which a health care facility can adequately continue to provide "hands on" patient care services during such work stoppages.

When District 1199, National Union of Hospital and Health Care Employees struck New York City hospitals and nursing homes in July 1976, the hospitals and homes continued to operate, albeit at different levels of occupancy, throughout the strike's 11-day duration. Employing strike contingency plans, the hospitals and homes continued operations at near-normal levels, utilizing the services of supervisors, volunteers, and professional employees. These nonstriking employees virtually worked around the clock and maintained patient care operations. An earlier strike—in November 1973—by District 1199 against the same hospitals and homes, while of lesser duration, had a more negative effect on the delivery of patient care. In that strike, both the Committee of Interns and Residents and the New York State Nurses Association sympathized with the strikers and instructed their members to perform only the duties of their classifications.[1]

In contrast to strikes by nonnursing personnel, a 13-day nursing strike at two Youngstown, Ohio hospitals, a 16-day strike by nurses at West Shoshone General Hospital in Kellogg, Idaho, the much publicized 570-day "longest nurses strike on record" at Ashtabula General Hospital in Ohio, and, most recently, a 14-day nurses strike against Staten Island Hospital in New York forced the hospitals involved to handle only emergency cases and/or to curtail census and services significantly.

The critical importance to patient care of the attending physician and the house staff is readily recognized. Too often the role of the nurse is less appreciated. Professional nurses contribute significantly to patient care. They play an unusual role in the patient care family—more equal than others and, therefore, more essential. City and state health codes mandate a nurse's presence in many phases and areas of patient care. New York City health codes, for instance, require that a circulating nurse be present in an operating room where Caesarean section deliveries are performed and that at least one registered nurse be on staff for every ten maternity patients on day shift and every twenty patients on other shifts. No less important is the matter of patient perception. Many patients view nurses as more important to their total recuperation process than their own attending physicians. Hospital patients recognize the essential role that physicians play, but they see them only periodically. In contrast, the nurse is by the patient's side daily, comforting and assisting his or her recovery.

A personnel administrator of an institution that experienced a nursing walkout lasting 98 days stated that, "One of our major considerations from the strike's very beginning was assuring the remaining patient population (those who could not be discharged or relocated), that care would continue to be provided by physicians, supervisory nurses, replacement nurses, LPNs and aides." He added that, "Patient fear, for the most part, centered on a loss of personalized daily health care services provided by the nurse who, to the patient, was always there." Patients generally do not recognize the contribution of the other very dedicated and hard-working, but often unseen, employees, such as porters, painters, aides, food service workers, guards, or clerks. Patients perceive the nurse as the primary provider of care and comfort during their time of need. An antediluvian image of "angels of mercy" still exists. This phenomenon is widely known as "Nightingalism," so named for the 19th century health crusader, Florence Nightingale. Strictly interpreted, Nightingalism is self-sacrifice, that is, service given without concern for economic reward or job conditions.[2] Notwithstanding the outdated nature of such perception, it is one of the important factors that distinguishes strikes of nurses from those of other employee groups. Present in most nurse confrontations with health care institutions are the pressures on nurses, not to abandon their patients; pressure on the hospital administrator to act responsibly to avoid such walkouts; and finally, the lack of understanding and, therefore, lack of support of such action by the patients and the public.

## A SERIES OF CONFLICTS

Obvious conflicts exist in perceptions of what nurses are and/or should be; how they should conduct themselves professionally while attempting to improve their working conditions and wages; and to what extent nurses should act collectively to control their own destiny. These conflicts weave the intricately complex web of irony and agony that ensnares nurses, patients, hospital administrators, unions, and the public.

Based on sheer numbers alone, nurses have greater potential power than any other health professional group.[3] Most nurses know this to be inherently true. Then why, with all this power, do nurses largely agree with the position of the National Alliance for Fair Licensure of Foreign Nursing Graduates[4] that nurses are overworked, underpaid, and, having no time for themselves, socially alienated? An interesting paradox? According to a study measuring levels of satisfaction and dissatisfaction of union and nonunion professional nurses conducted by Management Science Associates, Inc. and displayed here in Appendix 4-A, the degree to which nurses feel that the job they do is satisfying is high. Yet dissatisfaction abounds in nursing,[5] and turnover rates are high. In 1980 the National Association of Nurse Recruiters reported a national nurse turnover rate of 30 percent; the New York State Health Advisory Council set the 1980 statewide nurse turnover rate at 20 percent. Another paradox? High nursing turnover seriously affects a health care institution's goal of providing quality care for its patients.[6] Yet most nurses believe that hospital administration and physicians are largely responsible for this condition. They claim that administrators ignore the frustrations of the nurse, while physicians persist in regarding them not as valued health care coprofessionals, but rather as handmaidens.

These are perceptions; whether valid or not, they are factors in the distressingly high rate of dropouts from the nursing profession. Further, some nurses have critically viewed administrators and physicians as often paying "lip service." They say that nurses are fellow professionals having significant input in matters of patient care; yet they do little to enhance their professional development. Often cited as a prime example to support this claim is the wide variance that exists between the salaries of physicians and nurses. Physicians' salaries are, on the average, four times that of nurses. This significant difference, many nurses contend, is perpetuated by hospital administrators and physicians in their attempts to preserve traditional roles, their general resistance to women's drive for comparable worth, their desire to maintain established levels of authority, and the inordinate amount of attention they pay to balanced budgets.

The American Nurses' Association (ANA) contends—and hospital administrators agree—that nurses are professionals. Why then, the nurses ask, are other professional groups given more decision-making input on questions of staffing, scheduling, education, unit management, and patient care? A study conducted by Management Science Associates surveyed the attitudes, morale, and opinions of more than 20,000 nurses. The Study defined their job needs as follows:

- Need for more individual job freedom.
- Need for greater input in matters that affect their jobs.
- Need for greater control over the work schedule.
- Need for more enlightened supervision and for top management to exhibit a more existential management style in their dealings with professional nurses.
- Need for more advancement and educational opportunities.[7]

There are those who contend, even in the face of a myriad of published studies, surveys, and analyses highlighting the nurses' frustration over denial of true professional status, that it is the nurse who practices sophistry. To these skeptics, nurses are ambivalent; they cannot make up their minds as to whether they wish to be recognized as health care professionals or as unionists (they claim an inherent conflict between the two). Antilabor philosophy? Not necessarily. Some union leaders share this view. They see unions as having played an important role in the shaping of wages and conditions for the traditional worker (blue collar), but they contend that a nurse is a professional, not a worker. The case for such differentiation is unfounded. Webster defines a profession as a ". . . field of endeavor in which individuals are engaged for gain; and . . . engaged in by persons receiving financial return." Further, professionalism is ". . . the following of a profession for gain or livelihood." There exists a definite relationship between professionals and other workers, as well as a common interest in bettering working conditions, which has sparked unionization of professionals.

Others profess that unionization of nurses is acceptable and understandable. The use of the strike, or even the threat of a strike is, however, seriously questioned as a "professional" option. But how effective is the collective bargaining process without the threat of a strike? Miller states that

> ". . . when the negotiation process is unsuccessful, the parties involved may be forced to use their relative economic strength. For the health care facility this means using its ability to withstand a strike. For the staff it means the ability to withstand forced unemployment. For the patients it may mean uncertain health care. Nevertheless, the use of economic strength may be the only means, although not necessarily the desirable means, of achieving bargaining or other objectives."[8]

This kind of thinking generated the withdrawal of the no-strike policy by the ANA at its national convention in 1968. Established in 1950, the no-strike pledge, for all of its 18-year existence, conflicted with the association's ability to conduct effective collective bargaining with health care employers. Barbara G. Shutt, editor of the *American Journal of Nursing*, stated in a 1968 journal article that the no-strike policy ". . . assumes that employers would demonstrate, on their part, a sense of obligation and good will by dealing with the nurses' representatives. With a few sterling exceptions, nurses' employers proved to be as unwilling as most other employers to negotiate with employee groups."[9]

## EARLY OBJECTIVES AND CHANGING DIRECTIONS

Prior to World War II, the ANA engaged in an economic security program; however, the policy of the program did not include collective bargaining. Although nurses' strikes and concerted efforts had occurred, the national organization did not sanction them.[10] Organized in 1896, the association's stated main purposes were to:

1. establish and maintain a code of ethics;
2. elevate the standards of nursing education; and
3. promote the financial and other interests of the nursing profession.[11]

In the latter purpose lay the roots of conflict that would surface 72 years later. In a pioneering position, the ANA stated that the nurses should not ". . . seriously consider forming, or participating in organizations which accept as a principle 'a collective withdrawal from work' even as a 'last resort.'"[12] Apparently the association founders did not comprehend the incongruity of attempting to promote financial interests of its members while forbidding those same members to join organizations that might exercise economic pressures to achieve such objectives. For a typical code of ethics, see Appendix 4-B, the text of the New York State Nurses Association ethics code.

The California Nurses Association (CNA) has been an innovator in protecting and improving the economic conditions of nurses.[13] In 1966, two years prior to similar action by the national association, the CNA rescinded its no-strike policy. In 1943, after securing a 15 percent salary increase from the National War Labor Board, the CNA implemented a total economic security program and signed its first contract with the San Francisco Bay area hospitals in 1946.[14] Its success, the acceleration of union organizing, and the persistent low level of nurse compensation led the House of Delegates of the ANA in 1946 to adopt an economic security program, including collective bargaining.[15] It issued the following policy statement:

> The American Nurses Association believes that the several state and district nurses associations are qualified to act and should act as the exclusive agents of their respective memberships in the important fields of economic security and collective bargaining. The Association . . . urges all state and district nurses associations to push such a program vigorously and expeditiously.[16]

By 1948, nurses associations in Washington, Minnesota, and Oregon had also been recognized as bargaining agents for their members, and in the same year 22 state associations adopted the ANA economic security program.[17] By 1957, associations in 43 states had adopted the program. By 1961 that number had risen to 48.

When the ANA adopted the no-strike policy in 1950, it also adopted a neutrality policy (which remained effective until 1970) in disputes that did not involve nurses.[18] The neutrality policy recommended that nurses remain neutral in conflicts involving other employee groups and that nurses not perform tasks outside their normal duties. The ANA reissued its policy subsequent to the 1958–1959 strikes throughout the country.[19] The no-strike pledge was adopted in anticipation that, as a *quid pro quo* for the continuation of work guarantee, the association would expect good faith collective bargaining from health care employers.

Unfortunately for nurses, collective bargaining was not the panacea for their problems. Even with mediation and fact-finding panels, nurses found many of their goals unrealized in the collective bargaining process. Without a measure of force—which was still banned by the ANA's no-strike policy—most nurses saw little chance of making major breakthroughs toward their objectives. Some claimed that employers abstained from meaningful give-and-take negotiations and adhered to whatever criteria they deemed reasonable.[20]

The 1950s and early 1960s proved frustrating to nurses. Many felt a sense of impotence in the collective bargaining arena. Prior to the rescission of the no-strike pledge by the CNA in 1966, the festering frustration began to push nurses into collective work action, and nurse employee groups emerged as formidable collective bargaining adversaries. From this time on, nurses harnessed and wielded power on a national level. The nightmare of nurses abandoning their patients turned into a stark reality. Nurses went out on strike in distressingly large numbers. The shock waves resounded throughout the health care industry.

In 1961 mass nurse resignations developed as a tool for realizing gains. In April of that year, the Illinois Nursing Association was refused a meeting with the administration of Keewanee Hospital, a voluntary not-for-profit hospital; the nurses turned in their resignations. Nurses at eight hospitals in Orange County, California also resigned en masse to demonstrate for recognition.[21] During the mid-1960s, the use of mass resignation and picketing increased substantially. Nurses became aggressive in their demands and enforced them by strikes, sick-outs, and mass resignations. These actions occurred in San Francisco, in Youngstown, Ohio, in New York City, and in Los Angeles, among other areas.[22] After 13 days, nurses in Youngstown, Ohio returned to work, having won a 19 percent raise.[23] In hospitals in other major cities, nurse resignations brought managements close to total submission to the demonstrating nurses' demands for improved benefits. In effect, resignation was achieving the same results as a strike.

Why did the nurses prefer resignation to strikes? There was still the matter of the ANA's no-strike pledge, and, more importantly, at that time nurses still believed that it was wrong to abandon their commitment to the patient by conducting job actions and picketing. They perceived this as unprofessional. Resignation was a means to an end "with honor." The nurses would, with a minimum amount of guilt, leave the hospital, or the profession for that matter, to eliminate the stress they were experiencing. They were not betraying their professional vows. They were merely "getting out of a bad situation." As Miller points outs,

> ". . . employees who hand in their resignations supposedly have no intention of returning to their jobs even if changes are made; . . . resignation concerns the right of individuals to work for the

employer they wish and under the circumstances they prefer. . . . Although the philosophy of mass resignation and striking are different . . . mass resignation functions in the same manner as a strike."[24]

The nurses did not want to resign their positions. They were frustrated and due to a sense of guilt could not indulge in a strike. Then the idea of a job action as a means of achieving desired working condition improvements began to be openly discussed and considered as an alternative to resignation. Nurses reasoned that while it might be considered unprofessional to walk out on patients, doing so might be the only effective means available to obtain changes, and further, such action would ultimately redound to the benefit of patient care.

Barbara Shutt's appointment in 1960 to the editorship of the *American Journal of Nursing* significantly boosted the collective action movement of nurses. Her appointment gave the economic security program a national platform. She used the journal to communicate to the nation's nurses, frequently and militantly. Prior to 1960, only about 3,000 nurses worked under ANA-negotiated contracts. By the end of 1960, approximately 18,000 nurses were under contract.[25]

**No-Strike Pledge Rescinded**

In its no-strike policy rescission statement, the ANA supported ". . . the efforts of the State Nurses Associations acting as bargaining representatives for members in taking necessary steps to achieve improved conditions, including use of concerted economic pressures which are lawful and consistent with the nurses' professional responsibilities and with the public need."[26] Shutt lauded the policy reversal and stated in the journal, "After eighteen agonizing and economically almost fruitless years, it finally became clear that the policy was unrealistic, practically unenforceable and at best misleading, if not dishonest.[27] The die was cast! The conflict resolved! Collective bargaining in the health care industry would never be quite the same.

In 1969 two noteworthy strikes occurred, one in Los Angeles and the other in San Francisco. The strikes are noteworthy because of the issue common to both. Both strikes, which collectively lasted 62 days, resulted in settlements that granted a demand aimed at improving deteriorating staffing conditions—the creation of the Professional Practice Committee. Common in nursing contracts today, the Professional Practice Committee provided for a joint-committee composition of members of management and nursing staff, which would meet periodically to discuss development of staffing patterns, problems in patient care, and existing conflict situations between physicians and nurses. These "non-economic demands," seen by many hospital administrators as erosive of management rights, would become common in the years that followed.

**The Calm before the Storm**

The early 1970s were essentially quiet years, but the atmosphere was to change. If we were to call this period "the calm before the storm," the atmospheric disturbance to come would be manifest in two major events: first, the 21-day strike by the CNA against hospitals and clinics in the San Francisco Bay area in 1974; and second, Public Law 93-360, effective August 25, 1974, which amended the National Labor Relations Act (NLRA) and repealed the exemption that had been incorporated into the act in 1947.[28] Under the 1974 amendments, the same rights and privileges would now be granted to all not-for-profit hospital workers—numbering 1.6 million and employed in 3,400 institutions—as had been legislated for most other workers 39 years earlier. The 1974 amendments intensified union activity among nurses, and by the early 1980s the number of ANA member nurses working under bargaining contracts had risen to about 80,000, a more-than-fourfold increase since 1960.

On June 7, 1974 approximately 4,400 registered nurses struck 41 hospitals and clinics in the San Francisco Bay area. Although the CNA, which represented the nurses, sought economic gains inclusive of pension improvements, its main demand was for a voice in staffing pattern decisions. During its annual convention in San Francisco, the CNA House of Delegates, while soliciting support from its member attendees, resolved to establish a special fund that would assist its striking members. The crippled hospitals submitted to almost all of the CNA's demands, ending the 21-day-old strike. The nurses achieved two major inroads into patient care decision making:

1. Registered nurses (RNs) have a right to take part in determining how many nurses are needed for intensive care, renal dialysis, postanesthesia recovery, and other nursing units. Boards of directors composed solely of doctors and hospital administrators cannot make decisions on staffing these units without input from knowledgeable nurses.
2. The hospital boards must establish procedures so that nurses can advise on staffing needs for medical-surgical and other patients requiring special nursing care. Hospitals will pay the nurses for participation on these professional performance committees.[29]

On July 12, 1976 approximately 1,800 nurses struck 15 Seattle, Washington area hospitals. Area newspapers defined the issues as demands for RN input into patient care, ongoing inservice education, limited shift rotation, mandatory Washington State Nurses' Association (WSNA) membership, a cost-of-living salary increase, recognition of the increased complexity of patient care, and a shift differential.[30] The strike lasted approximately 68 days, cutting patient population by 50 percent during that time.

**A BREED APART**

One group of researchers determined that, "In collective bargaining, the nurses' definition of a situation might be quite different from that of health service management; thus, their reasons for striking and their assessment of the bargaining issues would not be congruent with those of management."[31] While many hospital administrators feel that industrial-sector bargaining issues, such as wages and job security, are critical problems for nurses, in reality the nurses are more concerned about communication with management and participation in organizational decision making. In fact, the latter two issues have important implications in their impact on predicting strike behavior. Again and again, studies point out that an overwhelmingly large number of nurses have concerns quite different from other employees, and these concerns spill over into collective bargaining. They are:

1. inability to communicate concerns to management;
2. authoritarian behavior on the part of management;
3. understaffing;
4. lack of respect from physicians;
5. lack of control over nursing practice;
6. lack of support from nursing administration; and
7. dissatisfaction with shift assignments, rotations, weekend scheduling, and mandatory overtime.

A marked difference between traditional collective bargaining and collective bargaining with nurses is the ability to take "several bites of the apple." It is a hallowed concept of traditional collective bargaining that management makes the "deal" at the bargaining table, that all issues are aired, and that a settlement, once arrived at, concludes the bargain. This is not always true with professional groups. Because of market pressures, nursing shortages, and turnover, midyear, midcontract adjustments are not unusual.

The Taft-Hartley Act requires the parties to bargain about "wages, hours, and other terms and conditions of employment." These are the traditional issues addressed at the collective bargaining table. They may not always be amenable to early settlement, but the process of collective bargaining has proved to be well suited to their resolution. With nurses a variety of other issues complicate the bargain. Shortly after the Health Care Amendments to the Act, an article appeared in the *American Journal of Nursing,* which stated:

> The jurisdictional expansion of the NLRA to include employees of private health care institutions can become an opportunity for the nursing profession to increase its influence and control over the practice of nursing. The labor contract . . . becomes a legal instrument *through* which the profession can implement standards of care. . . . Collective bargaining can be an effective process for bringing about a redistribution of the base of power within the health service organization.[32]

This analysis proved to be a self-fulfilling prophecy. Such an interpretation pervaded nursing associations, which organized RNs in the years following the passage of the amendments.

Nurses seek shared governance, i.e., a role in shaping rights and responsibilities to determine the nature of the delivery of patient care. Such issues have proved extremely difficult to resolve in the collective bargaining arena. Institutions usually do not have the resources to resolve these concerns, and the parties sometimes, in the end, seek resolution through legal channels. However, as most experienced labor relations practitioners know, few contracts are resolved and few strikes surrendered as a result of legal decisions.

**THE BARGAINING PROCESS**

Collective bargaining with nurses has proved to be extremely complex and fraught with the danger of impasse and ensuing strikes. The frustrations expressed by Candice Owley, chairperson of the Federation of Nurses and Health Professions of the American Federation of Teachers–United Federation of Teachers, at a seminar on collective bargaining are exemplary. She explained why nurses are angry: "We don't like our working conditions, we don't like the image that is portrayed, and we don't like each other, and we don't like the doctors. . . ." Such frustrations are common and are often brought to the bargaining table with growing militancy, chaos, and ill will. Strikes result. In such situations, the community is at risk.

It is not only the nurses who are frustrated within the collective bargaining process. Often management participants find the difference between traditional bargaining and nurse bargaining frustrating and difficult to handle. Settlements are hammered out, only to be rejected quickly by rank-and-file nurses. The immediate analysis of management is that units represented by nursing associations often are uncontrollable. A knee-jerk management condemnation of the leadership of nurses' associations follows, but when clearer heads look around they find a similar rejection of settlements by units represented by traditional trade unions. It is clear that even given the most skilled labor negotiators and the best of intentions on both sides, settlement rejections can still proliferate and strikes can still result. The commitments made on and off the record by union representatives have frittered away in the face of rank-and-file rejection. These votes of "no confidence" in their union leadership reflect a broader problem than individual rejection. This inability of nurse union leadership to translate the real concerns of nurses into acceptable settlements has played a role in the proliferation of strikes of professional nurses.

**Anatomy of Three Nursing Strikes**

Several years ago three separate bargaining units at three separate hospitals, made up of several thousand professional nurses, reached bargaining impasses and went out on strike.

Upon receiving the ten-day strike notice, the first institution immediately curtailed occupancy. It halted elected admissions, and doctors examined their patients by service, recommending, where appropriate, discharge or transfer. This strike lasted five full days. Occupancy rates declined from an average of 92 percent to 25 percent. The institution did not lay off any other employees, union or nonunion. Nonunion registered nurses (nurse supervisors and administrative nurses), LPNs, aides, and housestaff provided nursing services. Some unionized nurses, even though part of the bargaining unit out on strike, came in to staff critical care areas. It took six full days after the strike to reach normal occupancy. The hospital lost an estimated $4 million. This hospital had a high RN to LPN/nursing aide ratio.

Believing that the strike would last only one or two days, the administrator of the second hospital decided not to curtail occupancy. When the strike ensued, nurse supervisors, LPNs, and aides provided the nursing services. The hospital did screen admissions to identify the more acutely ill patients. Some consolidation of units took place. On the third and last day of the strike, the hospital discharged many patients and curtailed admissions. However, curtailment of services never exceeded 20 percent. The financial impact of the strike was minimal. Interestingly, both the first and second hospitals have attempted since the strikes to hire more LPNs and have made concerted efforts to exclude head nurses from bargaining units.

The third hospital suffered a disastrous strike. It was one of the longest strikes on record at that time. One of the key issues was the union's position regarding floating. The hospital had a policy that provided for floating employees throughout the hospital. The union wanted this policy eliminated. During the strike supervisors, clinical coordinators, head nurses, and assistant head nurses provided the nursing services. The hospital began to recruit per diems and full-time replacements. They sought assistance from private agencies and paid premium salaries to nurses who would cross the picket line to replace striking nurses. Occupancy, which had been at 90 percent or better before the strike, moved sharply downward to approximately 50 percent. Patients were discharged immediately after receipt of the ten-day strike notice. Elective admissions were discontinued. By the first week of the strike, only 300 of the hospital's 550 beds were occupied. By the third week of the strike, occupancy was at 225 beds. A total of 140 nurses provided services for these 225 patients.

Negotiations were suspended as soon as the strike occurred, and no meetings were scheduled for the first two weeks of the strike. Positions hardened. Negotiations began again in the third week. Federal mediation was involved, but a board of inquiry was not appointed because both parties rejected the idea. The union brought new issues to the table once negotiations resumed, and issues that were withdrawn by the union in negotiations prior to the strike were reintroduced. Positions hardened further. A settlement was fashioned, but the membership overwhelmingly turned it down. Once again the ugly difference in nurse negotiations reared its head: The negotiating group did not speak for the membership.

Negotiations floundered. The hospital continued to operate with only 225 beds occupied. Because no other group of employees at the hospital was organized, the hospital did not lay off anyone, hoping that its nonunionized employees would see this effort at saving their jobs as a symbol. Financial losses were staggering, and pressure was placed on the hospital to settle. After one of the longest nursing strikes on record at that time, a settlement was hammered out and overwhelmingly approved.

The hospital lost more than $1 million. It took more than a month after the strike ended to get back to the original 95 percent occupancy. The returning nurses were extremely militant. As one hospital administrator pointed out, "We went through an earthquake, and we are now feeling the aftershock." The hospital agreed to bring all the striking nurses back, but it also retained any new nurses hired during the strike. Antagonism between the two groups was high, and grievances increased.

## STRIKE IMPACT

Nursing strikes are different. Their impact is dramatically greater than strikes of nonnurses. The issues often are different and less amenable to settlement across the collective bargaining table. Whether legally mandatory items for bargaining or not, the issues are put on the table and become threshold issues, frequently blocking settlements. Bargaining leadership is often permissive and unable to reflect the real concerns of the bargaining unit and, more often, unwilling to exercise control. Salary source replacements for strikers are readily available, a fact that further sets nurses apart from other labor groups.

---

**NOTES**

1. *Hospital Strike* (New York: League of Voluntary Hospitals and Homes of New York, 1973), p. 1.
2. Norma K. Grand, "Nightingalism, Employeeism and Professional Collectivism," *Nursing Forum,* Vol. 10, 1971, p. 289.
3. L.Y. Kelly, "The Revolt of Nurses," *Nursing Outlook,* Vol. 26, No. 10, June 1978, pp. 356–360.
4. A Critical Analysis of the Nursing Profession and the Role of Unions, by the National Alliance for Fair Licensure of Foreign Nursing Graduates, *Philippine Journal of Nursing,* Vol. 51, No. 1 (January–March 1981).
5. M. Godfrey, "Job Satisfaction—Or Should That Be Dissatisfaction?" How Nurses Feel About Nursing, Parts I and II, *Nursing 78* (1978), pp. 90, 105.
6. J.L. Price and C.W. Mueller, "How to Reduce the Turnover of Hospital Nurses," *Handbook of Health Care Human Resources Management,* Norman Metzger, ed. (Rockville, Md.: Aspen Systems Corp., 1981), p. 381.
7. K.B. Stickler and J.C. Velghe, "Why Nurses Join Unions," *Hospital Forum* (March 1980). Reprinted by permission of the Association of Western Hospitals.
8. Michael H. Miller, "Nurses Right to Strike," *The Journal of Nursing Administration,* Vol. 5, No. 2 (February 1975), pp. 35–39.
9. Barbara G. Shutt, "The Right to Strike." Copyright 1968. American Journal of Nursing Company. Reprinted with permission from *American Journal of Nursing,* Vol. 26, No. 10 (July 1968).
10. D. Wood, "They Live and Learn with Unions," *The Modern Hospital,* Vol. 93, No. 1 (July 1959), pp. 73–74.
11. G.J. Griffin and J. Griffin, *Jensen's History and Trends of Professional Nursing,* 6th ed. (St. Louis, Mo.: C.V. Mosby Co., 1969), p. 116.

12. "Nurses' Unions?" Copyright 1936. American Journal of Nursing Company, Reprinted with permission from *American Journal of Nursing*, Vol. 36 (November 1968), p. 1122.
13. Norman Metzger and Dennis Pointer, *Labor-Management Relations in the Health Services Industry, Theory and Practice* (Washington, D.C.: The Science and Health Publications, Inc., 1972), p. 37.
14. Ronald L. Miller, "Development and Structure of Collective Bargaining Among Registered Nurses," *Personnel Journal* 5 (February 1971), p. 134.
15. Lyndia Flanagan, *One Strong Voice: The Story of the American Nurses' Association* (Kansas City, Mo.: American Nurses' Association, 1976), p. 168.
16. *American Nurses' Association Major Official Policies Relating to the Economic Security Program* (New York: American Nurses' Association, 1965), p. 1.
17. "The Economic Security Program." Copyright 1947. American Journal of Nursing Company. Reprinted with permission from *American Journal of Nursing*, Vol. 47, Nos. 70–73 (April 1947), p. 190.
18. J. Seidman, "Nurses and Collective Bargaining," *Industrial and Labor Relations Review*, Vol. 23, No. 3 (April 1970), p. 342.
19. "If A Hospital Strike Occurs." Copyright 1960. American Journal of Nursing Company. Reprinted with permission from *American Journal of Nursing*, Vol. 60, No. 3 (March 1960), pp. 344–347.
20. Michael H. Miller, *supra*, p. 35.
21. Metzger and Pointer, *supra*, p. 36.
22. Dorothy Peters, "The Keewanee Story." Copyright 1961. American Journal of Nursing Company. Reprinted with permission from *American Journal of Nursing*, Vol. 61, No. 10 (October 1961), pp. 74–79.
23. "Youngstown Nurses End Thirteen Day Walkout; Michigan Nurses Sign First Agreement," *White Collar Report*, Vol. 74, No. 5 (December 15, 1966).
24. Michael H. Miller, *supra*, pp. 35–39.
25. "Program Briefs." Copyright 1961. American Journal of Nursing Company. Reprinted with permission from *American Journal of Nursing*, Vol. 61, No. 9 (September 1961), p. 74.
26. American Nurses' Association, *ANA's Economic and General Welfare Program: Philosophy, Goals, Policies, Positions* (Kansas City, Mo.: American Nurses' Association, 1976), p. 5.
27. Shutt, *supra*.
28. S.M. Kaynard, "Health Care Industry Under the National Labor Relations Act," *Handbook of Health Care Human Resources Management*, Norman Metzger, ed. (Rockville, Md.: Aspen Systems Corp., 1981), p. 537.
29. "Nurses Set Precedent in Gains from San Francisco Strike," *RN*, Vol. 37, No. 9 (September 1974).
30. "Mini on the Scene; Seattle, Washington," *Nursing Administration Quarterly*, Vol. 6, No. 2 (Winter 1982), pp. 41–58.
31. Joan R. Bloom, G. Nicholas Parlette, and Charles A. O'Reilly, "Collective Bargaining by Nurses: A Comparative Analysis of Management and Employee Perceptions," *Health Care Management Review*, Vol. 5, No. 1 (Winter 1980), pp. 25–33.
32. Virginia Cleland, "The Professional Model," *American Journal of Nursing*, Vol. 75, No. 2 (February 1975), p. 288.

# Appendix 4-A

# Collective Bargaining and the Professional Nurse: Does It Work?

**STATISTICAL METHODOLOGY USED FOR COMPARING THE OPINION SURVEY SCORES OF UNION VERSUS NONUNION REGISTERED NURSES**

On the following pages are several pie charts and bar graphs. Based on a scientific opinion study of 15,538 registered nurses (RNs) working in hospitals throughout the United States between January 1, 1979 and April 1, 1982, the graphs (Figures 4A-1–4A-13) provide information regarding nurse demographics and professional satisfaction. The text preceding the table and graphs describes the statistical methodology used to compile the facts disclosed here. It also provides in tabular format a look at job satisfaction levels among nurses.

**The Analysis of Variance**

To test the difference between the attitudes of two or more groups of respondents, the statistical procedure Analysis of Variance is used. Analysis of Variance (ANOVA) is similar to the T-Test statistical technique, but with two decided differences. First, ANOVA allows for more than two groups to be compared simultaneously (which is not relevant in this study), while T-Test allows for only two groups to be compared. Second, ANOVA makes no assumptions that the groups being compared come from the same population, i.e., that the groups have the same standard deviation. The T-Test is generally used to compare two sets of observa-

---

*Note:* All figures in Appendix 4-A are reprinted with permission of Management Science Associates, Inc., Kansas City, Missouri, copyright © 1982.

*Source:* Reprinted from "Collective Bargaining and the Professional Nurse—Does It Work?" by permission of Management Science Associates, Inc., Kansas City, Missouri, copyright © 1982.

tions from the same sample (there are corrections which allow the T-Test to be used on observations from different samples). All in all, the ANOVA is generally accepted as a more powerful or "robust" statistical test than the T-Test. Furthermore, the results of the ANOVA and T-Test should almost always yield the same conclusions regarding presence or absence of statistical differences.

The ANOVA is used to determine whether or not two groups of employees, union RNs and nonunion RNs, hold differing levels of satisfaction and dissatisfaction on the 15 attitude areas measured by the Management Science Associates Employee Relations Improvement Survey. The average score on an attitude area is compared for nonunion and union nurses to determine whether nonunion nurses are significantly more or less satisfied than union nurses. Levels of statistical significance are used to conclude whether differences exist.

The level of statistical significance tells us how confident one can be that the difference found is the result of a "true" difference in attitude rather than a chance occurrence. The greater the significance, the higher our degree of confidence. It would be incorrect to state that the greater the significance, the greater the difference.

Following generally accepted statistical practice, a significance level equal to or exceeding .95, on a scale from 0 to 1.00, represents a statistically significant difference between nonunion and union RNs. Any significance below that point would indicate that the difference found may be a result of random variation in respondent answers.

**Job Satisfaction Numerical Survey Results**

Following is a scientific study of 15,538 registered nurses working in hospitals throughout the United States during the period of January 1, 1979 through April 1, 1982.

1. Job Satisfaction

| Average for Nonunion RNs | Average for Union RNs | Difference |
|---|---|---|
| 2.40 | 2.49 | .09 |

Level of Significance = .99
Conclusion: Nonunion nurses are significantly more satisfied with their jobs.

2. Satisfaction with Administration

| Average for Nonunion RNs | Average for Union RNs | Difference |
|---|---|---|
| 3.11 | 3.38 | .27 |

Level of Significance = .99
Conclusion: Nonunion RNs are significantly more satisfied with administration.

3. Satisfaction with Supervisors

| Average for Nonunion RNs | Average for Union RNs | Difference |
|---|---|---|
| 2.90 | 2.95 | .05 |

Level of Significance = .95
Conclusion: Nonunion RNs are significantly more satisfied with supervisors.

4. Satisfaction with Evaluation

| Average for Nonunion RNs | Average for Union RNs | Difference |
|---|---|---|
| 3.11 | 3.26 | .15 |

Level of Significance = .99
Conclusion: Nonunion nurses are significantly more satisfied with their evaluations.

5. Satisfaction with Participation

| Average for Nonunion RNs | Average for Union RNs | Difference |
|---|---|---|
| 3.68 | 3.86 | .18 |

Level of Significance = .99
Conclusion: Union RNs are significantly more dissatisfied with participation than are nonunion RNs.

6. Satisfaction with Communication

| Average for Nonunion RNs | Average for Union RNs | Difference |
|---|---|---|
| 3.54 | 3.55 | .01 |

Level of Significance = .17
Conclusion: No difference exists between union and nonunion RNs in their satisfaction with communications.

7. Satisfaction with Personnel Policies

| Average for Nonunion RNs | Average for Union RNs | Difference |
|---|---|---|
| 3.30 | 3.32 | .02 |

Level of Significance = .42
Conclusion: No difference exists in satisfaction with personnel policies.

8. Satisfaction with Job Mobility

| Average for Nonunion RNs | Average for Union RNs | Difference |
|---|---|---|
| 3.19 | 3.30 | .11 |

Level of Significance = .99
Conclusion: Nonunion RNs are significantly more satisfied with job mobility than are union RNs.

9. Satisfaction with Salary

| Average for Nonunion RNs | Average for Union RNs | Difference |
|---|---|---|
| 3.38 | 3.70 | .32 |

Level of Significance = .99
Conclusion: Nonunion RNs are satisfied with salary while union RNs are dissatisfied. The difference is highly significant.

10. Job Security

| Average for Nonunion RNs | Average for Union RNs | Difference |
|---|---|---|
| 2.19 | 2.21 | .02 |

Level of Significance = .53

Conclusion: Both nonunion and union RNs feel secure in their jobs, and there is no significant difference between them.

11. Satisfaction with Physical Working Conditions

| Average for Nonunion RNs | Average for Union RNs | Difference |
|---|---|---|
| 2.74 | 2.80 | .06 |

Level of Significance = .98
Conclusion: Nonunion RNs are significantly more satisfied with the physical working conditions.

12. Satisfaction with Benefits

| Average for Nonunion RNs | Average for Union RNs | Difference |
|---|---|---|
| 3.05 | 3.20 | .15 |

Level of Significance = .99
Conclusion: Nonunion RNs are significantly more satisfied with their benefits.

13. Satisfaction with Job Demands

| Average for Nonunion RNs | Average for Union RNs | Difference |
|---|---|---|
| 3.01 | 2.93 | .08 |

Level of Significance = .97
Conclusion: Union RNs are significantly more satisfied with job demands.

14. Satisfaction with Peer Working Relationships

| Average for Nonunion RNs | Average for Union RNs | Difference |
|---|---|---|
| 2.15 | 2.08 | .07 |

Level of Significance = .97
Conclusion: While both union and nonunion RNs are highly satisfied with peer working relationships, union RNs are significantly more satisfied.

15. Satisfaction with Resource Utilization

| Average for Nonunion RNs | Average for Union RNs | Difference |
|---|---|---|
| 2.62 | 2.62 | .00 |

Level of Significance = .00
Conclusion: No difference exists in satisfaction with resource utilization.

**Figure 4A-1** Employment Status

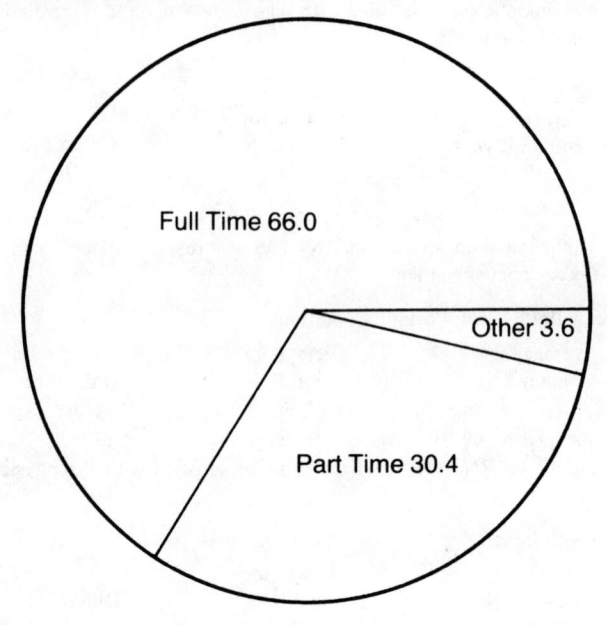

Full Time 66.0
Other 3.6
Part Time 30.4

**Figure 4A-2** Race-Sex

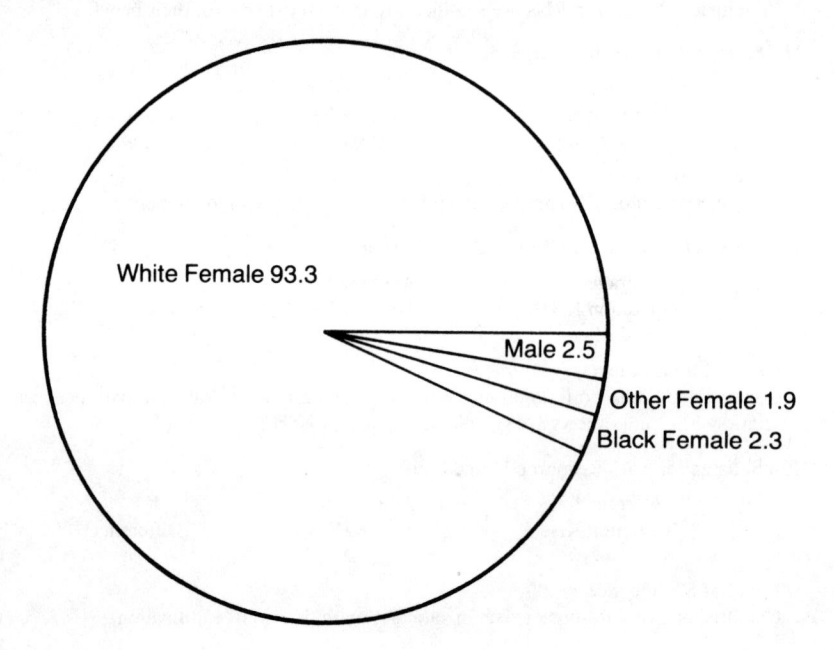

White Female 93.3
Male 2.5
Other Female 1.9
Black Female 2.3

**Figure 4A-3** Shift

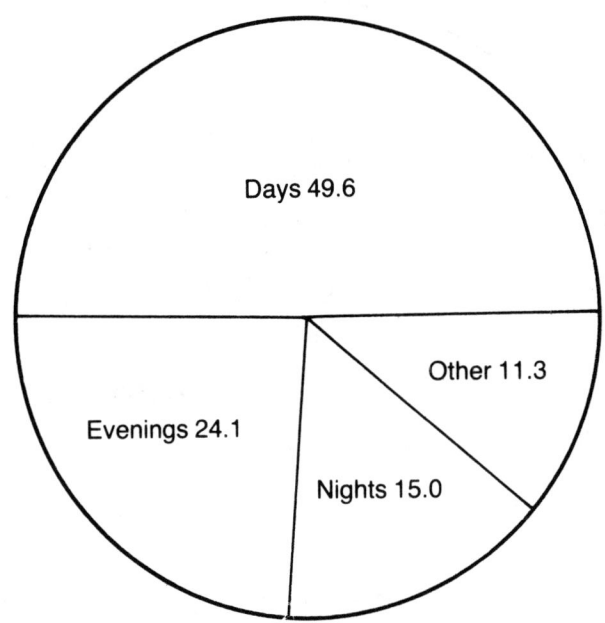

Days 49.6
Other 11.3
Evenings 24.1
Nights 15.0

**Figure 4A-4** Years of Service

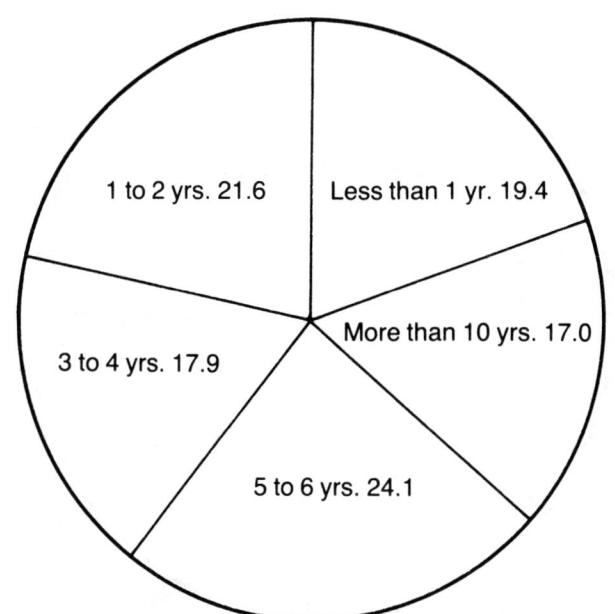

1 to 2 yrs. 21.6
Less than 1 yr. 19.4
3 to 4 yrs. 17.9
More than 10 yrs. 17.0
5 to 6 yrs. 24.1

110   WHEN HEALTH CARE EMPLOYEES STRIKE

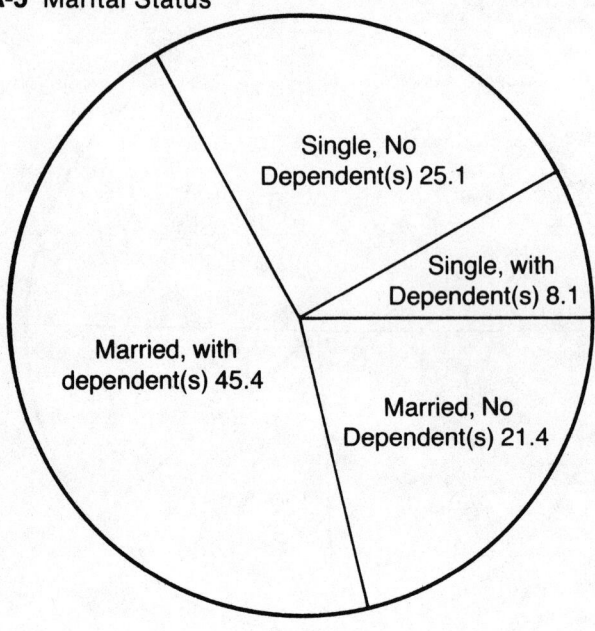

**Figure 4A-5** Marital Status

- Single, No Dependent(s) 25.1
- Single, with Dependent(s) 8.1
- Married, No Dependent(s) 21.4
- Married, with dependent(s) 45.4

**Figure 4A-6** Age

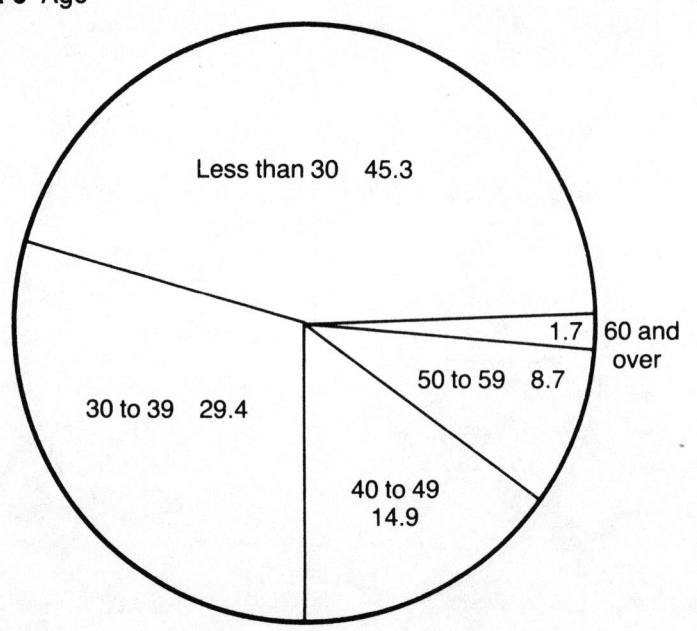

- Less than 30    45.3
- 30 to 39    29.4
- 40 to 49    14.9
- 50 to 59    8.7
- 60 and over    1.7

*Nursing Strikes* 111

**Figure 4A-7** Education

- Diploma 45.6
- Associate Degree 23.6
- Graduate Degree 4.1
- BSN 26.7

**Figure 4A-8** Union/Nonunion

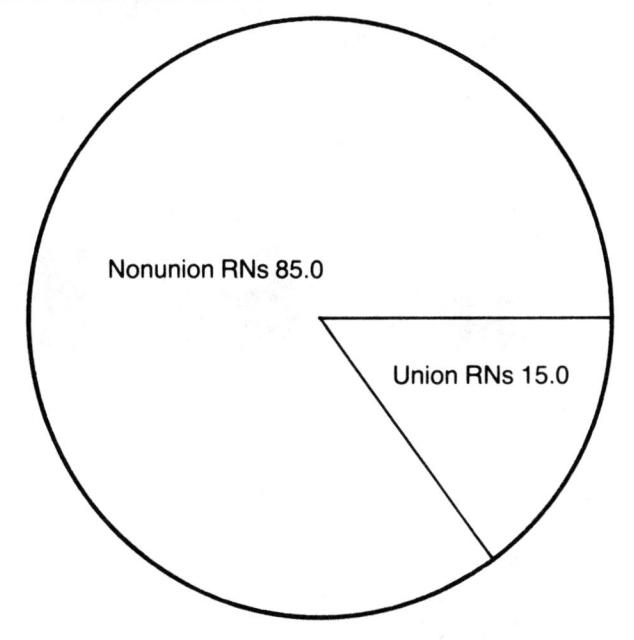

- Nonunion RNs 85.0
- Union RNs 15.0

**Figure 4A-9** Nonunion and Union Opinions on Job Satisfaction, Administration, and Supervision

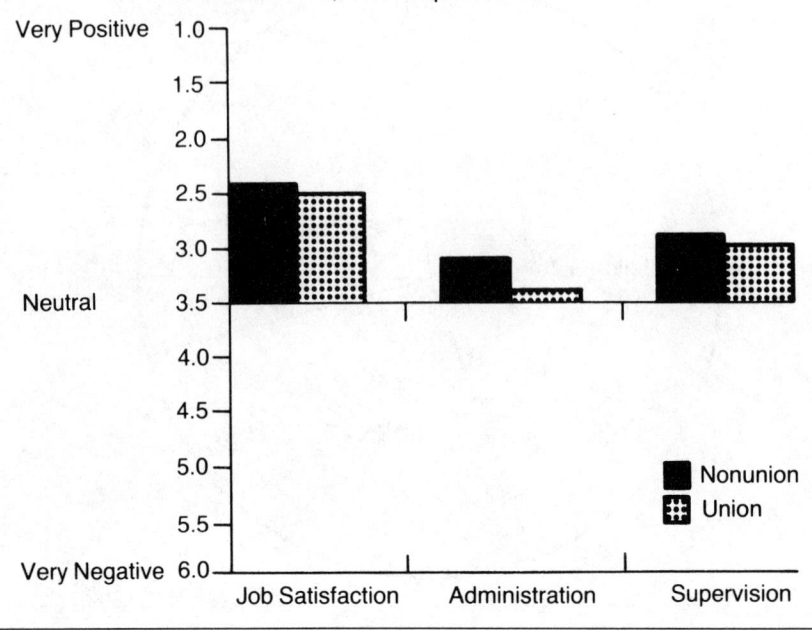

**Figure 4A-10** Nonunion and Union Opinions on Job Demands, Peer Relationships, and Resource Utility

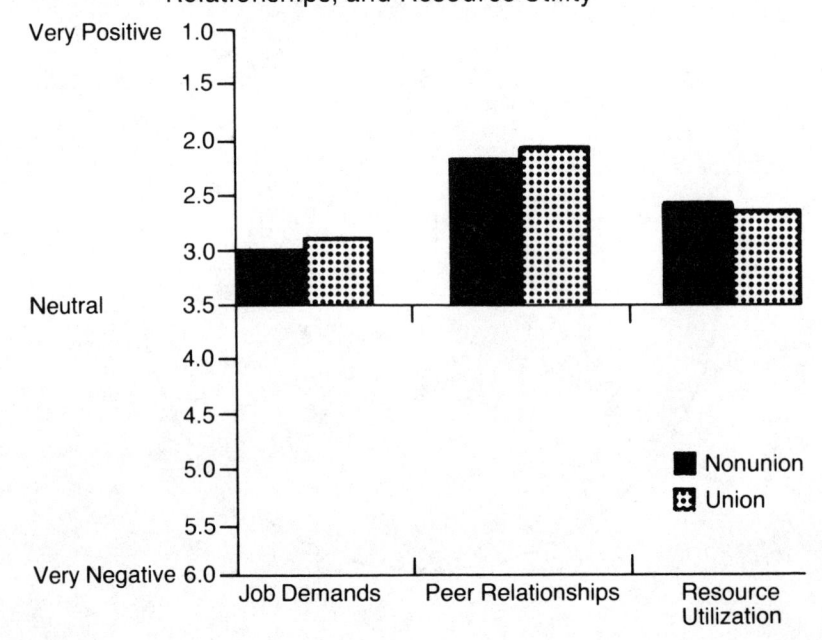

Nursing Strikes 113

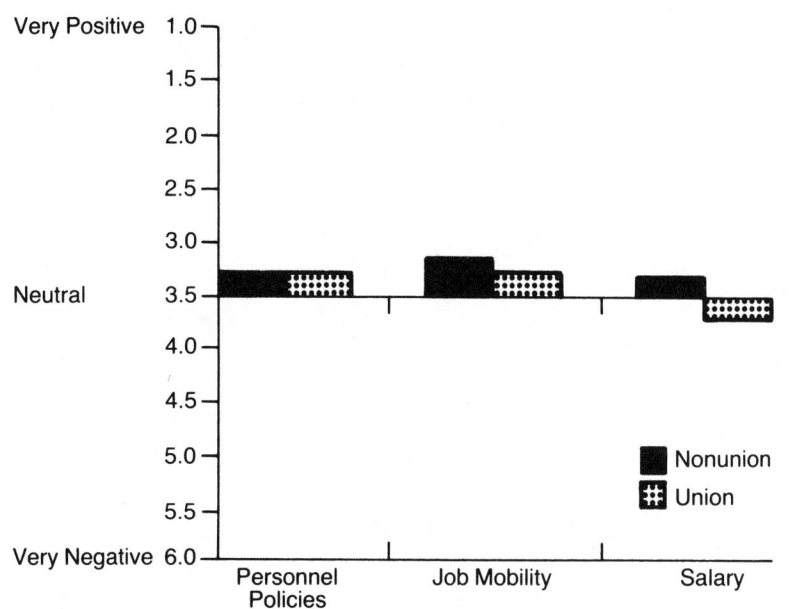

**Figure 4A-11** Nonunion and Union Opinions on Job Security, Work Conditions, and Benefits

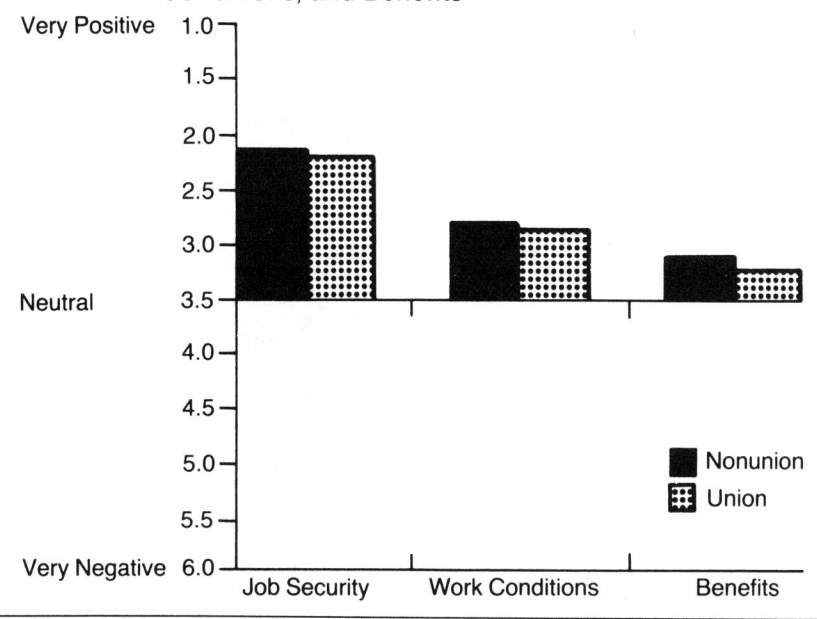

**Figure 4A-12** Nonunion and Union Opinions on Personnel Policies, Job Mobility, and Salary

**Figure 4A-13** Nonunion and Union Opinions on Job Evaluation, Participation, and Communication

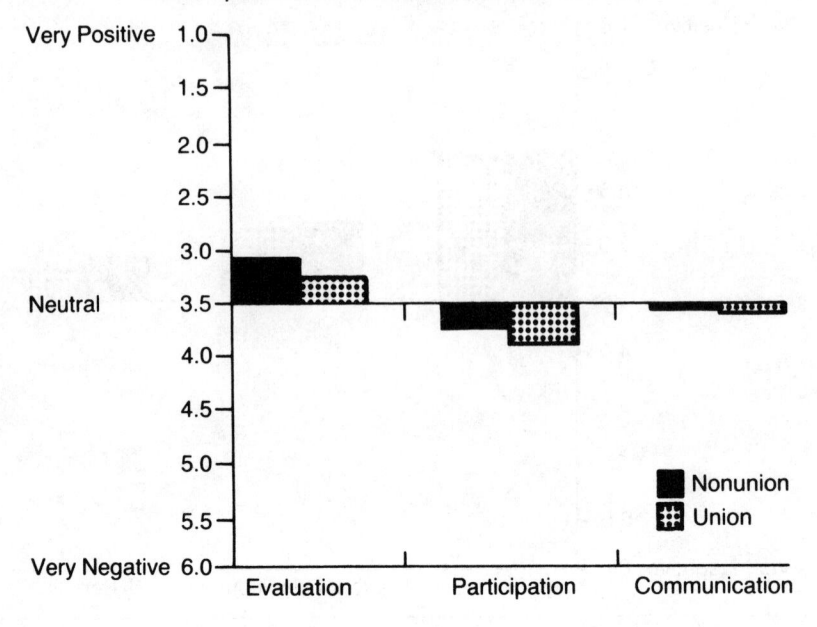

# Appendix 4-B

# New York State Nurses Association Council on Ethical Practice

## RELATIONSHIP OF NYS NURSE PRACTICE ACT, CODE FOR NURSES, AND NYS PROFESSIONAL CONDUCT LAWS

### Preamble

The New York State Nurses Association Council on Ethical Practice recognizes that:

- historically, nursing has been a humanistic profession recognizing the intrinsic worth of each individual and his or her right to health care;
- the nurse comes to his or her professional role with individual values and integrity developed in response to a particular, earlier setting;
- the nurse's prior values are synthesized with a commitment to the humanistic values of nursing education and nursing practice;
- the nurse's authority derives from and is conferred by the patient in conjunction with the values and beliefs associated with the nursing role;
- these nursing values are documented in:
  - •• New York State Nurse Practice Act, Title VIII, Article 139;
  - •• American Nurses' Association Code for Nurses;
  - •• New York State Education Law, Title VIII, Article 130;
  - •• New York State Rules of the Board of Regents Relating to Definitions of Unprofessional Conduct.

*Note:* Approved by the NYSNA Board of Directors September 26, 1980.

*Source:* Reprinted from NEW YORK STATE NURSES ASSOCIATION COUNCIL ON ETHICAL PRACTICE, Relationship of NYS Nurse Practice Act ANA Code for Nurses and NYS Professional Conduct Laws by permission of New York State Nurses Association, © 1981.

The intent of this study is to demonstrate the interrelationship of these documents and to present [them] to the Nursing Community as a ready reference. (See Table 4-B1.)

## NYSNA COUNCIL ON ETHICAL PRACTICE

Josephine Rizzo, R.N., M.A.
Elsie L. Bandman, R.N., Ed.D.
Virginia P. Bartoszek, R.N., M.S.
Josephine Goldberg, R.N.
Elizabeth M. Maloney, R.N., Ed.D.
M. Janice Nelson, R.N., Ed.D.
Betty Zavon, R.N., C.O.H.N.
Sister Marie Celeste Allen, R.N., M.S., Director of Nursing Practice and Services Program

**Table 4B-1** Relationship of NYS Nurse Practice Act, ANA Code for Nurses, and NYS Professional Conduct Laws

| Nurse Practice Act<br>Title VIII, Article 139 | American Nurses' Association Code for Nurses | Professional Conduct<br>Title VIII, Article 130 | Professional Conduct Rules of the NYS Board of Regents |
|---|---|---|---|
| § 6900—Introduction<br>This article applies to the profession of nursing. The general provisions for all professions contained in article 130 of this title apply to this article.<br>§ 6901—Definitions<br>As used in § 6902:<br>1) *"Diagnosing"* in the context of nursing practice means that identification of and discrimination between physical and psychosocial signs and symptoms essential to effective execution and management of the nursing regimen. Such diagnostic privilege is distinct from a medical diagnosis.<br>2) *"Treating"* means selection and performance of those therapeutic measures essential to the effective execution and management of the nursing regimen, and execution of any prescribed medical regimen. | 1) The nurse provides services with respect for human dignity and the uniqueness of the client unrestricted by considerations of social or economic status, personal attributes, or the nature of health problems.<br>1.1 Self-determination of clients.<br>1.2 Social and economic status of clients.<br>1.3 Personal attributes of clients.<br>1.4 The nature of health problems.<br>1.5 The setting for health care.<br>1.6 The dying person.∎ | § 6509—Definitions of Professional Misconduct<br>Each of the following is professional misconduct, and any licensee found guilty of such misconduct under the procedures prescribed in § 6510 shall be subject to the penalties prescribed in § 6511:<br>●●●<br>6) Refusing to provide professional service to a person because of such person's race, creed, color, or national origin;∎ | § 29.1—General Provisions for all Professions<br>§ 29.1 (a)<br>Unprofessional conduct shall be the conduct prohibited by this section. The provisions of these rules applicable to a particular profession may define additional acts or omissions as unprofessional conduct and may establish exceptions to these general prohibitions.<br>(b) Unprofessional conduct in the practice of any profession licensed or certified pursuant to Title VIII of the Education Law shall include:<br>*(follows as applicable)*<br>●●●<br>§ 29.2—General provisions for health and professions.<br>*(follows as applicable)*<br>●●● |

**Table 4B-1** continued

| Nurse Practice Act Title VIII, Article 139 | American Nurses' Association Code for Nurses | Professional Conduct Title VIII, Article 130 | Rules of the NYS Board of Regents |
|---|---|---|---|
| 3) "*Human Responses*" means those signs, symptoms, and processes that denote the individual's interaction with an actual or potential health problem.<br><br>§ 6902—Definition of practice of nursing<br><br>1) The practice of the profession of nursing as a registered professional nurse is defined as diagnosing and treating human responses to actual or potential health problems through such services as casefinding, health teaching, health counseling, and provision of care supportive to or restorative of life and well-being, and executing medical regimens prescribed by a licensed or otherwise legally authorized physician or dentist. A nursing regimen shall be consistent with and shall not vary any existing medical regimen.<br><br>2) The practice of nursing as a licensed practical nurse is | | | § 29.2 (a)<br><br>(1) abandoning or neglecting a patient or client under and in need of immediate professional care without making reasonable arrangements for the continuation of such care, or abandoning a professional employment by a group practice, hospital, clinic or other health care facility, without reasonable notice and under circumstances which seriously impair the delivery of professional care to patients or clients;<br><br>(2) willfully harassing, abusing or intimidating a patient either physically or verbally;■ |

defined as performing tasks and responsibilities within the framework of casefinding, health teaching, health counseling, and provision of supportive and restorative care under the direction of a registered professional nurse or licensed or otherwise legally authorized physician or dentist.■

2) The nurse safeguards the client's right to privacy by judiciously protecting information of a confidential nature.

2.1 Disclosure to the health team.

2.2 Disclosure for quality assurance purposes.

2.3 Disclosure to others not involved in the client's care.

2.4 Disclosure in a court of law.

2.5 Access to records.■

§ 29.1 (b)

(7) failing to make available to a patient or client, upon request, copies of documents in the possession or under the control of the licensee which have been prepared for and paid for by the patient or client;

(8) revealing of personally identifiable facts, data or information obtained in a professional capacity without the prior consent of the patient or client, except as authorized or required by law;■

§ 29.2 (a)

(7) guaranteeing that satisfaction or a cure will result from the performance of professional services;■

**Table 4B-1** continued

| Nurse Practice Act<br>Title VIII, Article 139 | American Nurses'<br>Association<br>Code for Nurses | Professional Conduct<br>Title VIII, Article 130 | Rules of the NYS Board<br>of Regents |
|---|---|---|---|
| | 3) The nurse acts to safeguard the client and the public when health care and safety are affected by incompetent, unethical, or illegal practice of any person.<br><br>3.1 Role of advocate.<br>3.2 Initial action.<br>3.3 Follow-up action.<br>3.4 Peer review. ■ | 1) Obtaining the license fraudulently;<br><br>2) Practicing the profession fraudulently, beyond its authorized scope, with gross incompetence, with gross negligence on a particular occasion or negligence or incompetence on more than one occasion;<br><br>3) Practicing the profession while the ability to practice is impaired by alcohol, drugs, physical disability or mental disability;<br><br>4) Being habitually drunk or being dependent on, or a habitual user of narcotics, barbiturates, amphetamines, hallucinogens, or other drugs having similar effects;<br><br>6) Refusing to provide professional service to a person because of such person's race, creed, color, or national origin;<br><br>7) Permitting, aiding or abetting | § 29.1 (b)<br><br>(1) willful or grossly negligent failure to comply with substantial provisions of Federal, State or local laws, rules or regulations governing the practice of the profession;<br><br>(9) practicing or offering to practice beyond the scope permitted by law, or accepting and performing professional responsibilities which the licensee knows or has reason to know that he or she is not competent to perform, or performing without adequate supervision professional services which the licensee is authorized to perform only under the supervision of a licensed professional, except in an emergency situation where a person's life or health is in danger;<br><br>(10) delegating professional responsibilities to a person when |

Nursing Strikes 121

an unlicensed person to perform activities requiring a license;

8) Practicing the profession while the license is suspended, or willfully failing to register or notify the department of any change of name or mailing address, or, if a professional service corporation willfully failing to comply with § 1503 and § 1514 of the business corporation law; or

9) Committing unprofessional conduct, as defined by the board of regents in its rules or by the commissioner in regulations approved by the board of regents; ■

the licensee delegating such responsibilities knows or has reason to know that such person is not qualified, by training, by experience or by licensure, to perform them; ■

§ 6901—Definitions
As used in § 6902:

1) *"Diagnosing"* in the context of nursing practice means that identification of and discrimination between physical and psychosocial signs and symptoms essential to effective execution and management of the nursing regimen. Such diagnostic privilege is distinct from a medical diagnosis.

2) *"Treating"* means selection and performance of those ther-

4) The nurse assumes responsibility and accountability for individual nursing judgments and actions.

4.1 Acceptance of responsibility and accountability.
4.2 Responsibility.
4.3 Accountability.
4.4 Evaluation of performance. ■

§ 29.1 (b)

(1) willful or grossly negligent failure to comply with substantial provisions of Federal, State or local laws, rules or regulations governing the practice of the profession;

(9) practicing or offering to practice beyond the scope permitted by law, or accepting and performing professional responsibilities which the licensee knows or has reason to know that he or she is not competent to

3) Practicing the profession while the ability to practice is impaired by alcohol, drugs, physical disability or mental disability;

4) Being habitually drunk or being dependent on, or a habitual user of narcotics, barbiturates, amphetamines, hallucinogens, or other drugs having similar effects.

7) Permitting, aiding or abetting an unlicensed person to perform activities requiring a license; ■

**Table 4B-1** continued

| Nurse Practice Act<br>Title VIII, Article 139 | American Nurses'<br>Association<br>Code for Nurses | Professional Conduct<br>Title VIII, Article 130 | Rules of the NYS Board<br>of Regents |
|---|---|---|---|
| apeutic measures essential to the effective execution and management of the nursing regimen, and execution of any prescribed medical regimen.<br><br>3) *"Human Responses"* means those signs, symptoms, and processes which denote the individual's interaction with an actual or potential health problem.<br><br>§ 6902—Definition of practice of nursing<br><br>1) The practice of the profession of nursing as a registered professional nurse is defined as diagnosing and treating human responses to actual or potential health problems through such services as casefinding, health teaching, health counseling, and provision of care supportive to or restorative of life and well-being, and executing medical regimens prescribed by a licensed or otherwise legally | | | perform, or performing without adequate supervision professional services which the licensee is authorized to perform only under the supervision of a licensed professional, except in an emergency situation where a person's life or health is in danger;<br><br>(10) delegating professional responsibilities to a person when the licensee delegating such responsibilities knows or has reason to know that such person is not qualified, by training, by experience or by licensure, to perform them;<br><br>(11) performing professional services which have not been duly authorized by the patient or client or his or her legal representative;■<br><br>§ 29.2 (a)<br><br>(1) abandoning or neglecting a patient or client under and in |

authorized physician or dentist. A nursing regimen shall be consistent with and shall not vary any existing medical regimen.

2) The practice of nursing as a license practical nurse is defined as performing tasks and responsibilities within the framework of casefinding, health teaching, health counseling, and provision of supportive and restorative care under the direction of a registered professional nurse or licensed or otherwise legally authorized physician or dentist. ■

need of immediate professional care without making reasonable arrangements for the continuation of such care, or abandoning a professional employment by a group practice, hospital, clinic or other health care facility, without reasonable notice and under circumstances which seriously impair the delivery of professional care to patients or clients;

(2) willfully harassing, abusing or intimidating a patient either physically or verbally;

(3) failing to maintain a record for each patient which accurately reflects the evaluation and treatment of the patient. Unless otherwise provided by law, all patient records must be retained for at least six years. Obstetrical records and records of minor patients must be retained for at least six years, and until one year after the minor patient reaches the age of 21 years. ■

5) The nurse maintains competence in nursing.

5.1 Personal responsibility for competence.

2) Practicing the profession fraudulently, beyond its authorized scope, with gross incompetence, with gross negligence

§ 29.1 (b)

(1) willful or grossly negligent failure to comply with substantial provisions of Federal, State

**Table 4B-1** continued

| Nurse Practice Act Title VIII, Article 139 | American Nurses' Association Code for Nurses | Professional Conduct Title VIII, Article 130 | Rules of the NYS Board of Regents |
|---|---|---|---|
| | 5.2 Measurement of competence in nursing practice.<br><br>5.3 Continuing education for continuing competence.<br><br>5.4 Intraprofessional responsibility for competence in nursing care. ■ | on a particular occasion or negligence or incompetence on more than one occasion;<br><br>3) Practicing the profession while the ability to practice is impaired by alcohol, drugs, physical disability or mental disability;<br><br>4) Being habitually drunk or being dependent on, or a habitual user of narcotics, barbiturates, amphetamines, hallucinogens, or other drugs having similar effects; ■ | or local laws, rules or regulations governing the practice of the profession;<br><br>(9) practicing or offering to practice beyond the scope permitted by law, or accepting and performing professional responsibilities which the licensee knows or has reason to know that he or she is not competent to perform, or performing without adequate supervision professional services which the licensee is authorized to perform only under the supervision of a licensed professional, except in an emergency situation where a person's life or health is in danger;<br><br>(10) delegating professional responsibilities to a person when the licensee delegating such responsibilities knows or has reason to know that such person is not qualified, by training, by |

experience or by licensure, to perform them;

§ 29.2 (a)

(1) abandoning or neglecting a patient or client under and in need of immediate professional care without making reasonable arrangements for the continuation of such care, or abandoning a professional employment by a group practice, hospital, clinic or other health care facility, without reasonable notice and under circumstances which seriously impair the delivery of professional care to patients or clients;

(5) failing to exercise appropriate supervision over persons who are authorized to practice only under the supervision of the licensed professional;

(9) claiming or using any secret or special method of treatment which the licensee refuses to divulge to the State Board for the profession.■

§ 29.1 (b)

(1) willful or grossly negligent failure to comply with substantial provisions of Federal, State

6) The nurse exercises informed judgment and uses individual competence and qualifications as criteria in seeking consulta-

7) Permitting, aiding or abetting an unlicensed person to perform activities requiring a license;■

**Table 4B-1** continued

| Nurse Practice Act<br>Title VIII, Article 139 | American Nurses'<br>Association<br>Code for Nurses | Professional Conduct<br>Title VIII, Article 130 | Rules of the NYS Board<br>of Regents |
|---|---|---|---|
| | tion, accepting responsibilities, and delegating nursing activities to others.<br><br>6.1 Changing functions.<br>6.2 Joint policy statements.<br>6.3 Seeking consultation.<br>6.4 Accepting responsibilities or delegating activities.<br>6.5 Accepting responsibility.■ | | or local laws, rules or regulations governing the practice of the profession;<br><br>(9) practicing or offering to practice beyond the scope permitted by law, or accepting and performing professional responsibilities which the licensee knows or has reason to know that he or she is not competent to perform, or performing without adequate supervision professional services which the licensee is authorized to perform only under the supervision of a licensed professional, except in an emergency situation where a person's life or health is in danger;<br><br>(10) delegating professional responsibilities to a person when the licensee delegating such responsibilities knows or has reason to know that such person is not qualified, by training, by experience or by licensure, to perform them; |

## Nursing Strikes 127

(11) performing professional services which have not been duly authorized by the patient or client or his or her legal representative;■

§ 29.2 (a)

(5) failing to exercise appropriate supervision over persons who are authorized to practice only under the supervision of the licensed professional;■

7) The nurse participates in activities that contribute to the ongoing development of the profession's body of knowledge.

7.1 The nurse and research.

7.2 General guidelines for participating in research.

7.3 The protection of human rights in research.

7.4 The practitioner's rights and responsibilities in research.■

8) The nurse participates in the profession's efforts to implement and improve standards of nursing.

8.1 Responsibility to the public.

8.2 Responsibility to the discipline.

2) Practicing the profession fraudulently, beyond its authorized scope, with gross incompetence, with gross negligence on a particular occasion or negligence or incompetence on more than one occasion;

§ 29.1 (b)

(1) willful or grossly negligent failure to comply with substantial provisions of Federal, State or local laws, rules or regulations governing the practice of the profession;

**Table 4B-1** continued

| Nurse Practice Act Title VIII, Article 139 | American Nurses' Association Code for Nurses | Professional Conduct Title VIII, Article 130 | Rules of the NYS Board of Regents |
|---|---|---|---|
| | 8.3 Responsibility to nursing students. ■ | 3) Practicing the profession while the ability to practice is impaired by alcohol, drugs, physical disability or mental disability; <br><br> 4) Being habitually drunk or being dependent on, or a habitual user of narcotics, barbiturates, amphetamines, hallucinogens, or other drugs having similar effects; <br><br> 5) Being convicted of committing an act constituting a crime under: <br> (a) New York State law or <br> (b) Federal law or, <br> (c) The law of another jurisdiction and which, if committed within this state, would have constituted a crime under New York State law; <br><br> 6) Refusing to provide professional services to a person because of such person's race, creed, color, or national origin; | (5) conduct in the practice of a profession which evidences moral unfitness to practice the profession; <br><br> (6) willfully making or filing a false report, or failing to file a report required by law or by the Education Department, or willfully impeding or obstructing such filing, or inducing another person to do so; <br><br> (9) practicing or offering to practice beyond the scope permitted by law, or accepting and performing professional responsibilities which the licensee knows or has reason to know that he or she is not competent to perform, or performing without adequate supervision professional services which the licensee is authorized to perform only under the supervision of a licensed professional, except in an emergency situation where a |

7) Permitting, aiding or abetting an unlicensed person to perform activities requiring a license;

person's life or health is in danger;

(10) delegating professional responsibilities to a person when the licensee delegating such responsibilities knows or has reason to know that such person is not qualified, by training, by experience or by licensure, to perform them;

(11) performing professional services which have not been duly authorized by the patient or client or his or her legal representative;

§ 29.2 (a)

(1) abandoning or neglecting a patient or client under and in need of immediate professional care without making reasonable arrangements for the continuation of such care, or abandoning a professional employment by a group practice, hospital, clinic or other health care facility, without reasonable notice and under circumstances which seriously impair the delivery of professional care to patients or clients;

(2) willfully harassing, abusing

**Table 4B-1** continued

| Nurse Practice Act<br>Title VIII, Article 139 | American Nurses'<br>Association<br>Code for Nurses | Professional Conduct<br>Title VIII, Article 130 | Rules of the NYS Board<br>of Regents |
|---|---|---|---|
| | | | or intimidating a patient either physically or verbally;<br><br>(3) failing to maintain a record for each patient which accurately reflects the evaluation and treatment of the patient. Unless otherwise provided by law, all patient records must be retained for at least six years. Obstetrical records and records of minor patients must be retained for at least six years, and until one year after the minor patient reaches the age of 21 years.<br><br>(5) failing to exercise appropriate supervision over persons who are authorized to practice only under the supervision of the licensed professional;<br><br>(6) upon a patient's written request, failing to make available to a patient, or, to another licensed health practitioner consistent with that practitioner's authorized scope of practice, copies of the record required |

by paragraph (3) of this subdivision and copies of reports, test records, evaluations or X rays relating to the patient which are in the possession or under the control of the licensee, or failing to complete forms or reports required for the reimbursement of a patient by a third party. Reasonable fees may be charged for such copies, forms or reports, but prior payment for the professional services to which such records relate may not be required as a condition for making such records available. A practitioner may, however, withhold information from a patient if, in the reasonable exercise of his or her professional judgment, he or she believes release of such information would adversely affect the patient's health, and this section shall not require release, to the parent or guardian of a minor, of records or information relating to venereal disease or abortion except with the minor's consent. This provision shall apply in lieu of section 29.1 (b) (7) of this Part;

(9) claiming or using any secret

## Table 4B-1 continued

| Nurse Practice Act Title VIII, Article 139 | American Nurses' Association Code for Nurses | Professional Conduct Title VIII, Article 130 | Rules of the NYS Board of Regents |
|---|---|---|---|
| | 9) The nurse participates in the profession's efforts to establish and maintain conditions of employment conducive to high quality nursing care.<br><br>9.1 Responsibility for conditions of employment.<br><br>9.2 Collective action.<br><br>9.3 Individual action.<br><br>10) The nurse participates in the profession's effort to protect the public from misinformation and misrepresentation and to maintain the integrity of nursing. ■ | 1) Obtaining the license fraudulently;<br><br>2) Practicing the profession fraudulently, beyond its authorized scope, with gross incompetence, with gross negligence on a particular occasion or negligence or incompetence on more than one occasion;<br><br>3) Practicing the profession while the ability to practice is impaired by alcohol, drugs, physical disability or mental disability;<br><br>4) Being habitually drunk or being dependent on, or a habitual user of narcotics, barbitu- or special method of treatment which the licensee refuses to divulge to the State Board for the profession.<br><br>(11) entering into an arrangement or agreement with a pharmacy for the compounding and/or dispensing of coded or specially marked prescriptions. ■ | § 29.1 (b)<br><br>(1) willful or grossly negligent failure to comply with substantial provisions of Federal, State or local laws, rules or regulations governing the practice of the profession;<br><br>(3) directly or indirectly offering, giving, soliciting, or receiving or agreeing to receive, any fee or other consideration to or from a third party for the referral of a patient or client or in connection with the performance of professional services; ■ |

rates, amphetamines, hallucinogens, or other drugs having similar effects;

5) Being convicted of committing an act constituting a crime under:

(a) New York State law or

(b) Federal law or,

(c) The law of another jurisdiction and which, if committed within this state, would have constituted a crime under New York State law;

6) Refusing to provide professional services to a person because of such person's race, creed, color, or national origin;

7) Permitting, aiding or abetting an unlicensed person to perform activities requiring a license;

8) Practicing the profession while the license is suspended, or willfully failing to register or notify the department of any change of name or mailing address, or, if a professional service corporation willfully failing to comply with § 1503 and § 1514 of the business corporation law; or

9) Committing unprofessional conduct, as defined by the board

**Table 4B-1** continued

| Nurse Practice Act<br>Title VIII, Article 139 | American Nurses' Association<br>Code for Nurses | Professional Conduct<br>Title VIII, Article 130 | Rules of the NYS Board of Regents |
|---|---|---|---|
| § 6903—Practice of nursing and use of title *"registered professional nurse"* or *"licensed practical nurse"*<br><br>Only a person licensed or otherwise authorized under this article shall practice nursing and only a person licensed under § 6905 shall use the title *"registered professional nurse"* and only a person licensed under § 6906 of this article shall use the title *"licensed practical nurse."* ■ | 10) The nurse participates in the profession's effort to protect the public from misinformation and misrepresentation and to maintain the integrity of nursing.<br>10.1 Advertising services.<br>10.2 Use of titles and symbols.<br>10.3 Endorsement of commercial products or services.<br>10.4 Protecting the client from harmful products.<br>10.5 Reporting infractions. ■ | of regents in its rules or by the commissioner in regulations approved by the board of regents;<br>10) A willful violation by a licensed physician of subdivision 11 of § 230 of the public health law. ■<br>§ 6509 NOS. 1 through 10 *(see previous section)* | § 29.1 (b)<br>(1) willful or grossly negligent failure to comply with substantial provisions of Federal, State or local laws, rules or regulations governing the practice of the profession;<br>(2) exercising undue influence on the patient or client, including the promotion of the sale of services, goods, appliances or drugs in such manner as to exploit the patient or client for the financial gain of the practitioner or of a third party;<br>(6) willfully making or filing a false report, or failing to file a report required by law or by the |

Education Department, or willfully impeding or obstructing such filing, or inducing another person to do so;

(10) delegating professional responsibilities to a person when the licensee delegating such responsibilities knows or has reason to know that such person is not qualified, by training, by experience or by licensure, to perform them;

(12) advertising or soliciting for patronage that is not in the public interest;

(i) Advertising or soliciting not in the public interest shall include but not be limited to advertising that:

(a) is false, fraudulent, deceptive, misleading, sensational or flamboyant;

(b) represents intimidation or undue pressure;

(c) uses testimonials;

(d) guarantees any service;

(e) offers gratuitous services or discounts in connection with professional services; but this clause shall not be construed to relate to the negotia-

**Table 4B-1** continued

| Nurse Practice Act<br>Title VIII, Article 139 | American Nurses'<br>Association<br>Code for Nurses | Professional Conduct<br>Title VIII, Article 130 | Rules of the NYS Board<br>of Regents |
|---|---|---|---|
| | | | tion of fees between professionals and patients or clients, or to prohibit the rendering of professional services for which no fee is charged;<br><br>(f) makes claims of professional superiority which cannot be substantiated by the licensee, who shall have the burden of proof; or<br><br>(g) states or includes prices for professional services, except as provided for in clause (b) of subparagraph (ii) of this paragraph;<br><br>(ii) The following shall be deemed appropriate means of informing the public of the availability of professional services:<br><br>(a) informational advertising not contrary to the foregoing prohibitions, and<br><br>(b) the advertising in a newspaper, periodical or professional directory or on radio |

or television of fixed prices, or a stated range of prices, for specified routine professional services, provided

(iv) No demonstrations, dramatizations or other portrayals of professional practice shall be permitted in advertising on radio or television;

§ 29.2 (a)

(4) using the word "Doctor" in offering to perform professional services without also indicating the profession in which the licensee holds a doctorate;

(5) failing to exercise appropriate supervision over persons who are authorized to practice only under the supervision of the licensed professional;

(8) ordering of excessive tests, treatment, or use of treatment facilities not warranted by the condition of the patient;

(10) failing to wear an identifying badge, which shall be conspicuously displayed and legible, indicating the practitioner's name and professional title authorized pursuant to the Education Law, while practicing as

## Table 4B-1 continued

| Nurse Practice Act<br>Title VIII, Article 139 | American Nurses'<br>Association<br>Code for Nurses | Professional Conduct<br>Title VIII, Article 130<br>Rules of the NYS Board<br>of Regents |
|---|---|---|
| | (11) The nurse collaborates with members of the health professions and other citizens in promoting community and national efforts to meet the health needs of the public.<br><br>11.1 Quality Health Care as a right.<br>11.2 Responsibility to the consumer of health care.<br>11.3 Relationships with other disciplines.<br>11.4 Relationship with medicine.<br>11.5 Conflict of interest.■ | an employee or operator of a hospital, clinic, group practice or multiprofessional facility, or at a commercial establishment offering health services to the public.<br><br>(11) performing professional services which have not been duly authorized by the patient or client or his or her legal representative;■ |

**REFERENCES**

The Nurse Practice Act of New York State, as contained in Articles 130 and 139 of Title VIII of the Education Law from *McKinney's Consolidated Laws of New York State Annotated* (Book 16), Including Amendments enacted through 1978 ($1.50).

American Nurses' Association, *Code for Nurses With Interpretive Statements,* Kansas City, Mo., 1977, (G-56R, 25¢).

"Rules of the New York State Board of Regents Relating to Definitions of Unprofessional Conduct," *Official Compilation Codes, Rules, Regulations of the State of New York,* Title VIII, Chapter I, Part 29.1–29.2, 1978.

New York State Nurses Association:
  "Policies and Procedures Governing Violations of the Code for Nurses,"
  "Form for Reporting Alleged Violations of the Code for Nurses,"
  "Operational Definitions in Evaluating Allegations of Professional Misconduct in Nursing,"
  "Overview of Peer Review."

Chapter 5

# The Future: Proposals for Change

The traditional view subscribed to by both management and union practitioners as to the place of strikes in the collective bargaining arena was expressed by Karsh.

> The strike is among the most highly publicized and the least studied social phenomena of our time . . . (It) is the mechanism which produces that increment of pressure necessary to force agreement where differences are persistent and do not yield to persuasion or argument around the bargaining table . . . The alternate to such a system might result in the demise of the collective bargaining system as we know it; some form of coercion exercised by a supreme authority whether it be a government board, an industrial relations court, compulsory arbitrations, or some other of the many proposals which have been advanced from time to time, would supplant the voluntarism implicit in the American collective bargaining experience. Thus, the strike, or threat of strike, is the ultimate device whereby the competing interests of antagonistic parties are expediently resolved, leading to a modus operandi which permits both sides to accommodate their differences and live with one another.[1]

As in other industries, strikes and strike threats are integral parts of the total industrial collective bargaining experience in the health care industry. It is not unusual for administrators of nonunion institutions to believe that union recognition is a direct invitation to strikes. Where contract terms are not settled to a union's satisfaction, strikes will be used to force management to compromise its position and meet either entirely or partially the union's demands. Labor law requires that management and labor bargain "in good faith," but it does not compel them to agree to proposals made by either side. Unions can and do strike to support their positions in negotiations. The strike is part of the arsenal of weapons available to the union, which intends to make it expensive and inconvenient for the employer not to agree to its proposals.[2]

The right to strike continues to be defended by many experts but the general strife on the health care labor front and in other industrial areas, including the discomforting strikes of transit workers, teachers, police officers, firefighters, and other public sector employees, has given rise to a hue and cry from the public.[3] Public approval of stoppages is waning, as unemployed workers look askance at those with the opportunity to work during economically depressed times but who withhold their services.

Some observers feel that health care unions, by striking, do not punish their employers but rather the patients and, of course, the public. That same public has now found that the strike, in seeking to apply pressure if not to cause injury to the employer, has many byproducts that affect the broader community, including inconvenience and final transfer of higher costs for products or services to the public. Far more important is the awareness that the strike of health care workers may well be a threat to the continued uninterrupted delivery of lifesaving services.

**THE EFFECT OF STRIKES**

The impact of any strike on consumers of the product involved is related to three considerations: the cultural necessity of the product, the stock effect, and the possibility of substitution.[4] The term "cultural necessity" is defined as the importance of the product in the lives of those who consume it. Products that are dispensable or deferrable may be considered unnecessary; other products must be available if hardship is to be avoided; and at the top of the scale, some products are necessary for health and safety.

The "stock effect" is the extent to which consumption declines, owing to diminishing stocks. In a milk strike, for example, as the stock of milk declines in the stores, the impact increases.

The third factor, the possibility of substituting other products for the "struck" products, ranges from a completely acceptable substitute at the lower end of the scale to the top of the scale where no acceptable substitute is available.

A strike of a hospital or nursing home produces a high impact because the end product, patient care, is necessary for health and safety. It is absolutely necessary; this is not debatable. As to the stock effect, a strike removes beds from the available stock in the community, thus extending waiting lists, and mitigates the provision of emergency services. Regarding the last factor, it is not difficult to appreciate the limit of acceptable substitutes in most communities.

The real losers in strikes in health care institutions are the patients, their families, and prospective patients. The patients will be underserved, may be moved from the struck hospital or home, or may be discharged earlier than they should be. Families of patients will be subjected to anxieties over the limited care that is available and may be forced to administer home care. Prospective patients will be troubled by the limited available beds, operations will be delayed and outpatient care discontinued.

## HEALTH CARE STRIKES: ARE THEY DEFENSIBLE?

The appropriateness of collective bargaining as it is now practiced in health care institutions is suspect. Are strikes, walkouts, or the threat of either of these traditional labor weapons necessary or acceptable when, in the final analysis, they directly or indirectly impact on patient care? Charles Darwin commented that he had steadily endeavored to keep his mind free so as to give up any hypothesis, however much beloved (and he further commented that he could not resist forming one on every subject), as soon as facts are shown to be opposed. The facts are, indeed, clearly opposed to the old hypothesis of the rationalization of the need for strikes in health care collective bargaining. The pendulum has swung in the health care industry from a minimal concern for employee relations to an almost distracting overemphasis on that area. Concern for employees is, of course, an essential part of quality health care. The unions have been instrumental in directing our focus on the needs of employees. But who represents the patients? Who speaks for the sick? The seriously ill? The concerned patients who need the full attention of our medical staff? What comfort is it to patients to know that a strike is threatened, that a walkout may take place when they are in desperate need of attention? How are the fears of the elderly allayed when the workers at a home for the aged walk out over contract negotiations?

Many practitioners point to the low incidence of strikes in our society, but the possibility of a strike and the threat of strikes are still realities in the health care industry. In many areas the style of unions, as nurtured by management and governmental representatives, is brinkmanship, which puts the patients ill at ease. Someone once said that in labor relations affairs an industry gets the kind of labor relations it deserves. Do we truly deserve the industrial model? Is confrontation necessary, or even permissible, where patient care is involved? Health care collective bargaining must be more than an adversarial relationship built upon an aggression-containment model. It must be more than a fist fight. Only children and incomplete adults think that life is a continuous test of strength, and think that one side must always prevail. Mills believes that managers and union officials must always have at the top of their agenda the broadening of cooperation and consensus.[5] We must attempt to move the collective bargaining process beyond continual confrontation and into a more constructive mode. Some new approaches should be developed to minimize crisis bargaining. Relationships should be altered. Management must be a partner in this review of alternative approaches to the present model. The unions, of course, should seek innovative remedies and take the lead in designing an equitable arbitration system that would settle the contract disputes of public and health care employees without destructive strikes.[6] Both unions and management must be willing to take a chance and pay the price. They have not been willing in the past.

## ALTERNATIVES TO THE STRIKE

The quest for impasse procedures that will make strikes unnecessary in the health care industry is a relatively new undertaking. Some health care labor contracts contain interest arbitration clauses that prohibit strikes, and some states have such provisions for public sector employees and have included health care employees under such jurisdiction, but such provisions and laws are generally opposed by both parties to the collective bargaining agreement. This is difficult to understand, for binding arbitration laws have been relatively successful in the public sector. Arguments against binding arbitration are mostly theoretical in nature, and are based upon the premise of the chilling effect of such provisions on collective bargaining. Attempts to consider any mechanism that prohibits strikes in the health care industry have been stymied in the past for much the same reasons that such attempts have been stalled in the public sector. Beamer[7] points out that despite the relative success of binding arbitration laws, a large number of individuals are unable or unwilling to consider alternatives to the strike. They support their opposition to binding arbitration with arguments from the past, positions taken before the laws were really tested, arguments that are, in essence, more fiction than fact. The health care industry can learn a great deal from the successful experiments with alternatives to strikes in public employment. (See Appendix 5-A.)

Impasse resolution methods include fact finding, conventional interest arbitration, final-offer arbitration, and mediation-arbitration.

**Fact Finding**

Fact finding is a discipline quite different from mediation. The mediator often provides the parties with a method to communicate without face-to-face confrontations. The mediator often is a messenger, but not one without effect. The mediator attempts to clarify arguments and channel the parties into positions of compromise. Fact finders, either in a panel or singularly, are responsible for establishing relevant facts in a dispute and often recommend compromise positions. Tripartite panels usually consist of a representative from the employer, one from the union, and an agreed-upon neutral representative selected by both parties. A fact finder can be a single party as well. In either case, panel or individual, the fact finder is charged with developing the facts of the dispute through a hearing with, in some cases, the rights to subpoena and to render an opinion or to recommend a settlement of the dispute based upon the acquired information.[8]

There are four types of fact finding. The first is fact finding without recommendations. A fact finder who is not empowered to give recommendations examines the events that have transpired and evaluates the areas of factual difference. This process is usually an exercise in futility because most labor disputes are so complicated that a mere portrayal of facts does not create the basis for a settlement.[9] The second type of fact finder also makes no recommendations. This kind of fact finding takes place well in advance of the actual negotiations. In such cases an impartial person or agency is appointed before negotiations have begun to develop a factual background for future use by the bargainers. For example, impartial actuaries or insurance experts can provide a single set of facts about the costs of a variety of hypothetical pension and insurance benefits. President Kennedy's Advisory Committee on Labor-Management Policy recommended this system in 1962. It normally precedes a stalemate and helps avoid a strike.[10]

Another type of fact finding involves recommendations on procedures or direction without recommendations on issue. The Taylor-Higgins-Reedy Board used this method when handling the 1967–68 nonferrous disputes. During the negotiations the parties were stalemated over a demand by the union for coordinated bargaining. The board did not attempt to examine the specific economic and noneconomic issues. It did, however, review the history of the bargaining structure and then recommended a structure that best fit the companies and unions in light of the facts uncovered and the current positions of the parties involved. This type of fact finding results in recommendations as to the criteria or procedural device to get the parties around a road block to bargain.[11]

Finally, there is fact finding with recommendations on issues as well as on procedure. Here the fact finders are charged with making specific recommendations on the disputed issues after finding the facts. The procedural aspects are somewhat similar to arbitration in that formal hearings usually occur and the fact finder may believe that it is improper to confer with one party in the absence of the other. After the fact finder has secured the facts through evidence and testimony, he or she will prepare a set of recommendations that are not binding to the parties. This, in effect, is the manner in which boards of inquiry operate in the health care industry.

In most cases, the recommendations of fact-finding panels are only advisory, but they are sometimes made public by either the fact finder or the parties. With the findings of the panel made public it is hoped that public opinion will cause the parties to resolve the dispute.[12]

> Although the fact finder's recommendations are advisory there is, theoretically, an obligation on the part of both parties to attempt to arrive at an agreement based on the recommendations.
> In fact, it has been held that an employer has an obligation to bargain in good faith following the issuance of the fact finders' recommendation.[13]

Fact finding with recommendations allows the parties to review their positions in relation to the recommendations set forth by that fact finder. It should be clear that either party, or both parties, can reject the recommendations.

**Conventional Interest Arbitration**

Conventional interest arbitration involves the establishment of a panel or a single arbitrator, whose recommendations go far beyond those of mediators or fact finders—they are final and binding. This neutral person or committee reviews the facts much like a fact finder, and issues a decision for settlement on all outstanding issues. In most cases, such panels or individuals make decisions in terms of adjustment, accommodation, and acceptability, rather than win-lose. The arbitrator in many cases compromises between the positions of the parties.

Conventional interest arbitration has been opposed on the grounds that if either party anticipates that it will get more from an arbitrator than through negotiations, that party will avoid the necessary trade offs and compromises inherent in good-faith collective bargaining. It has been argued that interest arbitration stifles negotiations. The system's opponents point out that both parties make a sham of bargaining, because they are hesitant to make even a modest offer for fear of raising the bargaining floor from which the arbitrator begins deliberations. An early observer pointed out that,

> Under free collective bargaining final authority rests with union and management officials. Their freedom includes freedom to disagree with the consequent risks of strikes. The possibility of a strike . . . hangs over every bargaining conference and without it, bargaining would have little meaning . . . [Compulsory arbitration] leads . . . to a withering away of collective bargaining and the assumption of full government control of the wages and conditions of employment. . . . If collective bargaining is desirable, one must accept the occasional inconvenience caused by work stoppages.[14]

Still others oppose binding arbitration inasmuch as the arbitrator may issue a monetary award that is binding on the parties but not necessarily on the public or third party payors.

In New York state tripartite interest arbitration is mandated in police and fire fighter impasses, and the so-called "chilling" effect of that procedure has been neither obvious nor evident. In 1981 only 18 police and firefighter cases went to arbitration, and they represented 11 percent of the total negotiations involving police officers and firefighters that took place in the state during that year. It is interesting to note that arbitration awards provided smaller wage settlements for police and firefighters than those that were achieved by the unions at the bargaining table.[15]

Iowa has implemented a statute for all its public employees, providing for final and binding arbitration of interest disputes. In the reporting years 1977–1978, 1978–1979, and 1979–1980, less than 5 percent of the total number of collective bargaining agreements were settled by arbitration.

**Final-Offer Arbitration**

Final-offer arbitration, also referred to as last offer, final position, and forced choice arbitration, is, among other things, a process whereby an arbitrator chooses between the final offers of the two parties involved. In this process, final positions of the parties to unresolved issues are presented to the arbitrator. The arbitrator must decide between the two. There is no flexibility in the process to vary items within the package or to modify the terms presented by the parties to what the arbitrator might consider more fair and reasonable. Such rigid final-offer procedures usually require that the parties' final offers be certified in writing in advance of the arbitration procedure, and cannot later be changed. It has been noted that such a draconian procedure may discourage a resort to arbitration and force more voluntary settlements during negotiations.[16] Many arbitrators have objected to rigid final-offer proceedings on the basis of the inflexible choice thrust upon the arbitrator to select from the parties' alternative settlement packages the one that seems to be more appropriate based on the facts and, in some instances, only on one or two important points. It is winner take all! Enormous risks are indeed involved in this procedure, but there are also possible benefits. Final-offer arbitration attempts to motivate the parties to develop more reasonable positions prior to the arbitrator's decision. In theory, the parties, in an effort to win the arbitrator's approval, should be so close together that they will either reach settlement on their own, or narrow the area of disagreement to such an extent that the arbitrator's award, no matter which package is chosen, will be a reasonable one. Fear that the arbitrator will select the other party's offer causes a mechanism likened to a strike by creating the possibility of severe financial impacts due to continued disagreement.[17]

Another form of final-offer arbitration provides more flexibility. The arbitrator makes an award on each separate issue. Currently the last-offer-by-issue system is provided for by the Policemen's and Firemen's Act of 1972 in Michigan, and in the Public Employment Relations Act of 1974 in Iowa. Major league baseball has also voluntarily adopted this system for the resolution of salary disputes. In Michigan, the parties may submit or change their final offers during the hearing or wait until the close of the hearing to submit a final offer. A final offer statute in New Jersey was recently held by the new Jersey Supreme Court to permit changes in the parties' economic package offers during the proceedings.[18] Issue-by-issue final offer arbitration permits flexibility and prevents a winner-take-all phenomenon, which is destructive to the overall collective bargaining relationship.

Still another form of final-offer arbitration provides for a third choice, in addition to the employer's final offer of settlement and the union's final offer of settlement. This added choice is the recommendation of prior fact-finding panels. The arbitrator using this procedure has a strong though not invariable tendency to take the earlier fact finder's recommendations as a basis for settlement.[19]

### Mediation-Arbitration (Med-Arb)

Mediation-Arbitration (Med-Arb) offers the best of all worlds, or at least it appears to. It combines the role of the mediator with that of the arbitrator.

This individual participates throughout the negotiations in anticipation of the possibility of an impasse. The mediator-arbitrator's efforts are directed toward producing a settlement; therefore, he or she acts in the traditional role of a mediator. Failing in that role at a specific point (and only the experienced mediator can identify this point), he or she assumes the role of an arbitrator. The obvious advantage in Med-Arb is that the individual, the third party neutral, who finally must assume the role of arbitrator is fully cognizant and has broad appreciation of events preceding the impasse. The mediator-arbitrator can, therefore, evaluate the importance of positions and make a valid judgment as to those issues that are truly critical.

This process was developed during negotiations between the California Nurses Association (CNA) and hospitals in the San Francisco Bay area. The parties voluntarily accepted it in place of a strike. It proved a successful alternative.

These negotiations took place in 1970–1971. Interestingly, the CNA was pleased with the results, but hospital management representatives were not and refused to use the process during negotiations taking place in 1974. These negotiations ended in a three-week strike.

The third party in Med-Arb serves primarily as a mediator, and only after all mediation efforts fail is a final and binding decision made on all unresolved issues. Every effort is made to enable the parties to reach an agreement on their own. It is during this period that the mediator establishes neutrality and gains the respect of the parties, two achievements that are essential to the success of his or her later role as an arbitrator. Of course, the parties have a strong incentive to settle their differences on their own, for they know that if they fail to do so the Med-Arb will make an agreement for them.

The role of Med-Arb is a complex and demanding one, requiring far more sophistication than needed to play either role separately. There are risks; as one observer points out:

> Although mediators and arbitrators are both in the business of resolving disputes, some successful arbitrators do not possess the skills, abilities and characteristics to effectively function as mediators, and the converse is true for mediators. Med-Arbiters must be able to gain the trust and respect of the parties in a negotiating setting, especially where their presence has been mandated by an outside administrative agency. This requires an understanding of contract negotiations, a sense of timing, and the ability to induce the parties to change their positions through reasoning and persuasion. In addition, where mediation techniques prove unsuccessful, the Med-Arbiter may be required to

make face-to-face, on-the-spot decisions after providing the parties with an opportunity to fully present their arguments. Mediators and arbitrators, by virtue of a need to maintain their neutrality and acceptability are well aware of the risks attended to functioning in the emotion laden atmosphere of contract negotiations. Because of the high visibility of contract negotiations neutrals must consider the potential effects of their involvement in a Med-Arb proceeding on their continued acceptability to the labor and management communities.[20]

## PROPOSAL FOR THE FUTURE

Arvid Anderson, chairman of the Office of Collective Bargaining in New York City, wrote:

> I am under no illusion that there can be an absolute guarantee against strikes in a free society, or that arbitration is a panacea for all collective bargaining problems. But I do believe that we can substitute the rule of reason for trial by combat, that we can use the power of persuasion rather than the persuasion of power to settle disputes, and that interest arbitration is by far a better way to resolve public sector bargaining impasses.[21]

Anderson's eloquent statement reflects an enlightened view of the troubled collective bargaining arena in the health care industry. Interest arbitration may well be the answer.

The most preferred method for the resolution of disputes between unions and employees is the collective bargaining process. During collective bargaining negotiations one party may threaten the other with a work stoppage or lockout for the purpose of making the price of disagreement greater than that of agreement. The use of arbitration for dispute resolution will preclude the use of these economic weapons by either side. Moreover, arbitration does not preclude collective bargaining. To wit:

> Collective bargaining promotes labor peace because the affected parties have the capacity to express their concerns and the ability to have an impact upon the decision-making process on issues that vitally concern them. Arbitration does not limit this discussion which is a prerequisite to the final step of an arbitrator's determination. The ultimate mechanism for resolving a dispute is the only procedural change. The parties retain their capacity

to put forth their positions on conditions of employment. They merely lose ultimate economic control in the current round of negotiations to determine the outcome, should impasse occur. Furthermore, continued input occurs during the tripartite arbitration panel discussions, where both parties designate an arbitrator. Nonneutral arbitrators educate the arbitrator and attempt to form a consensus to reach an agreement. The give and take of collective bargaining continues even under arbitration through party representatives.[22]

The threat of strike imposes various potential costs on both parties. These potential costs act as incentives for the parties to reach settlement. The parties should then develop a range of potential settlements that they both consider preferable to strike. The range of potential settlements is called a "contract zone."[23]

Assuming that arbitration does not impose any direct costs on the parties, it must create (define) a contract zone through a mechanism that is fundamentally different from that of a strike. The major source of arbitration leverage is derived from the uncertainty of the parties regarding the behavior of the arbitrator: the parties are willing to give up some of the expected gains from an arbitrated settlement in order to avoid the attendant uncertainty.[24]

The uncertainty of an award has been defined as "the probability that interest arbitration would result in an outcome to a party less desirable than the party could have obtained through a bilateral settlement."[25] The "chilling" or narcotic effect of arbitration on the collective bargaining process is related to the degree of uncertainty associated with the method of arbitration to be used. If the parties believe that the cost of disagreement is less because of the compromise nature of the method, they will be more likely to use that method, thus creating a "chilling" or "narcotic" effect on the bargaining process.

Each type of interest arbitration has varying degrees of "uncertainties." The nature of mediation-arbitration requires the individual involved to act as both a mediator and an arbitrator, if necessary. Mediation requires the direct exchange of information between the potential arbitrator and the parties. The parties may then become familiar with the reasoning process of the potential arbitrator, thus reducing the uncertainty associated with a potential arbitration award.[26]

These considerations suggest that, in order to preserve the uncertainty surrounding the arbitration process and to encourage real bargaining, allowing the arbitrator to act as a mediator and other mechanisms that provide flows of information from the arbitrator to the parties will be counterproductive.[27]

In many cases, an arbitrator attempts to mediate a settlement between the parties prior to proceeding with conventional interest arbitration. The actual arbitration process is basically the same in both methods. (See Appendix 5-B.)

The degree of uncertainty attributed to conventional interest arbitration is minimal due to its compromising nature. When asked whether conventional interest arbitration resulted in a compromise, Jesse Simons, a well-known arbitrator, replied, "I believe in most instances the arbitrator or panel obtain from the employer what it can afford to give and from the union what its members want and then compromise."[28]

A 1978 laboratory-simulation study of the relative impact of final-offer and conventional arbitration on a bargainer's aspiration level, bargaining behavior, and feeling of responsibility for outcomes under conditions of high and low conflict indicated that in comparison to the subjects in the conventional arbitration condition, the subjects in the final-offer condition had significantly lower aspiration levels immediately before bargaining, were closer to agreement at the conclusion of the bargaining, and felt a greater personal responsibility for the outcome of the negotiations.[29]

The overall utilization of conventional arbitration, as shown in Table 5-1, is greater than final-offer arbitration, thus indicating less of an incentive to reach a negotiated agreement in those systems using conventional interest arbitration.

The state of Michigan provides an interesting comparison between conventional and final-offer arbitration. The state used conventional arbitration from 1969 until 1972 for impasses involving police, firefighters, and deputy sheriffs. Since 1972, final-offer arbitration has been used for economic matters. Under the conventional arbitration system, 39 percent of all arbitration petitions were settled prior to an award being issued, and under the final-offer arbitration system 61 percent of all arbitration petitions were settled prior to an award being issued.[30]

The uncertainty associated with the last-offer-by-issue system of interest arbitration is similar to that of conventional interest arbitration. Negotiators from either side usually expect the arbitrator to issue an award favoring some of its demands and some of its opponent's demands. The award, therefore, would compromise the interests of both parties, making the cost of disagreeing with the opponent less than the cost of agreeing. The dif-

**Table 5-1** Impasse Procedures and the Incentive To Negotiate

| Domain | Years | Type of Impasse Procedure | Total Number of Negotiation Cases | Cases Employing Stated Impasse Procedure | Procedure Usage as a Percentage of Total Negotiation Cases |
|---|---|---|---|---|---|
| Baseball | 1974–1975 | Final-offer | 1,000 | 43 | 4.3 |
| Iowa | 1975–1976 | Final-offer | 372 | 25 | 6.7 |
| Massachusetts | 1975–1976 | Final-offer | 548 | 36 | 6.6 |
| Wisconsin | 1973–1976 | Final-offer | 549 | 64 | 11.6 |
| Michigan | 1973–1976 | Final-offer | 540 | 88 | 16.3 |
| Pennsylvania | 1969–1974 | Conventional | 276 | 83 | 30.1 |
| New York | 1974–1976 | Conventional | 118 | 34 | 28.8 |
| Canadian Federal Government | 1967–1974 | Conventional | 305 | 55 | 18.0 |
| British Columbia Schools | 1969–1973 | Conventional | 389 | 163 | 41.9 |

*Source:* Baseball data are from Dworkin (1976). Data for Iowa, Massachusetts, Wisconsin, Michigan, Pennsylvania, and New York from Lipsky and Barocci (1975b). Data for U.S. manufacturing from Kaufman (1977). See James R. Chellus and James B. Dworkin, "An Economic Analysis of Final-Offer Arbitration as a Conflict Resolution Device," *Journal of Conflict Resolution*, Vol. 24 (June 1980), p. 398. Reprinted with permission from Sage Publications, Inc.

ference between the last offers of the parties in this system at the end of the negotiations is also expected to be large.[31]

A laboratory-simulation test of the impact of various forms of arbitration on negotiating behaviors indicated a higher degree of concessions for those using the final-offer system than those using the last-offer-by-issue system. At the end of the negotiations, those using the final-offer system were closer to settlement than those using the last-offer-by-issue system.[32]

> The results of this research indicate that the difference in impact on negotiations between the final-offer . . . and last-offer-by-issue systems is significant. The former system generates genuine bargaining while the latter subverts free negotiations. In other words, the last-offer-by-issue system may have the same "narcotic" effect on negotiators as that of "conventional" arbitration.[33]

The final-offer system is uncertain in that the arbitrator must award the final package of offers of one of the parties. The threat of this type of arbitration should, therefore, generate concessions from the other if it is expected that the cost of disagreeing will be greater than the expected cost of agreeing on such terms. If one party expects its offer to be awarded, then the cost of disagreement is minimal. However, if the offer by the other party is expected to be awarded, then the cost of disagreement is high. Negotiators will, therefore, reduce the expected costs of disagreement through concessions and compromises until the expected cost of disagreements are perceived as equal. The differences between these offers should, therefore, be small.[34]

When Jesse Simons was asked whether final-offer arbitration provided an incentive to bargain, he said, "Yes, there is a terror that the adversary will win before the arbitrator. However, it doesn't always work because occasionally either party reaches a conclusion it has to win as a matter of principle."[35]

In developing the binding arbitration statutes in Iowa, which include fact finding, significant reliance was placed upon information presented by Robert Helsby, chairman of the New York Public Relations Employment Board (PERB) in 1973. He stated that a system where the arbitrator could select either the final position of one of the parties or the fact finder's recommendation on each impasse item would place great emphasis on fact finding and increase the possibility of settlement at that stage rather than at arbitration. Statistical evidence in Iowa has borne out Dr. Helsby's prophesy.[36] The Iowa system has provided a balance between the need for cooperative relationships between government and its employees and the right of the public to be assured the effective and orderly function of government. It appears that there is a direct relationship of that experience on the health care industry: the third party payors, the public, and, certainly, the patients.

Any alternatives to the strike in health care collective bargaining must be flexible enough to bend to the circumstances in a particular impasse situation. Genuine collective bargaining must be encouraged; it will lessen the need for the extreme impasse resolution recommendations where all else fails. Longer periods of time for the negotiations of contracts may be the answer. The law provides for a notice of 90 days before a contract expires, the notice to be issued by the party wishing to change the conditions in the operative contract. Most negotiations start later and move at a snail's pace, with an unwritten acknowledgment that "nothing will happen until the ten-day strike notice is sent out." This often is a self-fulfilling prophesy. The parties should meet during the life of the contract to identify issues that have been unresolved in prior negotiations, or that have developed during the life of the contract. Such committees would operate with the goal of improving industrial relations, being fully cognizant of the effects of crisis bargaining, educating each other as to the problems, positions, and proposed solutions that may well be part of the next round of collective bargaining. Once negotiations begin, that is, the formal negotiations 90 days before the termination of the contract, the identification of a mediator-arbitrator should be the first order of business. Initially, this individual will not be present at the negotiations. He or she will appear 60 days before the termination of the contract. This person's role will be that of a traditional mediator with one difference; both parties are fully aware that this individual, at some point in the negotiations (when an impasse is reached), will assume the role of arbitrator. The mediator must become knowledgeable about all of the issues, attempt to identify common grounds, and work feverishly to prevent having to take on the role of arbitrator. Absent an agreement 15 days before the contract expires, a fact finder will be appointed. This could well be the normal appointment of a board of inquiry under present Federal Mediation and Conciliation Service regulations. The fact finder's report will be available to both parties and to the mediator within ten days; that is, five days before the contract expires. This fact-finding procedure will have a far greater effect on the negotiations and the possibility of a collectively bargained settlement than such reports issued by traditional boards of inquiry. Both parties are fully aware that the fact finder's report will be an alternate to their last position as far as the arbitrator is concerned. If an impasse is reached, the mediator-arbitrator—after the fact finder's report is issued—will make a selection, on an issue-by-issue basis, from three choices: the management's last position, the union's last position, and the fact finder's recommendation. This will encourage the parties to endeavor to negotiate a settlement on their own. The mediator-arbitrator will continue during this period and up until the time an award is issued to try to bring the parties together on all issues; at the very least, such efforts may result in the reduction of open issues and/or the narrowing of differences on issues that will be submitted to arbitration.

This may be an imperfect system and variations are to be encouraged, but in the final analysis there are many added incentives for the parties to agree on their own: the mediator who may well become an arbitrator; the fact finder; and the choice of the most realistic position on an issue-by-issue basis.

---

**NOTES**

1. Bernard Karsh, *Diary of a Strike* (Champaign, Ill.: University of Illinois Press, 1958), *passim*.
2. Edwin F. Beal and Edward D. Wickersham, *The Practice of Collective Bargaining* (Homewood, Ill.: Richard D. Irwin, Inc., 1959), p. 289.
3. Karsh, *supra*.
4. Neil W. Chamberlain and Jane M. Schilling, *The Impact of Strikes* (New York: Harper & Brothers, 1954), *passim*. Metzger and Pointer, *Labor Relations in the Health Service Industry, Theory and Practice* (Washington, D.C.: The Science and Health Publications Inc., 1972), p. 220.
5. D. Quinn Mills, *Collective Bargaining for a New Era,* speech presented at a Labor Relations Conference, NAALMC and FMCS, Washington, D.C., September 9, 1982.
6. Editorial, *Labor Day,* New York Times, September 6, 1982.
7. John E. Beamer, "Fact or Fiction Regarding Interest Arbitration: The Iowa Experience," *Selected Proceedings of the 30th Annual Conference of the Association of Labor Relations Agencies* (Fort Washington, Pa.: Labor Relations Press, 1981), p. 50.
8. Reid C. Richardson, *Collective Bargaining by Objectives* (Englewood Cliffs, N.J.: Prentice-Hall, Inc., 1977), p. 288.
9. William E. Simkin, *Mediation and the Dynamics of Collective Bargaining* (Washington, D.C.: Bureau of National Affairs, 1971), pp. 238–239.
10. *Id.*, pp. 239–240.
11. *Id.*, p. 240.
12. Richardson, *supra*, p. 258.
13. R. Theodore Clark, Jr., *Coping With Mediation Fact Finding and Forms of Arbitration* (Chicago, Ill.: International Personnel Management Association, 1974), p. 248.
14. Lloyd C. Reynolds, *Labor Economics and Labor Relations* (Englewood Cliffs, N.J.: Prentice-Hall, Inc., 1956), *passim*. Reprinted with permission from Prentice-Hall, Inc.
15. Harold Newman, "Interest Arbitration: Impressions of a PERB Chairman," *The Arbitration Journal*, Vol. 37, No. 4, December 1982, p. 8.
16. Charles M. Rehmus, "Varieties of Final Offer Arbitration," *The Arbitration Journal*, Vol. 37, No. 4, December 1982, p. 5.

17. Peter Fueille, *Final Offer Arbitration* (Chicago, Ill.: International Personnel Management Association, 1975), p. 13.

18. Rehmus, *supra*, note 16.

19. Rehmus, *supra*, p. 6.

20. Jerome H. Ross, *The Med-Arb Process in Labor Agreement Negotiations* (SPIDR Committee on Research and Education, Occasional Paper #82-1, February 1982).

21. Arvid Anderson, "Interest Arbitration in New York City," *The Arbitration Journal*, Vol. 37, No. 4, December 1982, p. 20.

22. Clifford Scharman, "Interest Arbitration in the Private Sector," *The Arbitration Journal*, Vol. 36, No. 3, September 1981, p. 20. Reprinted with permission from the American Arbitration Association.

23. Reprinted, with permission, from Henry S. Farber and Harry C. Katz, "Interest Arbitration, Outcomes, and the Incentive to Bargain," *Industrial & Labor Relations Review*, Vol. 33, No. 1 (October 1971), p. 55.

24. *Id.*, p. 56.

25. A.V. Subbarao, "The Impact of Binding Interest Arbitration on Negotiation and Process Outcome," *Journal of Conflict Resolution*, Vol. 22, No. 2 (March 1978), p. 84. Reprinted by permission of Sage Publications, Inc.

26. Farber and Katz, *supra*, p. 63.

27. *Id.*, p. 63.

28. Statement by Jesse Simons, arbitrator, in a personal interview, New York, New York, February 10, 1982.

29. William W. Notz and Frederick A. Starke, "Final-Offer versus Conventional Arbitration as a Means of Conflict Management," *Administrative Science Quarterly*, Vol. 23, No. 2 (June 1978), pp. 189–202.

30. J. Joseph Loewenberg, Walter J. Gershenfeld, H.J. Glasbeek, B.A. Hepple, and Kenneth F. Walker, *Compulsory Arbitration* (Lexington, Mass.: D.C. Heath and Company, 1976), p. 161.

31. Subbarao, *supra*, p. 85. Reprinted by permission of Sage Publications, Inc.

32. *Id.*, p. 98. Reprinted by permission of Sage Publications, Inc.

33. *Id.*, p. 98. Reprinted by permission of Sage Publications, Inc.

34. *Id.*, p. 84. Reprinted by permission of Sage Publications, Inc.

35. Statement by Jesse Simons, arbitrator, in a personal interview, New York, New York, February 10, 1982.

36. Beamer, *supra*, p. 52.

# Appendix 5-A

# Labor Relations and the Nursing Leader

## ALTERNATIVES TO THE STRIKE IN COLLECTIVE BARGAINING

In the spring of 1973 the Steelworkers' union and the major steel companies announced that agreement had been reached on a plan which would mean that there would be no nationwide steel strike in 1974. Instead, under the terms of the Experimental Negotiating Agreement (ENA), the parties would rely on voluntary arbitration if no agreement was reached at the bargaining table in 1974.

Pressure from two sources brought about the agreement. First, competition from foreign steel companies which had moved into the American markets was hurting the companies and the union's members. In the event of a lengthy strike many steel users would rely on imported steel and would probably continue to import after the strike—creating a permanent loss of jobs for the union's members.

The other pressure was the traditional stockpiling by the companies who built up inventories in preparation for a possible strike. In past years, this meant that union members worked considerable amounts of overtime in the last year of the agreement while the companies built their inventories. After bargaining was over there would be lengthy layoffs while inventories were being depleted. Even with the 116-day strike in 1959 inventories were still high, and many steelworkers did not return to work for several months because the companies filled orders from their stockpiled supplies.

## WHAT WAS ENA?

The terms of ENA were worked out in negotiating sessions which started in 1969 and continued until the announcement of the plan in the spring of

---

*Source:* Reprinted from *Journal of Nursing Administration*, Vol. 5, January 1975, by Norman E. Amundson by permission of Concept Development, Inc., ©1975.

1973. In addition to the clause that provided for voluntary arbitration of the national agreement, ENA also included provisions for a 3 percent increase in wages during each of the three years of the agreement, retention of a cost-of-living clause, safeguards for management prerogatives, and protection for employee benefit plans.

The basic element in the ENA has been talked about in industrial relations for many years under the term *continuous negotiation*. The usual practice in collective bargaining is for the parties to sign two-three-or more-year agreements with a reopening clause requiring the parties to exchange demands 60 days prior to the expiration of the current agreement. This often results in the parties attempting to come to agreement on a host of issues without sufficient time for careful consideration. Working against the deadline of the contract expiration, they are unable to prepare adequate contract language understandable to both sides. Important items are dropped or set aside for further discussion which never takes place. In contrast to this, *continuous negotiation* means that labor and management meet on a regular basis with the goal of achieving better and more complete agreements on troublesome issues. This is actually what happened in the steel industry and it worked for them.

The participants began their bargaining in January of 1974 and reached final agreement on April 11. The contract did not expire until September of 1974, which meant that the parties had reached agreement five months before their deadline and ensured industrial peace in steel until the fall of 1977. The union did retain the right to strike on local issues in the plant bargaining that follows national bargaining. But the spirit of cooperation at the top level had an effect on local bargaining, which proceeded smoothly with disruptions.

## COMPULSORY ARBITRATION

A system of *compulsory arbitration* is utilized when there is a legal prohibition on strikes and the parties are required by law to take unresolved issues to an impartial third party. The impartial arbitrator hears the case and renders a decision binding on both parties. This system is in effect in Australia and New Zealand. During World War II it was also in effect in the United States since all of the unions except the miners had subscribed to a no-strike pledge for the duration of the emergency. It has not eliminated strikes, however, in those countries where it is used. It has resulted in strikes in defiance of the law by a union or by dissident members. Strikes tend to be shorter but more frequent under their system.

In the United States compulsory arbitration is in effect in a few states, and applies to government agencies where a vital service, such as police protection and firefighting, is involved. It does hamper the development of successful collective bargaining because the parties frame their demands on the basis of how an arbitrator will view the situation rather than holding the goal of coming to agreement at the bargaining table.

## FACT FINDING

This is a procedure whereby the parties agree to call in an impartial person or persons to hear the arguments of both sides. Based upon the evidence presented to him the fact finder will prepare a series of recommendations for settlement. The parties are not required to accept these recommendations. There will be considerable pressure upon them to conform, however, because of the public nature of the process and the pressures engendered by having sought an impartial expert's opinion.

*Fact finding* was used by the California Nurses Association in the summer of 1966. The nurses voted not to go on strike but to submit the strike issues to a panel of three experienced, well-known experts in industrial relations. The parties were under no obligation to accept the fact finders' recommendations, and could have rejected them if they had chosen to do so. They did not, however, and the recommendations of the fact finders were put into effect.

Fact finding as an alternative to striking has gained some acceptance in this country, mostly in the public sector. Most often the report and recommendations of the fact finders are accepted as a basis for settlement. The process differs from binding arbitration in that the parties are free to reject the recommendations, but in practice they rarely do.

## MEDIATION-ARBITRATION

This is a new approach to settling which has been tried in a few situations. It involves a neutral, experienced arbitrator sitting in on the negotiations. If an *impasse* is reached he tries to mediate between the parties and bring about an agreement voluntarily. If he is unable to achieve agreement by mediation at whatever point he feels is appropriate, he assumes the role of an arbitrator and issues an award which both parties must accept as the settlement of the issue at *impasse*.

The most successful use of this process to date was in the 1970–1971 negotiations of the California Nurses Association and the hospitals in the San Francisco Bay area, which involved about 5,000 RNs covered by collective bargaining agreements. Prior to the beginning of negotiations the involved nurses met and voted not to go on strike but to use "Med-Arb" as the process for bargaining.

It was a successful alternative to the use of a strike to resolve an *impasse* at the bargaining table. At the conclusion of the bargaining sessions the nurses association was pleased with the results and felt that they would not be averse to using the process in future negotiations. The hospital management representatives were not as pleased as the association. They felt the process was entirely too lengthy and wasted much valuable time. For these and other reasons they went back to the traditional collective bargaining procedures in 1974 negotiations. These ended in a three-week strike by the RNs, principally over the issue of patient care. The nurses wanted a voice in establishing staffing patterns and in the assignment of nurses to work in special units such as ICU and CCU. The settlement required all the hospitals to develop a system for the determination of nurse staffing which must be discussed with the CNA and which must include staff nurse participation in assessing patients' daily needs for nursing care. In addition, the hospitals agreed that, except in cases of emergency, nurses without appropriate training or experience would not be assigned to special care units.

## LAST-OFFER ARBITRATION

This is a new technique which has been used in a few situations for resolving *impasses* in collective bargaining. The parties jointly select an arbitrator. Then each side presents to him the package of proposals which is the least they will settle for. The arbitrator then studies the two proposals and selects one of them as the final agreement. The principle involved here is that parties who know they have to prepare what could be the terms of settlement will be very realistic in what they propose.

## MEDIATION AND CONCILIATION

*Mediation* and *conciliation* are steps used in traditional bargaining rather than strike alternatives *per se*. The mediator enters the process and tries to achieve voluntary agreement. If he is particularly skilled and brings considerable experience and status to the bargaining table, he can operate in such a manner as to avert a strike.

In 1966 President Johnson used what he called "mediation to finality" to resolve a bargaining impasse in the airlines. He called the two parties to a meeting in the White House, locked them in a room with a mediator, and said that they would not be allowed out until they reached a settlement. It worked because the parties knew the President meant it.

There is a need for imaginative, creative methods for averting strikes, particularly in the sensitive areas of an economy such as police protection, firefighting, and health care. No one method will be appropriate in all instances. The circumstances surrounding any *impasse* situation dictate what solution might be proper at that time. I believe that serious negotiation by experienced, competent, responsible, and honest negotiators is the best alternative to a strike. Too often the lack of these qualities in negotiators is the reason that a strike occurs.

## Appendix 5-B

# The Use of Interest Arbitration in the Public Sector

*Daniel G. Gallagher*

A review of the literature on public sector collective bargaining reveals considerable research and comment on interest dispute resolution procedures. Why is there this fascination with public sector impasse resolution procedures, and especially with compulsory arbitration?

Perhaps one answer is that public sector impasse resolution mechanisms, such as fact finding or compulsory arbitration, are rather foreign concepts in the private sector. They are a major departure from our understanding of the dynamics of conventional bargaining and may generate a need to reformulate existing theories of the bargaining process.

Second, the number of jurisdictions adopting compulsory arbitration as the terminal step for disputes has grown, thus increasing the opportunities for both intra- and interjurisdictional studies of various compulsory arbitration schemes: conventional, final offer (FOA) on an issue package basis, and mediation-arbitration (med-arb). The primary concern in these studies then often becomes identification of the most effective procedural scheme. Closely related to this concern is the considerable attention being devoted by the so-called "interventionist tinkerers" to making the arbitration process more effective in encouraging voluntary settlements.

There may be other reasons for this increasing concern with compulsory arbitration. Narrative essays on the advantages and disadvantages of compulsory arbitration may multiply as more practitioners and neutrals become involved in negotiations that terminate in arbitration and as the gradual increase in the number of public sector laws that allow strike action permits comparative studies of arbitration, not only with the weaker advisory forms of dispute resolution but with the recent experience in some jurisdictions where public employees have the right to strike.

*Source:* Proceedings of the 1982 Spring Meeting, April 28–30, 1982, Milwaukee, Wisconsin. Reprinted with permission from Industrial Relations Research Association.

The focus here is twofold. We begin with a brief review of the effectiveness of compulsory arbitration and then discuss a few selected concerns regarding the use and/or availability of arbitration as a dispute resolution procedure. The arbitration systems highlighted are those in Iowa, Michigan, Minnesota, and Wisconsin. By using these states we give a regional focus to our discussion and take advantage of the fact that, although they are geographically contiguous, their impasse resolution procedures, which involve compulsory arbitration for some or all categories of public employees, are both structurally and operationally diverse.

However, when evaluating the effectiveness of compulsory arbitration, a realistic appraisal of politically and operationally feasible alternatives is required. The common normative assumption is that the public both wants and needs to be protected against strikes by protective service or "essential" employees.[1] Thus, despite criticism of requiring compulsory arbitration in interest disputes involving these employees, the political reality is that they are not likely to be granted the right to strike.

In contrast, it is reasonable to compare the results under compulsory arbitration procedures and right to strike legislation, which is currently available in some ten jurisdictions. But, it is not reasonable to compare arbitration results with those under advisory procedures, such as fact finding, since the latter exclude the bilateral risk that is necessary to encourage the parties to reach a voluntary settlement.

## EFFECTIVENESS OF COMPULSORY ARBITRATION

The literature reflects different approaches to evaluating the effectiveness of compulsory arbitration as a dispute resolution technique. In a comprehensive study, Anderson identified the key issue when he said, "We really don't know . . . how effective . . . compulsory arbitration [is]."[2] In fact, as Anderson noted, the evaluations tend to focus on only a few dimensions, primarily that bargaining incentives should be protected.[3] In other words, considerable empirical research on the "effectiveness" of arbitration has attempted to determine if the infamous, but poorly defined, "chilling effect" is associated with arbitration as evidenced by the frequency of arbitrated settlements relative to voluntary agreements.

Using this conventional measure of usage rates, we may be tempted to reach conclusions about the effectiveness of the various impasse procedures in Iowa, Michigan, Minnesota, and Wisconsin. For example, in Iowa, where the statutory impasse procedure is mediation, fact finding, and tri-offer FOA, arbitration awards have been limited to between 4.5 and 7.1 percent of all contract negotiations over the first six years of experience.[4] Available data on the Michigan experience indicate that about

10 to 15 percent of all public safety employee negotiations resulted in arbitrated awards.[5] In Wisconsin, 9 to 18 percent of public-safety negotiations have been settled by the issuance of an FOA package award, while approximately 5.4 percent of nonessential employee impasses were settled by arbitration during 1978 and 1979 under the 1978 mutual-choice-of-procedures statute.[6] Between 1973 and 1980 in Minnesota, about 30 percent of all negotiations requesting mediation for essential-service employee disputes resulted in arbitrated settlements.[7]

Although these findings do indicate various jurisdictions' reliance on arbitrated settlements, it is often inappropriate to compare both intra- and interjurisdictional usage of arbitration and to suggest that one compulsory arbitration system works better than another based on the extent to which the parties rely upon voluntary compared to arbitrated settlements. Comparability among systems may be hampered by the number of statutory steps preceding arbitration, the category of employees who have access to arbitration, and, quite often, the very basic difference between state agencies in reporting impasses.

Another major limitation is the failure of most studies to account for various exogenous and endogenous variables that may affect not only the bargaining process, but also the parties' inclination to arbitrate disputes. In other words, the relatively lower reliance on arbitrated settlements in Iowa compared with other midwestern jurisdictions may reflect not only the availability of fact finding prior to issue-by-issue FOA, but also the considerable difference of the bargaining environment of rural Iowa from that of urbanized areas in Michigan and Minnesota. Even if such environmental factors are controlled, the explanatory power of the models that examine the effectiveness of arbitration through usage rates is often limited and erratic.

## ALTERNATIVES

A few studies have used alternative approaches to measure the effectiveness of arbitration. One, by Kochan *et al.*, used position convergence to measure the effect of the change in New York State's terminal impasse step from fact finding to arbitration. The results showed a significantly higher probability of impasse but no substantial impact on position convergency by those parties utilizing arbitration.[8] This tended to confirm prior research, which suggested that, regardless of the terminal step, position modification prior to impasse apparently is limited. But such results on position convergence should be interpreted carefully since they are based on a sample of bargaining relationships where adjudicative intervention occurred.

An alternative measure of the effectiveness of arbitration is issue reduction. The rather fragmented studies appear to suggest little difference in the number of unresolved issues presented at fact finding compared to arbitration when they are terminal steps.[9] However, most studies of the relationship between arbitration and issue reduction tend to focus on the relative effectiveness of different arbitration schemes.

Once again, due to methodological limitations and procedural differences among jurisdictions, such as steps prior to impasse, two-tier mediation efforts, and scope of issues, our conclusions about the effectiveness of different compulsory arbitration schemes are limited to comparing the procedures. Among our four midwestern jurisdictions, the mean number of issues submitted to arbitration ranges from three in Iowa (tri-offer, issue FOA) and Wisconsin (package FOA) to seven under conventional arbitration in Minnesota and eight or more economic items under the Michigan issue-by-issue FOA.

Perhaps one of the most salient concerns in attempting to evaluate the effectiveness of arbitration is identifying its effect on wage settlements—primarily whether arbitrated wage awards tend to exceed negotiated wage settlements. But measuring the effect of arbitration on wages is not an easy task. In a Michigan study, a joint governmental agency that attempted to measure this effect had difficulty in reaching a conclusion because of problems in identifying a standard against which arbitrated wages would be judged excessive.[10] Thus, in order to estimate the effect of arbitration on wages, it is necessary to control the multitude of factors, aside from arbitration, which may influence wages. The results of multiple regression studies generally show a slight or nonsignificant relationship between arbitration and wage levels, except where comparatively lower wage-rate units were brought closer to the wage settlement in similarly situated jurisdictions. Finally, the effect of arbitrated wage levels in jurisdictions with the right-to-strike option has not been explored in depth.

Thus, it seems that we know a great deal about the extent to which the negotiating parties in different jurisdictions and under various forms of arbitration rely on arbitrated awards and, to a lesser degree, about position convergence and issue reduction. But methodological concerns often make the existing comparative evaluations suspect and provide us with only limited measures of the effectiveness of arbitration. Even well-structured and comprehensive studies may not assist in resolving the controversy over the effectiveness of arbitration as a dispute-resolution technique. As Feuille noted, the same objective data may be interpreted differently depending upon personal preferences.[11]

An excellent illustration of the difficulties in reaching policy decisions based on empirical research emerged from the study of New York State's

Taylor Law by Kochan *et al.*[12] Despite the rather detailed empirical research, unions and managements, after interpreting the data, reached rather different conclusions about the effectiveness of compulsory arbitration and the desirability of extending the arbitration statute to cover police and firefighters.

Furthermore, different statistical analyses of a single data set may produce different results. Focusing on a "narcotic effect," Butler and Ehrenberg used substantially different statistical techniques in their reexamination of the data used in Kochan and Baderschneider's study and reach fundamentally different conclusions.[13] The issue raised by these illustrations is that interpretations of effectiveness are subject not only to the practitioner community's approval and experience, but also to differences in analytical approaches used by academicians who provide much of the quantitative measures of compulsory experiences.

## CONCERNS

Judging the effectiveness of compulsory arbitration also involves some subjective, less quantifiable issues. Much of the literature, especially on FDA, addresses the desirability of structuring impasse procedures to maximize "mutual anxiety" so that the parties will reach a voluntary rather than an adjudicated settlement. In practice, this pressure appears to differ among various arbitration schemes.

The Iowa statute requires the parties to submit final offers and prohibits the arbitration from mediating. Since the parties expect nothing other than an award, there appears to be a limited tactical advantage for the parties to hold back on an issue proceeding to arbitration.

In contrast, the med-arb process in Wisconsin and particularly in Michigan is more flexible, but it raises the concern that the pressure of "mutual anxiety" may be seriously eroded, since an adjudicative decision is not initially expected. Although disputes in both states have been successfully resolved by second-tier mediation efforts at or prior to arbitration, the concern remains over the extent to which the parties' ability to modify final offers reduces the incentive to negotiate prior to arbitration. This ability to modify final offers seems contradictory to the underlying theory of FOA, even if justified on the basis of the sanctity of a voluntary agreement.

Judgments of the effectiveness of these various approaches depend on whether arbitration is considered a terminal adjudicative process at which a final decision is expected and rendered or a forum for the initiation of bona fide negotiations. The goal of promoting voluntary settlements, as in

Michigan, must be weighed against the drawback of prolonging the bargaining process when disputes are remanded to further negotiations and final offers are resubmitted. At issue is the balance between the benefits of a voluntary settlement even if the process is prolonged with the benefits of a bargaining agreement that coincides with the parties' current employment needs and fiscal conditions rather than one that is retroactively applied.

A problem that has arisen in Iowa and Wisconsin flows from the statutes' distinction between mandatory and permissive bargaining items. Since both statutes imply that there must be mutual agreement to discuss permissive items, either party can exclude such items from arbitral review if the parties fail to reach a voluntary settlement. In addition, one party may be able to impose a cost on the other party which may be seeking an agreement on these items by using its willingness to agree to a permissive item or to maintain contract language about a permissive subject as a means of forcing concessions on other items that are in the mandatory category.

In the short run, the strategy of withholding concessions on permissive items may give a tactical advantage to one party. However, in the long run it may impair the effectiveness of compulsory arbitration as a dispute resolution technique.

A third, but closely related, concern, as Kochan suggested, is that arbitration may be subject to a "half-life" effect.[14] One or both parties may view arbitration as a mechanism to maintain the status quo. Although critics of compulsory arbitration frequently suggest that a party may achieve through arbitration what it could not through the bargaining process, little if any effort has been directed toward determining if in fact arbitration serves as a vehicle for introducing substantial innovations or changes in the contract. If innovation and change are forthcoming only when one party has a comparative advantage, then the perceived effectiveness of compulsory arbitration may diminish especially when the party at a disadvantage seeks an innovative solution to a particularly important problem. Should arbitration come to be perceived as a barrier to innovative resolutions of the emerging employment problems of the 1980s, the attractiveness of strike action may increase.

An ancillary concern, also involving some subjectivity, is the economic impact of arbitration. Studies have concluded that the impact of compulsory arbitration on wages is limited or statistically nonsignificant. But these studies have not quantified the possible broader economic costs. Little is known about whether arbitrated awards substantially increase the total labor cost within the bargaining unit or if there is a significantly higher disemployment effect than under voluntary settlements.

Second, the spillover effect of an arbitrated economic award on other bargaining units needs to be considered. Again, little is known about whether an arbitrated economic award results in a similar pattern for other employee units in the employment relationship or if the economic settlements differ depending on whether the other employee units use an advisory procedure like fact finding or whether they can invoke arbitration or resort to strike action. All of these questions remain unanswered.

## CHOICE-OF-PROCEDURE SYSTEMS

A final question is whether arbitration is more effective if it is an option in a choice-of-procedure system. Minnesota management, for example, unilaterally selected either conventional arbitration or the strike in nonessential employee negotiations during the 1973–1980 period when it had those options. Wisconsin's choice-of-procedure system for nonessential employees, in effect since 1977, provides for strike action by mutual agreement. Based on the experience in these states, it appears questionable whether the choice-of-procedure approach alleviates many of the fundamental problems associated with impasse resolution systems.

According to Ponak and Wheeler's analysis of the Wisconsin and Minnesota experience with these systems, there was no mutual agreement to pursue the strike option in Wisconsin during 1978, whereas in Minnesota managements' unilateral selection of the strike option was relatively rare in school district negotiations but was frequent in municipal and county unit negotiations.[15] Although in Minnesota a substantially higher rate of voluntary settlements followed the selection of the strike option, compared to the selection of arbitration, the system had a number of fundamental drawbacks which may account for its management—it was empowered to select the impasse technique, thereby giving it a major tactical advantage in being able to choose an impasse technique that best met its needs. In fact, Minnesota managements did make use of that advantage.[16]

From the union's perspective, the perceived advantage of strike action may be suspect when it can only be exercised if management concurs. As Cullen stated, "It's not a very smart labor union that strikes when management wants you to."[17]

## CONCLUSION

This condensed review of a broad and complex issue identifies some concerns pertaining to compulsory arbitration that warrant further study before any definitive conclusions about the effectiveness of compulsory arbitration as a dispute resolution technique can be reached. But, during the course of such study we may expect that compulsory arbitration will continue to serve as a terminal impasse procedure in jurisdictions where it currently exists, particularly for negotiations involving essential service employees. For such employees, the normative assumption that the public wants and needs to be protected against strike action is both reasonable and sufficiently compelling that legislative action to exclude compulsory arbitration is unlikely. However, the increased willingness of many jurisdictions to permit strikes as a terminal step does suggest that the attraction of compulsory arbitration may be decreasing.

Given the volume of research studies and experiences, it does not appear that the questions concerning terminal impasse-resolution procedures are likely to be soon resolved. Debate and disagreement will continue as long as management and union representatives maintain fundamentally different perceptions of the relative advantages of compulsory arbitration and alternative terminal procedures. As a result, the focus in the future could shift from evaluating the effectiveness of compulsory arbitration relative to other terminal procedures toward identifying changes that might be made in the structure and implementation of steps prior to impasse in order to encourage voluntary settlements.

## NOTES

The author acknowledges Thomas Gilroy, Richard Pegnetter, and Peter Veglahn for their helpful comments on an earlier draft of this paper.

1. Peter Feuille, "Selected Benefits and Costs of Compulsory Arbitration," *Industrial and Labor Relations Review* 33 (October 1979), pp. 64–75.
2. John C. Anderson, "The Impact of Arbitration: A Methodological Assessment," *Industrial Relations* 20 (Spring 1981), p. 144.
3. *Id.*, pp. 144–145.
4. Iowa Public Employment Relations Board, "Impasse Statistics: Iowa's Collective Bargaining Law," Fall 1981 (mimeo).
5. James L. Stern *et al.*, *Final-Offer Arbitration* (Lexington, Mass.: D.C. Heath, 1975); Ernest Benjamin, "Final-Offer Arbitration Awards in Michigan, 1973–1977," 1978 (mimeo); and Michigan Department of Labor, *Labor Register*, Vol. 3 (April 1979) and Vol. 4 (September 1980).
6. Craig Olson, "Final-Offer Arbitration in Wisconsin After Five Years," *Proceedings of the 31st Annual Meeting*, IRRA (Madison, Wis.: 1979), pp. 111–119; Arvid Anderson, "Interest Arbitration: Still the Better Way," *CERL Review* 2 (Spring 1981), pp. 28–32.
7. Mario Bognanno and Fredric Champlin, *A Quantitative Description and Evaluation of Public Sector Collective Bargaining in Minnesota: 1973–1980*, report submitted to the Legislative Committee on Employee Relations (Minneapolis: University of Minnesota, 1981).
8. Thomas A. Kochan *et al.*, *Dispute Resolution Under Fact-Finding and Arbitration* (New York: American Arbitration Association, 1979).

9. Daniel G. Gallagher and Richard Pegnetter, "Impasse Resolution Under the Iowa Multistep Procedure," *Industrial and Labor Relations Review* 32 (April 1979), pp. 327–328.

10. *Government Employee Relations Report* 820 (July 23, 1979), pp. 20–22.

11. Peter Feuille, "Analyzing Compulsory Arbitration Experiences: The Role of Personnel Experience," *Industrial and Labor Relations Review* 27 (April 1975), pp. 432–435.

12. Thomas A. Kochan, "The Politics of Interest Arbitration," *Arbitration Journal* 33 (March 1978), pp. 5–9.

13. Thomas A. Kochan and Jean Baderschneider, "Dependence on Impasse Procedures: Police and Firefighters in New York State," *Industrial and Labor Relations Review* 31 (July 1979), pp. 431–449; Richard J. Butler and Ronald G. Ehrenberg, "Estimating the Narcotic Effect of Public Sector Impasse Procedures," *Industrial and Labor Relations Review* 35 (October 1981), pp. 3–20; and Thomas A. Kochan and Jean Baderschneider, "Estimating the Narcotic Effect: Choosing Techniques that Fit the Problem," *Industrial and Labor Relations Review* 33 (October 1981), pp. 21–28.

14. Thomas A. Kochan, "Dynamics of Dispute Resolution in the Public Sector," in *Public-Sector Bargaining,* eds. Benjamin Aaron, Joseph R. Grodin, and James L. Stern, IRRA Series (Washington, D.C.: BNA Books, 1979), pp. 150–190.

15. Allen Ponak and Hoyt N. Wheeler, "Choice of Procedures in Canada and the United States," *Industrial Relations* 19 (Fall 1980), pp. 292–308.

16. Such a tactical strategy also appears in Canadian federal service where the union selects the impasse resolution technique. See John C. Anderson and Thomas A. Kochan, "Impasse Procedures in the Canadian Federal Service: Effects on the Bargaining Process," *Industrial and Labor Relations Review* 30 (April 1977), pp. 283–301.

17. *Government Employee Relations Report* 738 (December 12, 1977), p. 13.

**Addendum 1**

# A Guide to Basic Law and Procedures under the National Labor Relations Act

*Source:* U.S. Government Printing Office, Washington, D.C., © 1978.

This is a revised edition of a pamphlet originally issued in 1962. It provides a basic framework for a better understanding of the National Labor Relations Act and its administration.

A special chart that arranges systematically the types of cases in which an employer or a labor organization may be involved under the Act, including both unfair labor practice cases and representation election proceedings, appears in the center fold of this booklet.

U.S. GOVERNMENT PRINTING OFFICE

WASHINGTON : 1978

For sale by the Superintendent of Documents, U.S. Government Printing Office
Washington, D.C. 20402

*A guide to basic law and procedures* under the **NATIONAL LABOR RELATIONS ACT**

Prepared in the Office of the General Counsel
NATIONAL LABOR RELATIONS BOARD

*Table of Contents*

**Summary of the Act** — 1-2

Purpose of the Act, 1 . . . What the Act provides, 1 . . . How the Act is enforced, 1 . . . How this material is organized, 1.

**The Rights of Employees** — 2-7

**The Section 7 Rights, 2 . . .**

Examples of Section 7 rights, 2.

**The Union Shop, 2 . . .**

Union-security agreements, 3 . . . Requirements for union-security agreements, 3 . . . Prehire agreements in the construction industry, 3.

**The Right To Strike, 4 . . .**

Lawful and unlawful strikes, 4 . . . Strikes for a lawful object, 4 . . . Economic strikers defined, 5 . . . Unfair labor practice strikers defined, 5 . . . Strikes unlawful because of purpose, 5 . . . Strikes unlawful because of timing—Effect of no-strike contract, 6 . . . Same—Strikes at end of contract period, 6 . . . Strikes unlawful because of misconduct of strikers, 6.

**The Right To Picket, 7.**

**Collective Bargaining and Representation of Employees** — 7-19

**Collective Bargaining, 7 . . .**

Duty to bargain imposed on both employer and union, 7 . . . Bargaining steps to end or change a contract, 8 . . . When the bargaining steps are not required, 8.

### The Employee Representative, 8 . . .

What is an appropriate bargaining unit, 9 . . . How the appropriateness of a unit is determined, 9 . . . Who can or cannot be included in a unit, 10 . . . Duties of bargaining representative and employer, 10.

### How a Bargaining Representative Is Selected, 10 . . .

Petition for certification of representatives, 11 . . . Petition for decertification election, 11 . . . Union-shop deauthorization, 11 . . . Purpose of investigation and hearing, 11 . . . Jurisdiction to conduct an election, 12 . . . Expedited elections under Section 8(b)(7)(C), 12 . . . Showing of interest required, 12 . . . Existence of question of representation, 12 . . . Who can qualify as bargaining representative, 13.

### Bars to Election, 13 . . .

Existing collective-bargaining contract, 13 . . . Time provisions, 14 . . . When a petition can be filed if there is an existing contract, 14 . . . Effect of certification, 15 . . . Effect of prior election, 15 . . . When a petition can be filed if there has been a prior election, 15.

### The Representation Election, 15 . . .

Consent-election agreements, 16 . . . Who determines election matters, 16 . . . Who may vote in a representation election, 16 . . . When strikers may be allowed to vote, 17 . . . When elections are held, 17 . . . Conduct of elections, 17.

## Unfair Labor Practices of Employers 19–29

### Section 8(a)(1)—Interference With Section 7 Rights, 19 . . .

Examples of violations of Section 8(a)(1), 19.

### Section 8(a)(2)—Domination or Illegal Assistance and Support of a Labor Organization, 19 . . .

Domination, 20 . . . Illegal assistance and support, 20 . . . Examples of violations of Section 8(a)(2), 20 . . . Remedy in cases of domination differs from that in cases of illegal assistance and support, 21 . . . When an employer can pay employees for union activity during working hours, 21.

**Section 8(a)(3)—Discrimination Against Employees, 21...**

The union-shop exception to Section 8(a)(3), 21 . . . The Act does not limit employer's right to discharge for economic reasons, 22 . . . Examples of violations of Section 8(a)(3), 23.

**Section 8(a)(4)—Discrimination for NLRB Activity, 23...**

Examples of violations of Section 8(a)(4), 26.

**Section 8(a)(5)—Refusal To Bargain in Good Faith, 26...**

Required subjects of bargaining, 26 . . . Duty to bargain defined, 26 . . . What constitutes a violation of Section 8(a)(5), 27 . . . Duty to meet and confer, 27 . . . Duty to supply information, 27 . . . Multiemployer bargaining, 27 . . . Duty to refrain from unilateral action, 27 . . . Duty of successor employers, 28 . . . Examples of violations of Section 8(a)(5), 28.

**Section 8(e)—Entering a Hot Cargo Agreement, 28....**

What is prohibited, 29 . . . Exceptions for construction and garment industries, 29.

---

# Unfair Labor Practices of Labor Organizations     29–44

**Section 8(b)(1)(A)—Restraint and Coercion of Employees, 30...**

Section 8(b)(1)(A) compared with Section 8(a)(1), 30 . . . What violates Section 8(b)(1)(A), 30 . . . Examples of violations of Section 8(b)(1)(A), 31.

**Section 8(b)(1)(B)—Restraint and Coercion of Employers, 32....**

Examples of violations of Section 8(b)(1)(B), 32.

**Section 8(b)(2)—Causing or Attempting To Cause Discrimination, 32....**

What violates Section 8(b)(2), 33 . . . Illegal hiring-hall agreements and practices, 33 . . . Illegal union-security agreements, 34 . . . Examples of violations of Section 8(b)(2), 34.

**Section 8(b)(3)—Refusal To Bargain in Good Faith, 34...**
  Examples of violations of Section 8(b)(3), 36.

**Section 8(b)(4)—Prohibited Strikes and Boycotts, 36...**
  Proscribed action: Inducing or encouraging a strike, work stoppage, or boycott, 36... Subparagraph (A)—Prohibited action: Threats, coercion, and restraint, 37... Subparagraph (A)—Prohibited object: Compelling membership in an employer or labor organization or compelling a hot cargo agreement, 37... Examples of violations of Section 8(b)(4)(A), 37 ... Subparagraph (B)—Prohibited object: Compelling a boycott or work stoppage, 38 ... Examples of violations of Section 8(b)(4)(B), 38 ... When an employer is not protected from secondary strikes and boycotts, 39 ... When a union may picket an employer who shares a site with another employer, 39 ... Picketing contractors' gates, 40... Subparagraph (B)—Prohibited object: Compelling recognition of an uncertified union, 40... Subparagraph (C)—Prohibited object: Compelling recognition of a union if another union has been certified, 41... Subparagraph (D)—Prohibited object: Compelling assignment of certain work to certain employees, 41 ... Publicity such as handbilling allowed by Section 8(b)(4), 41.

**Section 8(b)(5)—Excessive or Discriminatory Membership Fees, 41...**
  Examples of violations of Section 8(b)(5), 42.

**Section 8(b)(6)—"Featherbedding," 42.**

**Section 8(b)(7)—Organizational and Recognitional Picketing by Noncertified Unions, 42...**
  Publicity picketing, 43 ... Expedited elections under Section 8(b)(7)(C), 43 ... Examples of violations of Section 8(b)(7), 43.

**Section 8(e)—Entering a Hot Cargo Agreement, 44.**

**Section 8(g)—Striking or Picketing a Health Care Institution Without Notice, 44.**

## How the Act Is Enforced 44–54

### Organization of the NLRB, 44 . . .

The Board—The General Counsel—The Regional Offices, 44 . . . Functions of the NLRB, 44.

### Authority of the NLRB, 45 . . .

Enterprises whose operations affect commerce, 45 . . . What is commerce, 45 . . . When the operations of an employer affect commerce, 45 . . . The Board does not act in all cases affecting commerce, 46 . . . NLRB jurisdictional standards, 46 . . . The Act does not cover certain individuals, 48 . . . Supervisor defined, 49 . . . The Act does not cover certain employers, 49.

### NLRB Procedure, 49 . . .

Procedure in representation cases, 49 . . . Procedure in unfair labor practice cases. 50 . . . The 6-month rule limiting issuance of complaint, 51 . . . Appeal to the General Counsel if complaint is not issued, 51.

### Powers of the NLRB, 51 . . .

Powers concerning investigations, 51 . . . The Act is remedial, not criminal, 52 . . . Affirmative action may be ordered by the Board, 52 . . . Examples of affirmative action directed to employers, 52 . . . Examples of affirmative action directed to unions, 52.

### Special Proceedings in Certain Cases, 53 . . .

Proceedings in jurisdictional disputes, 53 . . . The investigation of certain charges must be given priority, 53 . . . Injunction proceedings under Section 10(l), 54 . . . Injunctive relief may be sought in other cases, 54.

**Court Enforcement of Board Orders, 54** ...
In the U.S. Court of Appeals, 54 . . . Review by the U.S. Supreme Court, 54.

**Conclusion** — 55

**Supplements**
Chart, "Types of Cases," 24 and 25 . . . Map showing regional areas and offices, 56 . . . List of Regional Directors and addresses of Regional Offices, 57.

## Foreword

The Regional Offices of the National Labor Relations Board have found that, after more than four decades, there is still a lack of basic information about the National Labor Relations Act. Staff members have expressed a need for a simply stated explanation of the Act to which anyone could be referred for guidance. To meet this demand, the basic law under the Act has been set forth in this pamphlet in a nontechnical way so that those who may be affected by it can better understand what their rights and obligations are.

Any effort to state basic principles of law in a simple way is a challenging and unenviable task. This is especially true about labor law, a relatively complex field of law. Anyone reading this booklet must bear in mind several cautions.

First, it must be emphasized that the Office of the General Counsel does not issue advisory opinions and this material cannot be considered as an official statement of law. It represents the view of the Office of the General Counsel as of the date of publication only. *It is important to note that the law changes and advances.* In fact, it is the duty of the Agency to keep its decisions abreast of changing conditions, yet within the basic statute. Accordingly, with the passage of time no one can rely on these statements as absolute until and unless he has checked to see whether the law may have been changed substantially or specifically.

Furthermore, these are broad general principles only and countless subprinciples and detailed rules are not included. Only by evaluation of specific fact situations in the light of current principles and with the aid of expert advice would a person be in a position to know definitely where his proposed conduct may take him under the statute. No basic primer or text can constitute legal advice in particular fact situations. This effort to improve basic education about the statute should not be considered as such. Many areas of the statute remain untested. Legal advisers and other experts can find the total body of "Board law" reported in other Agency publications.

One other caution: This material does not deal with questions arising under other labor laws, but only with the National Labor Relations Act, as amended. Laws administered by other Government agencies such as the Labor-Management Reporting and Disclosure Act of 1959, the Employee Retirement Income Security Act, the Occupational Safety and Health Act, the Railway Labor Act, the Fair Labor Standards, Walsh-Healey, and Davis-Bacon Acts, Title VII of the Civil Rights Act of 1964, and the Veterans' Preference Act, are not treated herein.

Lastly, this material does not reflect the view of the National Labor Relations Board as the adjudicating agency which in the end will decide each case as it comes before it.

It is hoped that with this cautionary note this booklet may be helpful to those in need of a better basic understanding of the National Labor Relations Act.

Revised October 1978

# A Guide to Basic Law and Procedures Under the National Labor Relations Act

## Summary of the Act

*Purpose of the Act*

It is in the national interest of the United States to maintain full production in its economy. Industrial strife among employees, employers, and labor organizations interferes with full production and is contrary to our national interest. Experience has shown that labor disputes can be lessened if the parties involved recognize the legitimate rights of each in their relations with one another. To establish these rights under law, Congress enacted the National Labor Relations Act. Its purpose is to define and protect the rights of employees and employers, to encourage collective bargaining, and to eliminate certain practices on the part of labor and management that are harmful to the general welfare.

*What the Act provides*

The National Labor Relations Act states and defines the rights of employees to organize and to bargain collectively with their employers through representatives of their own choosing. To ensure that employees can freely choose their own representatives for the purpose of collective bargaining, the Act establishes a procedure by which they can exercise their choice at a secret ballot election conducted by the National Labor Relations Board. Further, to protect the rights of employees and employers, and to prevent labor disputes that would adversely affect the rights of the public, Congress has defined certain practices of employers and unions as unfair labor practices.

*How the Act is enforced*

The law is administered and enforced principally by the National Labor Relations Board and the General Counsel acting through more than 45 regional and other field offices located in major cities in various sections of the country. The General Counsel and his staff in the Regional Offices investigate and prosecute unfair labor practice cases and conduct elections to determine employee representatives. The five-member Board decides cases involving charges of unfair labor practices and determines representation election questions that come to it from the Regional Offices.

*How this material is organized*

The rights of employees, including the rights to self-organization and collective bargaining that are protected by Section 7 of the Act, are presented first in this material. The Act's provisions concerning the union shop and the requirements for union-security agreements are covered in the same section which also includes a discussion of the right to strike and the right to picket. The obligations of collective bargaining and the Act's provisions for the selection of employee representatives are treated in the following section. Unfair labor practices of employers and of labor organizations are then presented in separate sections. The final section, entitled "How the Act Is Enforced," sets forth the organization of the NLRB; its authority and limitations; its procedures and powers in representation matters, in unfair labor practice cases, and in certain special proceedings under the Act; and the Act's provisions concerning enforcement of the Board's orders.

## The Rights of Employees
### The Section 7 Rights

The rights of employees are set forth principally in Section 7 of the Act, which provides as follows:

Sec. 7. Employees shall have the right to self-organization, to form, join, or assist labor organizations, to bargain collectively through representatives of their own choosing, and to engage in other concerted activities for the purpose of collective bargaining or other mutual aid or protection, and shall also have the right to refrain from any or all of such activities except to the extent that such right may be affected by an agreement requiring membership in a labor organization as a condition of employment as authorized in section 8(a)(3).

Examples of the rights protected by this section are the following:

*Examples of Section 7 rights*

- Forming or attempting to form a union among the employees of a company.
- Joining a union whether the union is recognized by the employer or not.
- Assisting a union to organize the employees of an employer.
- Going out on strike to secure better working conditions.
- Refraining from activity in behalf of a union.

### The Union Shop

The Act permits, under certain conditions, a union and an employer to make an agreement (called a union-security agreement) requiring all employees to join the union in order to retain their jobs (Section 8(a)(3)). However, the Act does not authorize such agreements in States where they are forbidden by state law (Section 14(b)).

Under certain circumstances an employee of a health care institution may not be required to pay dues or fees to a union where the employee has religious objections to the payment of such dues and fees.

A union-security agreement cannot require that applicants for employment be members of the union in order to be hired. The most that can be required is that all employees in the group covered by the agreement become members of the union within a certain period of time after the contract takes effect. This "grace period" cannot be less than 30 days except in the building and construction industry. New employees may be required to join the union at the end of a 30-day grace period after they are hired. The Act allows a shorter grace period of 7 full days in the building and construction industry (Section 8(f)). A union-security agreement that provides a shorter grace period than the law allows is invalid, and any employee discharged because of nonmembership in the union is entitled to reinstatement.

*Union-security agreements*

For a union-security agreement to be valid, it must meet all of the following requirements:
1. The union must not have been assisted or controlled by the employer (see Section 8(a)(2) under "Unfair Labor Practices of Employers" on pages 19–24).
2. The union must be the majority representative of the employees in the appropriate collective-bargaining unit covered by such agreement when made.
3. The union's authority to make such an agreement must not have been revoked within the previous 12 months by the employees in a Board election.
4. The agreement must provide for the appropriate grace period.

*Requirements for union-security agreements*

Section 8(f) of the Act allows an employer engaged primarily in the building and construction industry to sign a union-security agreement with a union without the union's having been designated as the representative of its employees as otherwise required by the Act. The agreement can be made before the employer has hired any employees for a project and will apply to them when they are hired. As noted above, new employees may be required to join the union *after* 7 full days. If the agreement is made while employees are on the job, it must allow nonunion employees the same 7-day grace period. As with any other union-security agreement, the union involved must be free from employer assistance or control.

*Prehire agreements in the construction industry*

Agreements in the building and construction industry can include, as stated in Section 8(f), the following additional provisions:
1. A requirement that the employer notify the union concerning job openings.

2. A provision that gives the union an opportunity to refer qualified applicants for such jobs.
3. Job qualification standards based on training or experience.
4. A provision for priority in hiring based on length of service with the employer, in the industry, or in the particular geographic area. Such hiring provisions may lawfully be included in collective-bargaining agreements which cover employees in other industries as well.

Section 7 of the Act states in part, "Employees shall have the right . . . to engage in other concerted activities for the purpose of collective bargaining or other mutual aid or protection." Strikes are included among the concerted activities protected for employees by this section. Section 13 also concerns the right to strike. It reads as follows:

Nothing in this Act, except as specifically provided for herein, shall be construed so as either to interfere with or impede or diminish in any way the right to strike, or to affect the limitations or qualifications on that right.

It is clear from a reading of these two provisions that the law not only guarantees the right of employees to strike, but also places limitations and qualifications on the exercise of that right. See, for example, restrictions on strikes in health care institutions, page 44.

## The Right To Strike

The lawfulness of a strike may depend on the object, or purpose, of the strike, on its timing, or on the conduct of the strikers. The object, or objects, of a strike and whether the objects are lawful are matters that are not always easy to determine. Such issues often have to be decided by the National Labor Relations Board. The consequences can be severe to striking employees and struck employers, involving as they do questions of reinstatement and backpay.

It must be emphasized that the following is only a brief outline. A detailed analysis of the law concerning strikes, and application of the law to all of the factual situations that can arise in connection with strikes, is beyond the scope of this material. Employees and employers who anticipate being involved in strike action should proceed cautiously and on the basis of competent advice.

### Lawful and unlawful strikes

Employees who strike for a lawful object fall into two classes—"economic strikers" and "unfair labor practice strikers." Both classes continue as employees, but unfair labor practice strikers have greater rights of reinstatement to their jobs.

### Strikes for a lawful object

If the object of a strike is to obtain from the employer some economic concession such as higher wages, shorter hours, or better working conditions, the striking employees are called economic strikers. They retain their status as employees and cannot be discharged, but they can be replaced by their employer. If the employer has hired bona fide permanent replacements who are filling the jobs of the economic strikers when the strikers apply unconditionally to go back to work, the strikers are *not* entitled to reinstatement at that time. However, if the strikers do not obtain regular and substantially equivalent employment, they are entitled to be recalled to jobs for which they are qualified when openings in such jobs occur if they, or their bargaining representative, have made an unconditional request for their reinstatement.

*Economic strikers defined*

Employees who strike to protest an unfair labor practice committed by their employer are called unfair labor practice strikers. Such strikers can be neither discharged nor permanently replaced. When the strike ends, unfair labor practice strikers, absent serious misconduct on their part, are entitled to have their jobs back even if employees hired to do their work have to be discharged.

*Unfair labor practice strikers defined*

If the Board finds that economic strikers or unfair labor practice strikers who have made an unconditional request for reinstatement have been unlawfully denied reinstatement by their employer, the Board may award such strikers backpay starting at the time they should have been reinstated.

A strike may be unlawful because an object, or purpose, of the strike is unlawful. A strike in support of a union unfair labor practice, or one that would cause an employer to commit an unfair labor practice, may be a strike for an unlawful object. For example, it is an unfair labor practice for an employer to discharge an employee for lack of union membership where there is no union-security agreement in effect (Section 8(a)(3)). A strike to compel an employer to do this would be a strike for an unlawful object and, therefore, an unlawful strike. Strikes of this nature will be discussed in connection with the various unfair labor practices in a later section of this guide.

*Strikes unlawful because of purpose*

Furthermore, Section 8(b)(4) of the Act prohibits strikes for certain objects even though the objects are not necessarily unlawful if achieved by other means. An example of this would be a strike to compel Employer A to cease doing business with Employer B. It is not unlawful for Employer A voluntarily to stop doing business with Employer B, nor is it unlawful for a union merely to request that it do so. It is, however, unlawful for the union to strike with an object of forcing the employer to do so. These points will be covered in more detail in the explanation of Section 8(b)(4).

In any event, employees who participate in an unlawful strike may be discharged and are not entitled to reinstatement.

*Strikes unlawful because of timing—Effect of no-strike contract*

A strike that violates a no-strike provision of a contract is not protected by the Act, and the striking employees can be discharged or otherwise disciplined unless the strike is called to protest certain kinds of unfair labor practices committed by the employer. Also, an employee who is subject to a no-strike contract clause can be replaced for refusing to cross a picket line at the plant of another employer unless the contract specifically gives the employee the right not to cross a picket line. It should be noted that not all refusals to work are considered strikes and thus violations of no-strike provisions. A walkout because of conditions abnormally dangerous to health, such as a defective ventilation system in a spray-painting shop, has been held not to violate a no-strike provision.

*Same—Strikes at end of contract period*

Section 8(d) provides that where either party desires to terminate or change an existing contract, it must comply with certain conditions. (See page 7.) If these requirements are not met, a strike to terminate or change a contract is unlawful and participating strikers lose their status as employees of the employer engaged in the labor dispute. If the strike was caused by the unfair labor practice of the employer, however, the strikers are classed as unfair labor practice strikers and their status is not affected by failure to follow the required procedure.

*Strikes unlawful because of misconduct of strikers*

Strikers who engage in serious misconduct in the course of a strike may be refused reinstatement to their former jobs. This applies to both economic strikers and unfair labor practice strikers. Serious misconduct has been held to include, among other things, violence and threats of violence. The U.S. Supreme Court has ruled that a "sitdown" strike, where employees simply stay in the plant and refuse to work, thus depriving the owner of property, is not protected by the law. Where an unfair labor practice by the employer involved provokes an unfair labor practice strike, this fact may be considered in the determination of whether misconduct by strikers will bar their reinstatement. Examples of serious misconduct that could cause the employees involved to lose their right to reinstatement are:

- Strikers physically blocking persons from entering or leaving a struck plant.
- Strikers threatening violence against nonstriking employees entering a plant.
- Strikers attacking management representatives.

Likewise the right to picket is subject to limitations and qualifications. As with the right to strike, picketing can be prohibited because of its object or its timing, or misconduct on the picket line. In addition, Section 8(b)(7) declares it to be an unfair labor practice for a union to picket for certain objects whether the picketing accompanies a strike or not. This will be covered in more detail in the section on union unfair labor practices.

### The Right To Picket

## Collective Bargaining and Representation of Employees

Collective bargaining is one of the keystones of the Act. Section 1 of the Act declares that the policy of the United States is to be carried out "by encouraging the practice and procedure of collective bargaining and by protecting the exercise by workers of full freedom of association, self-organization, and designation of representatives of their own choosing, for the purpose of negotiating the terms and conditions of their employment or other mutual aid or protection."

Collective bargaining is defined in the Act. Section 8(d) requires an employer and the representative of its employees to meet at reasonable times, to confer in good faith about certain matters, and to put into writing any agreement reached if requested by either party. The parties must confer in good faith with respect to wages, hours, and other terms or conditions of employment, the negotiation of an agreement, or any question arising under an agreement.

These obligations are imposed equally on the employer and the representative of its employees. It is an unfair labor practice for either party to refuse to bargain collectively with the other. The obligation does not, however, compel either party to agree to a proposal by the other, nor does it require either party to make a concession to the other.

Section 8(d) provides further that where a collective-bargaining agreement is in effect no party to the contract shall end or change the contract unless the party wishing to end or change it takes the following steps:

### Collective Bargaining

*Duty to bargain imposed on both employer and union*

## Bargaining steps to end or change a contract

1. The party must notify the other party to the contract in writing about the proposed termination or modification 60 days before the date on which the contract is scheduled to expire. If the contract is not scheduled to expire on any particular date, the notice in writing must be served 60 days before the time when it is proposed that the termination or modification take effect.
2. The party must offer to meet and confer with the other party for the purpose of negotiating a new contract or a contract containing the proposed changes.
3. The party must, within 30 days after the notice to the other party, notify the Federal Mediation and Conciliation Service of the existence of a dispute if no agreement has been reached by that time. Said party must also notify at the same time any State or Territorial mediation or conciliation agency in the State or Territory where the dispute occurred.
4. The party must continue in full force and effect, without resorting to strike or lockout, all the terms and conditions of the existing contract until 60 days after the notice to the other party was given or until the date the contract is scheduled to expire, whichever is later.

(In the case of a health care institution, the requirement in paragraphs 1 and 4 is 90 days, and in paragraph 3 is 60 days. In addition, there is a 30-day notice requirement to the agencies in paragraph 3 when a dispute arises in bargaining for an initial contract.)

## When the bargaining steps are not required

The requirements of paragraphs 2, 3, and 4, above, cease to apply if the NLRB issues a certificate showing that the employees' representative who is a party to the contract has been replaced by a different representative or has been voted out by the employees. Neither party is required to discuss or agree to any change of the provisions of the contract if the other party proposes that the change become effective before the provision could be reopened according to the terms of the contract.

As has been pointed out, any employee who engages in a strike within the notice period loses status as an employee of the struck employer. This loss of status ends, however, if and when that individual is reemployed by the same employer.

## The Employee Representative

Section 9(a) provides that the employee representatives that have been "designated or selected for the purposes of collective bargaining by the majority of the employees in a unit appropriate for such purposes, shall be the exclusive representatives of all the employees in such unit for the purposes of collective bargaining."

A unit of employees is a group of two or more employees who share common employment interests and conditions and may reasonably be grouped together for purposes of collective bargaining. The determination of what is an appropriate unit for such purposes is, under the Act, left to the discretion of the NLRB. Section 9(b) states that the Board shall decide in each representation case whether, "in order to assure to employees the fullest freedom in exercising the rights guaranteed by this Act, the unit appropriate for the purposes of collective bargaining shall be the employer unit, craft unit, plant unit, or subdivision thereof."

*What is an appropriate bargaining unit*

This broad discretion is, however, limited by several other provisions of the Act. Section 9(b)(1) provides that the Board shall not approve as appropriate a unit that includes both professional and nonprofessional employees, unless a majority of the professional employees involved vote to be included in the mixed unit.

Section 9(b)(2) provides that the Board shall not hold a proposed craft unit to be inappropriate simply because a different unit was previously approved by the Board, unless a majority of the employees in the proposed craft unit vote against being represented separately.

Section 9(b)(3) prohibits the Board from including plant guards in the same unit with other employees. It also prohibits the Board from certifying a labor organization as the representative of a plant guard unit if the labor organization has members who are nonguard employees or if it is "affiliated directly or indirectly" with an organization that has members who are nonguard employees.

*How the appropriateness of a unit is determined*

Generally, the appropriateness of a bargaining unit is determined on the basis of the common employment interests of the employees involved. Those who have the same or substantially similar interests concerning wages, hours, and working conditions are grouped together in a bargaining unit. In determining whether a proposed unit is appropriate, the following factors are also considered:

1. Any history of collective bargaining.
2. The desires of the employees concerned.
3. The extent to which the employees are organized. Section 9(c)(5) forbids the Board from giving this factor controlling weight.

A unit may cover the employees in one plant of an employer, or it may cover employees in two or more plants of the same employer. In some industries where employers are grouped together in voluntary associations, a unit may include employees of two or more employers in any number of locations. It should be noted that a bargaining unit can include only persons who are "employees" within the meaning of the Act. The Act excludes certain individuals, such as agricultural laborers, independent contractors, supervisors, and persons in managerial positions, from the meaning of "employees." None of these individuals can be included in a bargaining unit established by the Board. In addition, the Board, as a matter of policy, excludes from bargaining units employees who act in a confidential capacity to an employer's labor relations officials.

Once an employee representative has been designated by a majority of the employees in an appropriate unit, the Act makes that representative the exclusive bargaining agent for all employees in the unit. As exclusive bargaining agent it has a duty to represent equally and fairly all employees in the unit without regard to their union membership or activities. Once a collective-bargaining representative has been designated or selected by its employees, it is illegal for an employer to bargain with individual employees, with a group of employees, or with another employee representative.

Section 9(a) provides that any individual employee or a group of employees shall have the right at any time to present grievances to their employer and to have such grievances adjusted without the intervention of the bargaining representative provided:

1. The adjustment is not inconsistent with the terms of any collective-bargaining agreement then in effect.
2. The bargaining representative has been given the opportunity to be present at such adjustment.

Although the Act requires that an employer bargain with the representative selected by its employees, it does not require that the representative be selected by any particular procedure so long as the representative is clearly the choice of a majority of the employees. As one of the methods by

*Who can or cannot be included in a unit*

*Duties of bargaining representative and employer*

**How a Bargaining Representative Is Selected**

which employees can select a bargaining representative the Act provides for the NLRB to conduct representation elections by secret ballot.

The NLRB can conduct such an election only when a petition has been filed requesting one.

*Petition for certification of representatives*

A petition for certification of representatives can be filed by an employee or a group of employees or any individual or labor organization acting on their behalf, or it can be filed by an employer. If filed by or on behalf of employees, the petition must be supported by a substantial number of employees who wish to be represented for collective bargaining and must state that their employer declines to recognize their representative. If filed by an employer, the petition must allege that one or more individuals or organizations have made a claim for recognition as the exclusive representative of the same group of employees.

*Petition for decertification election*

The Act also contains a provision whereby employees or someone acting on their behalf can file a petition seeking an election to determine if the employees wish to retain the individual or labor organization currently acting as their bargaining representative, whether the representative has been certified or voluntarily recognized by the employer. This is called a decertification election.

*Union-shop deauthorization*

Provision is also made for the Board to determine by secret ballot whether the employees covered by a union-shop agreement desire to withdraw the authority of their representative to continue the agreement. This is called a union-shop deauthorization election and can be brought about by the filing of a petition signed by 30 percent or more of the employees covered by the agreement.

If you will refer to the "Types of Cases" chart on pages 24 and 25 of this booklet you may find it easier to understand the differences between the six types of petitions that can be filed under the Act.

*Purpose of investigation and hearing*

The same petition form is used for any kind of Board election. When the petition is filed, the NLRB must investigate the petition, hold a hearing if necessary, and direct an election if it finds that a question of representation exists. The purpose of the investigation is to determine, among other things, the following:

1. Whether the Board has jurisdiction to conduct an election.

2. Whether there is a sufficient showing of employee interest to justify an election.
3. Whether a question of representation exists.
4. Whether the election is sought in an appropriate unit of employees.
5. Whether the representative named in the petition is qualified.
6. Whether there are any barriers to an election in the form of existing contracts or prior elections.

*Jurisdiction to conduct an election*

The jurisdiction of the NLRB to direct and conduct an election is limited to those enterprises that affect commerce. (This is discussed in greater detail at pages 45–49.) The other matters listed above will be discussed in turn.

*Expedited elections under Section 8(b)(7)(C)*

First, however, it should be noted that Section 8(b)(7)(C) provides, among other things, that when a petition is filed within a reasonable period, not to exceed 30 days, after the commencement of recognitional or organizational picketing, the NLRB shall "forthwith" order an election and certify the results. This is so if the picketing is not within the protection of the second proviso to Section 8(b)(7)(C). Where an election under Section 8(b)(7)(C) is appropriate, neither a hearing nor a showing of interest is required, and the election is scheduled sooner than under the ordinary procedure.

*Showing of interest required*

Regarding the showing of interest, it is the policy to require that a petitioner requesting an election for either certification of representatives or decertification show that at least 30 percent of the employees favor an election. The Act also requires that a petition for a union-shop deauthorization election be filed by 30 percent or more of the employees in the unit covered by the agreement for the NLRB to conduct an election for that purpose. The showing of interest must be exclusively by employees who are in the appropriate bargaining unit in which an election is sought.

*Existence of question of representation*

Section 9(c)(1) authorizes the NLRB to direct an election and certify the results thereof, provided the record shows that a question of representation exists. Petitions for certification of representatives present a question of representation if, among other things, they are based on a demand for recognition by the employee representative and a denial of recognition by the employer. The demand for recognition need not be made in any particular form; in fact, the filing of a petition by the representative itself is considered to be a demand for recognition. The NLRB has held that even a representative that is currently recognized by the employer can file a petition for certification and that such petition presents a question of representation provided the representative has not previously been certified.

A question of representation is also raised by a decertification petition which challenges the representative status of a bargaining agent previously certified or currently recognized by the employer. However, a decertification petition filed by a supervisor does not raise a valid question of representation and must be dismissed.

Section 2(4) of the Act provides that the employee representative for collective bargaining can be "any individual or labor organization." A supervisor or any other management representative may not be an employee representative. It is NLRB policy to direct an election and to issue a certification unless the proposed bargaining agent fails to qualify as a bona fide representative of the employees. In determining a union's qualifications as bargaining agent, it is the union's willingness to represent the employees rather than its constitution and bylaws that is the controlling factor. The NLRB's power to certify a labor organization as bargaining representative is limited by Section 9(b)(3) which prohibits certification of a union as the representative of a unit of plant guards if the union "admits to membership, or is affiliated directly or indirectly with an organization which admits to membership, employees other than guards."

*Who can qualify as bargaining representative*

The NLRB has established the policy of not directing an election among employees presently covered by a valid collective-bargaining agreement except in accordance with certain rules. These rules, followed in determining whether or not an existing collective-bargaining contract will bar an election, are called the NLRB contract-bar rules. Not every contract will bar an election. Examples of contracts that would *not* bar an election are:

**Bars to Election**

*Existing collective-bargaining contract*

- The contract is not in writing, or is not signed.
- The contract has not been ratified by the members of the union, if such is expressly required.
- The contract does not contain substantial terms or conditions of employment sufficient to stabilize the bargaining relationship.

- The contract can be terminated by either party at any time for any reason.
- The contract contains a clearly illegal union-security clause.
- The bargaining unit is not appropriate.
- The union that entered the contract with the employer is no longer in existence or is unable or unwilling to represent the employees.
- The contract discriminates between employees on racial grounds.
- The contracting union is involved in a basic internal conflict with resulting unstabilizing confusion about the identity of the union.
- The employer's operations have changed substantially since the contract was executed.

Under the NLRB rules a valid contract for a fixed period of 3 years or less will bar an election for the period covered by the contract. A contract for a fixed period of more than 3 years will bar an election sought by a contracting party during the life of the contract, but will act as a bar to an election sought by an outside party for only 3 years following its effective date. A contract of no fixed period will not act as a bar at all.

*Time provisions*

If there is no existing contract, a petition can bring about an election if it is filed before the day a contract is signed. If the petition is filed on the same day the contract is signed, the contract bars an election, unless the contract is effective immediately or retroactively and the employee has not been informed at the time of execution that a petition has been filed. Once the contract becomes effective as a bar to an election, no petition will be accepted until near the end of the period during which the contract is effective as a bar. Petitions filed not more than 90 days but over 60 days before the end of the contract-bar period will be accepted and can bring about an election. These time periods for filing petitions involving health care institutions are 120 and 90 days, respectively. Of course, a petition can be filed after the contract expires. However, the last 60 days of the contract-bar period is called an "insulated" period. During this time the parties to the existing contract are free to negotiate a new contract or to agree to extend the old one. If they reach agreement in this period, petitions will not be accepted until 90 days before the end of the new contract-bar period.

*When a petition can be filed if there is an existing contract*

*Effect of certification*

In addition to the contract-bar rules, the NLRB has established a rule that when a representative has been certified by the Board, the certification will ordinarily be binding for at least 1 year and a petition filed before the end of the certification year will be dismissed. In cases where the certified representative and the employer enter a valid collective-bargaining contract during the year, the contract becomes controlling, and whether a petition for an election can be filed is determined by the Board's contract-bar rules.

*Effect of prior election*

Section 9(c)(3) prohibits the holding of an election in any collective-bargaining unit or subdivision thereof in which a valid election has been held during the preceding 12-month period. A new election may be held, however, in a larger unit, but not in the same unit or subdivision in which the previous election was held. For example, if all of the production and maintenance employees in Company A, including draftsmen in the company engineering office, are included in a collective-bargaining unit, an election among all the employees in the unit would bar another election among all the employees in the unit for 12 months. Similarly, an election among the draftsmen only would bar another election among the draftsmen for 12 months. However, an election among the draftsmen would not bar a later election during the 12-month period among all the production and maintenance employees including the draftsmen.

It is the Board's interpretation that Section 9(c)(3) prohibits only the holding of an election during the 12-month period, but does not prohibit the filing of a petition. Accordingly, the NLRB will accept a petition filed not more than 60 days before the end of the 12-month period. The election cannot be held, of course, until after the 12-month period. If an election is held and a representative certified, that certification is binding for 1 year and a petition for another election in the same unit will be dismissed if it is filed during the 1-year period after the certification. If an election is held and no representative is certified, the election bars another election for 12 months. A petition for another election in the same unit can be filed not more than 60 days before the end of the 12-month period and the election can be held after the 12-month period expires.

*When a petition can be filed if there has been a prior election*

**The Representation Election**

Section 9(c)(1) provides that if a question of representation exists, the NLRB must make its determination by means of a secret ballot election. In a representation election employees are given a choice of one or more bargaining representatives or no representative at all. To be certified as the bargaining representative, an individual or a labor organization must receive a majority of the valid votes cast.

### Consent-election agreements

An election may be held by agreement between the employer and the individual or labor organization claiming to represent the employees. In such an agreement the parties would state the time and place agreed on, the choices to be included on the ballot, and a method to determine who is eligible to vote. They would also authorize the NLRB Regional Director to conduct the election.

If the parties are unable to reach an agreement, the Act authorizes the NLRB to order an election after a hearing. The Act also authorizes the Board to delegate to its Regional Directors the determination on matters concerning elections. Under this delegation of authority the Regional Directors can determine the appropriateness of the unit, direct an election, and certify the outcome. Upon the request of an interested party, the Board may review the action of a Regional Director, but such review does not stop the election process unless the Board so orders. The election details are left to the Regional Director. Such matters as who may vote, when the election will be held, and what standards of conduct will be imposed on the parties are decided in accordance with the Board's rules and its decisions.

### Who determines election matters

### Who may vote in a representation election

To be entitled to vote, an employee must have worked in the unit during the eligibility period set by the Board and must be employed in the unit on the date of the election. Generally, the eligibility period is the employer's payroll period just before the date on which the election was directed. This requirement does not apply, however, to employees who are ill, on vacation, or temporarily laid off, or to employees in military service who appear in person at the polls. The NLRB rules take into consideration the fact that employment is typically irregular in certain industries. In such industries eligibility to vote is determined according to formulas designed to permit all employees who have a substantial continuing interest in their employment conditions to vote. Examples of these formulas, which differ from case to case, are:

- In one case, employees of a construction company were allowed to vote if they worked for the employer at least 65 days during the year before the "eligibility date" for the election.

- In another case longshoremen who worked at least 700 hours during a specified contract year, and at least 20 hours in each full month between the end of that year and the date on which the election was directed, were allowed to vote.
- Radio and television talent employees and musicians in the television film, motion picture, and phonograph recording industries have been held eligible to vote if they worked in the unit 2 or more days during the year before the date on which the election was directed.

Section 9(c)(3) provides that economic strikers who have been replaced by bona fide permanent employees may be entitled to vote in "any election conducted within 12 months after the commencement of the strike." The permanent replacements are also eligible to vote at the same time. As a general proposition a striker is considered to be an economic striker unless found by the NLRB to be on strike over unfair labor practices of the employer. Whether the economic striker is eligible to vote or not is determined on the facts of each case.

*When strikers may be allowed to vote*

Ordinarily, elections are held within 30 days after they are directed. Seasonal drops in employment or any change in operations which would prevent a normal work force from being present may cause a different election date to be set. Normally an election will not be conducted when unfair labor practice charges have been filed based upon conduct of a nature which would have a tendency to interfere with the free choice of the employees in an election, except that, in certain cases, the Board may proceed to the election if the charging party so requests.

*When elections are held*

NLRB elections are conducted in accordance with strict standards designed to give the employee-voters an opportunity to freely indicate whether they wish to be represented for purposes of collective bargaining. Election details, such as time, place, and notice of an election, are left largely to the Regional Director who usually obtains the agreement of the parties on these matters. Any party to an election who believes that the Board election standards were not met may, within 5 days after the tally of ballots has been furnished, file objections to the election with the Regional Director under whose supervision the election was held. The Regional Director's rulings on these objections may be appealed

*Conduct of elections*

to the Board for decision except in the case of elections that are held by consent of the parties, in which case the Regional Director's rulings are final.

An election will be set aside if it was accompanied by conduct that the NLRB considers created an atmosphere of confusion or fear of reprisals and thus interfered with the employees' freedom of choice. In any particular case the NLRB does not attempt to determine whether the conduct actually interfered with the employees' expression of free choice, but rather asks whether the conduct tended to do so. If it is reasonable to believe that the conduct would tend to interfere with the free expression of the employees' choice, the election may be set aside. Examples of conduct the Board considers to interfere with employee free choice are:

- Threats of loss of jobs or benefits by an employer or a union to influence the votes or union activities of employees.
- Misstatements of important facts in the election campaign by an employer or a union where the other party does not have a fair chance to reply.
- An employer firing employees to discourage or encourage their union activities or a union causing an employer to take such action.
- An employer or a union making campaign speeches to assembled groups of employees on company time within the 24-hour period before the election.
- The incitement of racial or religious prejudice by inflammatory campaign appeals made by either an employer or a union.
- Threats or the use of physical force or violence against employees by an employer or a union to influence their votes.
- The occurrence of extensive violence or trouble or widespread fear of job losses which prevents the holding of a fair election, whether or not caused by an employer or a union.

## Unfair Labor Practices of Employers

The unfair labor practices of employers are listed in Section 8(a) of the Act; those of labor organizations in Section 8(b). Section 8(e) lists an unfair labor practice that can be committed only by an employer and a labor organization acting together. The "Types of Cases" chart at pages 24–25 may be helpful in getting to know the relationship between the various unfair labor practice sections of the Act.

### Section 8(a)(1)—Interference with Section 7 Rights

Section 8(a)(1) forbids an employer "to interfere with, restrain, or coerce employees in the exercise of the rights guaranteed in section 7." Any prohibited interference by an employer with the rights of employees to organize, to form, join, or assist a labor organization, to bargain collectively, or to refrain from any of these activities, constitutes a violation of this section. This is a broad prohibition on employer interference, and an employer violates this section whenever it commits any of the other employer unfair labor practices. In consequence, whenever a violation of Section 8(a)(2), (3), (4), or (5) is committed, a violation of Section 8(a)(1) is also found. This is called a "derivative violation" of Section 8(a)(1).

Employer conduct may of course independently violate Section 8(a)(1). Examples of such independent violations are:

*Examples of violations of Section 8(a)(1)*

- Threatening employees with loss of jobs or benefits if they should join or vote for a union.
- Threatening to close down the plant if a union should be organized in it.
- Questioning employees about their union activities or membership in such circumstances as will tend to restrain or coerce the employees.
- Spying on union gatherings, or pretending to spy.
- Granting wage increases deliberately timed to discourage employees from forming or joining a union.

### Section 8(a)(2)—Domination or Illegal Assistance and Support of a Labor Organization

Section 8(a)(2) makes it unlawful for an employer "to dominate or interfere with the formation or administration of any labor organization or contribute financial or other support to it." This section not only outlaws "company unions" that are dominated by the employer, but also forbids an employer to contribute money to a union it favors or to give a union improper advantages that are denied to rival unions.

*Domination*

A labor organization is considered dominated within the meaning of this section if the employer has interfered with its formation and has assisted and supported its operation and activities to such an extent that it must be looked at as the employer's creation instead of the true bargaining representative of the employees. Such domination is the result of a combination of factors and has been found to exist where there is not only the factor of the employer getting the organization started, but also such other factors as the employer deciding how the organization will be set up and what it will do, or representatives of management actually taking part in the meetings and activities of the organization and trying to influence its actions and policies.

Interference that is less than complete domination is found where an employer tries to help a union that it favors by various kinds of conduct, such as giving the favored union improper privileges that are denied to other unions competing to organize the employees, or recognizing a favored union when another union has raised a real representation claim concerning the employees involved. Financial support of unions violates the noninterference provision of this section whether it is a direct payment to the assisted union or indirect financial aid.

*Illegal assistance and support*

An employer violates Section 8(a)(2) by:

*Examples of violations of Section 8(a)(2)*

- Taking an active part in organizing a union or a committee to represent employees.
- Bringing pressure on employees to join a union, except in the enforcement of a lawful union-security agreement.
- Allowing one of several unions, competing to represent employees, to solicit on company premises during working hours and denying other unions the same privilege.
- Soliciting and obtaining from employees and applicants for employment, during the hiring procedure, applications for union membership and signed authorizations for the checkoff of union dues.

In remedying such unfair labor practices, the NLRB distinguishes between domination of a labor organization and conduct which amounts to no more than illegal assistance. When a union is found to be dominated by an employer, the Board has announced it will order the organization completely disestablished as a representative of employees. But, if the organization is found only to have been supported by employer assistance amounting to less than domination, the Board usually orders the employer to stop such support and to withhold recognition from the organization until such time as it has been certified by the Board as a bona fide representative of employees.

*Remedy in cases of domination differs from that in cases of illegal assistance and support*

It should be noted in connection with the last example, above, that Section 8(a)(2) provides that an employer may permit employees to confer with it on union business during working hours without loss of pay. This means that both the employee and the union representative who goes along to discuss a grievance with the employer during working hours may do so without loss of pay.

*When an employer can pay employees for union activity during working hours*

## Section 8(a)(3)—Discrimination Against Employees

Section 8(a)(3) makes it an unfair labor practice for an employer to discriminate against employees "in regard to hire or tenure of employment or any term or condition of employment" for the purpose of encouraging or discouraging membership in a labor organization. In general, the Act makes it illegal for an employer to discriminate in employment because of an employee's union or other group activity within the protection of the Act. A banding together of employees, even in the absence of a formal organization, may constitute a labor organization for purposes of Section 8(a)(3). It also prohibits discrimination because an employee has refrained from taking part in such union or group activity except where a valid union-shop agreement is in effect. Discrimination within the meaning of the Act would include such action as refusing to hire, discharging, demoting, assigning to a less desirable shift or job, or withholding benefits.

*The union-shop exception to Section 8(a)(3)*

As previously noted, Section 8(a)(3) provides that an employee may be discharged for failing to pay the required union initiation fees and dues uniformly required by the exclusive bargaining representative under a lawful union-shop contract. The section provides further, however, that no employer can justify any discriminatory action against an employee for nonmembership in a union if it has reason to believe that membership in the union was not open to the employee on the same terms and conditions that apply to others, or if it has reason to believe that the employee was denied membership in the union for some reason other than failure to pay regular dues and initiation fees.

Even where there is a valid union-security agreement in effect, an employer may not pay the union the dues and fees owed by its employees. The employer may, however, deduct these amounts from the wages of its employees and forward them to the union for each employee who has *voluntarily* signed a dues "checkoff" authorization. Such checkoff authorization may be made irrevocable for no more than a year. But employees may revoke their checkoff authorizations after a Board-conducted election in which the union's authority to maintain a union-security agreement has been withdrawn.

This section does not limit an employer's right to discharge, transfer, or lay off an employee for genuine economic reasons or for such good cause as disobedience or bad work. This right applies equally to employees who are active in support of a union and to those who are not. However, the fact that a lawful reason for the discharge or discipline of employees may exist does not entitle an employer to discharge or discipline them when the true reason is the employees' union or other activities protected by the law.

*The Act does not limit employer's right to discharge for economic reasons*

An employer who is engaged in good-faith bargaining with a union may lock out the represented employees, sometimes even before impasse is reached in the negotiations, if it does so to further its position in bargaining. But a bargaining lockout may be unlawful if the employer is at that time unlawfully refusing to bargain or is bargaining in bad faith. It is also unlawful if the employer's purpose in locking out its employees is to discourage them in their union loyalties and activities, that is, if the employer is motivated by hostility toward the union. Thus, a lockout to defeat a union's efforts to organize the employer's employees would violate the Act, as would the lockout of only those of its employees who are members of the union. On the other hand, lockouts are lawful which are intended to prevent any unusual losses or safety hazards which would be caused by an anticipated "quickie" strike.

Addendum 1    207

And a whipsaw strike against one employer engaged in multiemployer bargaining justifies a lockout by any of the other employers who are party to the bargaining.

Examples of illegal discrimination under Section 8(a)(3) include:

*Examples of violations of Section 8(a)(3)*

- Discharging employees because they urged other employees to join a union.
- Refusing to reinstate employees when jobs they are qualified for are open because they took part in a union's lawful strike.
- Granting of "superseniority" to those hired to replace employees engaged in a lawful strike.
- Demoting employees because they circulated a union petition among other employees asking the employer for an increase in pay.
- Discontinuing an operation at one plant and discharging the employees involved followed by opening the same operation at another plant with new employees because the employees at the first plant joined a union.
- Refusing to hire qualified applicants for jobs because they belong to a union. It would also be a violation if the qualified applicants were refused employment because they did not belong to a union, or because they belonged to one union rather than another.

## Section 8(a)(4)—Discrimination for NLRB Activity

Section 8(a)(4) makes it an unfair labor practice for an employer "to discharge or otherwise discriminate against an employee because he has filed charges or given testimony under this Act." This provision guards the right of employees to seek the protection of the Act by using the processes of the NLRB. Like the previous section, it forbids an employer to discharge, lay off, or engage in other forms of discrimination in working conditions against employees who have filed charges with the

## 1. CHARGES OF UNFAIR LABOR PRACTICES
### (C CASES)

| Charge Against Employer | Charge Against Labor Organization | |
|---|---|---|
| **CA** | **CB** | **CC** |
| *Section of the Act* | *Section of the Act* | *Section of the Act* |
| 8(a)(1) To interfere with, restrain, or coerce employees in exercise of their rights under Section 7 (to join or assist a labor organization or to refrain). | 8(b)(1)(A) To restrain or coerce employees in exercise of their rights under Section 7 (to join or assist a labor organization or to refrain). | 8(b)(4)(i) To engage in, or induce or encourage any individual employed by any person engaged in commerce or in an industry affecting commerce, to engage in a strike, work stoppage, or boycott, or (ii) to threaten, coerce, or restrain any person engaged in commerce or in an industry affecting commerce, where in either case an object is: |
| 8(a)(2) To dominate or interfere with the formation or administration of a labor organization or contribute financial or other support to it. | 8(b)(1)(B) To restrain or coerce an employer in the selection of its representatives for collective bargaining or adjustment of grievances. | (A) To force or require any employer or self-employed person to join any labor or employer organization or to enter into any agreement prohibited by Sec. 8(e). |
| 8(a)(3) By discrimination in regard to hire or tenure of employment or any term or condition of employment to encourage or discourage membership in any labor organization. | 8(b)(2) To cause or attempt to cause an employer to discriminate against an employee. | (B) To force or require any person to cease using, selling, handling, transporting, or otherwise dealing in the products of any other producer, processor, or manufacturer, or to cease doing business with any other person, or force or require any other employer to recognize or bargain with a labor organization as the representative of its employees unless such labor organization has been so certified. |
| 8(a)(4) To discharge or otherwise discriminate against employees because they have given testimony under the Act. | 8(b)(3) To refuse to bargain collectively with employer. | |
|  | 8(b)(5) To require of employees the payment of excessive or discriminatory fees for membership. | (C) To force or require any employer to recognize or bargain with a particular labor organization as the representative of its employees if another labor organization has been certified as the representative. |
| 8(a)(5) To refuse to bargain collectively with representatives of its employees. | 8(b)(6) To cause or attempt to cause an employer to pay or agree to pay money or other thing of value for services which are not performed or not to be performed. | |

### CD
*Section of the Act*

(D) To force or require any employer to assign particular work to employees in a particular labor organization or in a particular trade, craft, or class rather than to employees in another trade, craft, or class, unless such employer is failing to conform to an appropriate Board order or certification.

### CG
*Section of the Act*

8(g) To strike, picket, or otherwise concertedly refuse to work at any health care institution without notifying the institution and the Federal Mediation and Conciliation Service in writing 10 days prior to such action.

## Addendum 1

| Charge Against Labor Organization and Employer | 2. PETITIONS FOR CERTIFCATION OR DECERTIFICATION OF REPRESENTATIVES (R CASES) By or in Behalf of Employees | 2. PETITIONS FOR CERTIFCATION OR DECERTIFICATION OF REPRESENTATIVES (R CASES) By an Employer | 3. OTHER PETITIONS By or in Behalf of Employees | 3. OTHER PETITIONS By a Labor Organization or an Employer |
|---|---|---|---|---|
| **CP** *Section of the Act* 8(b)(7) To picket, cause, or threaten the picketing of any employer where an object is to force or require an employer to recognize or bargain with a labor organization as the representative of its employees, or to force or require the employees of an employer to select such labor organization as their collective-bargaining representative, unless such labor organization is currently certified as the representative of such employees: (A) where the employer has lawfully recognized any other labor organization and a question concerning representation may not appropriately be raised under Section 9(c), (B) where within the preceding 12 months a valid election under Section 9(c) has been conducted, or (C) where picketing has been conducted without a petition under 9(c) being filed within a reasonable period of time not to exceed 30 days from the commencement of the picketing; except where the picketing is for the purpose of truthfully advising the public (including consumers) that an employer does not employ members of, or have a contract with, a labor organization, and it does not have an effect of interference with deliveries or services. | **CE** *Section of the Act* 8(e) To enter into any contract or agreement (any labor organization and any employer) whereby such employer ceases or refrains or agrees to cease or refrain from handling or dealing in any product of any other employer, or to cease doing business with any other person. | **RC** *Section of the Act* 9(c)(1)(A)(i) Alleging that a substantial number of employees wish to be represented for collective bargaining and their employer declines to recognize their representative.* **RD** *Section of the Act* 9(c)(1)(A)(ii) Alleging that a substantial number of employees assert that the certified or currently recognized bargaining representative is no longer their representative.* | **RM** *Section of the Act* 9(c)(1)(B) Alleging that one or more claims for recognition as exclusive bargaining representative have been received by the employer.* *If an 8(b)(7) charge has been filed involving the same employer, these statements in RC, RD, and RM petitions are not required. | **UD** *Section of the Act* 9(e)(1) Alleging that employees (30 percent or more of an appropriate unit) wish to rescind an existing union-security agreement. | **UC** *Board Rules* *Subpart C* Seeking clarification of an existing bargaining unit. **AC** *Board Rules* *Subpart C* Seeking amendment of an outstanding certification of bargaining representative. |

Charges filed with the National Labor Relations Board are letter-coded and numbered. Unfair labor practice charges are classified as "C" cases and petitions for certification or decertification of representatives as "R" cases. This chart indicates the letter codes used for "C" cases, at left, and "R" cases, above, and also presents a summary of each section involved.

210   When Health Care Employees Strike

NLRB, given affidavits to NLRB investigators, or testified at an NLRB hearing. Violations of this section are in most cases also violations of Section 8(a)(3).

*Examples of violations of Section 8(a)(4)*

Examples of violations of Section 8(a)(4) are:

- Refusing to reinstate employees when jobs they are otherwise qualified for are open because they filed charges with the NLRB claiming their layoffs were based on union activity.
- Demoting employees because they testified at an NLRB hearing.

## Section 8(a)(5)—Refusal To Bargain in Good Faith

Section 8(a)(5) makes it illegal for an employer to refuse to bargain in good faith about wages, hours, and other conditions of employment with the representative selected by a majority of the employees in a unit appropriate for collective bargaining. A bargaining representative which seeks to enforce its right concerning an employer under this section must show that it has been designated by a majority of the employees, that the unit is appropriate, and that there has been both a demand that the employer bargain and a refusal by the employer to do so.

*Required subjects of bargaining*

The duty to bargain covers all matters concerning rates of pay, wages, hours of employment, or other conditions of employment. These are called "mandatory" subjects of bargaining about which the employer, as well as the employees' representative, must bargain in good faith, although the law does not require "either party to agree to a proposal or require the making of a concession." These mandatory subjects of bargaining include but are not limited to such matters as pensions for present and retired employees, bonuses, group insurance, grievance procedure, safety practices, seniority, procedures for discharge, layoff, recall, or discipline, and the union shop. On "nonmandatory" subjects, that is, matters that are lawful but not related to "wages, hours, and other conditions of employment," the parties are free to bargain and to agree, but neither party may insist on bargaining on such subjects over the objection of the other party.

*Duty to bargain defined*

An employer who is required to bargain under this section must, as stated in Section 8(d), "meet at reasonable times and confer in good faith with respect to wages, hours, and other terms and conditions of employment, or the negotiation of an agreement, or any question arising thereunder, and the execution of a written contract incorporating any agreement reached if requested by either party."

An employer, therefore, will be found to have violated Section 8(a)(5) if its conduct in bargaining, viewed in its entirety, indicates that the employer did not negotiate with a good-faith intention to reach agreement. However, the employer's good faith is not at issue where its conduct constitutes an out-and-out refusal to bargain on a mandatory subject. For example, it is a violation for an employer, regardless of good faith, to refuse to bargain about a subject which it believes is not a mandatory subject of bargaining, when in fact it is.

*What constitutes a violation of Section 8(a)(5)*

The duty of an employer to meet and confer with the representative of its employees includes the duty to deal with whoever is designated by the employees' representative to carry on negotiations. An employer may not dictate to a union its selection of agents or representatives and the employer must, in general, recognize the designated agent.

*Duty to meet and confer*

The employer's duty to bargain includes the duty to supply upon request information that is "relevant and necessary" to allow the employees' representative to bargain intelligently and effectively with respect to wages, hours, and other conditions of employment.

*Duty to supply information*

Where there is a history of bargaining between a union and a number of employers acting jointly, the employees who are thus represented constitute a multiemployer bargaining unit. Once such a unit has been established, any of the participating employers—or the union—may retire from this multiemployer bargaining relationship only by mutual assent or by a timely submitted withdrawal. Withdrawal is considered timely if unequivocal notice of the withdrawal is given near the termination of a collective-bargaining agreement but before bargaining begins on the next agreement. However, if the union agrees, an employer may also withdraw from a multiemployer unit and sign an individual contract with the union where there has been a breakdown in the multiemployer negotiations leading to an impasse and a resultant strike.

*Multiemployer bargaining*

Finally, the duty of an employer to bargain includes the duty to refrain from unilateral action, that is, taking action on its own with respect to matters concerning which it is required to bargain, and from making changes in terms and conditions of employment without consulting the employees' representative.

*Duty to refrain from unilateral action*

## Duty of successor employers

An employer who purchases or otherwise acquires the operations of another may be obligated to recognize and bargain with the union which represented the employees before the business was transferred. In general, these bargaining obligations exist—and the purchaser is termed a successor employer—where there is a substantial continuity in the employing enterprise despite the sale and transfer of the business. Whether the purchaser is a successor employer is dependent on several factors, including the number of employees taken over by the purchasing employer, the similarity in operations and product of the two employers, the manner in which the purchaser integrates the purchased operations into its other operations, and the character of the bargaining relationship and agreement between the union and the original employer.

## Examples of violations of Section 8(a)(5)

Examples of violations of Section 8(a)(5) are as follows:

- Refusing to meet with the employees' representative because the employees are out on strike.
- Insisting, until bargaining negotiations break down, on a contract provision that all employees will be polled by secret ballot before the union calls a strike.
- Refusing to supply the employees' representative with cost and other data concerning a group insurance plan covering the employees.
- Announcing a wage increase without consulting the employees' representative.
- Subcontracting certain work to another employer without notifying the union that represents the affected employees and without giving the union an opportunity to bargain concerning the change in working conditions of the employees.

## Section 8(e)—Entering a Hot Cargo Agreement

Section 8(e), added to the Act in 1959, makes it an unfair labor practice for any labor organization and any employer to enter into what is commonly called a "hot cargo" or "hot goods" agreement. It may also limit the restrictions that can be placed on the subcontracting of work by an employer. The typical hot cargo or hot goods clause in use before the 1959 amendment to the Act provided that employees would not be required by their employer to handle or work on goods or materials going to, or coming from, an employer designated by the union as "unfair." Such goods were said to be "hot cargo," thereby giving Section 8(e) its popular name. These clauses were most common in the construction and trucking industries.

Section 8(e) forbids an employer and a labor organization to make an agreement whereby the employer agrees to stop doing business with any other employer and declares void and unenforceable any such agreement that is made. It should be noted that a strike or picketing, or any other employee action, or the threat of it, to force an employer to agree to a hot cargo provision, or to force it to act in accordance with such a clause, has been held by the Board to be a violation of Section 8(b)(4). Exceptions are allowed in the construction and garment industries, and a union may seek, by contract, to keep within a bargaining unit work that is being done by the employees in the unit or to secure work which is "fairly claimable" in that unit.

In the construction industry a union and an employer in the industry may agree to a provision that restricts the contracting or subcontracting of work to be done at the construction site. Such a clause contained in the agreement between the employer and the union typically provides that if work is subcontracted by the employer it must go to an employer who has an agreement with the union. A union in the construction industry may engage in a strike and picketing to obtain, but not to enforce, contractual restrictions of this nature. Similarly, in the garment industry an employer and a union can agree that work to be done on the goods or on the premises of a jobber or manufacturer, or work that is part of "an intergrated process of production in the apparel and clothing industry," can be subcontracted only to an employer who has an agreement with the union. This exception, unlike the previous one concerning the construction industry, allows a labor organization in the garment industry not only to seek to obtain, but also to enforce, such a restriction on subcontracting by striking, picketing, or other lawful action.

*What is prohibited*

*Exceptions for construction and garment industries*

## Unfair Labor Practices of Labor Organizations

Section 8(b)(1)(A) forbids a labor organization or its agents "to restrain or coerce employees in the exercise of the rights guaranteed in section 7." The section also provides that it is not intended to "impair the rights of a labor organization to prescribe its own rules" concerning membership in the labor organization.

## Section 8(b)(1)(A)—Restraint and Coercion of Employees

### Section 8(b)(1)(A) compared with Section 8(a)(1)

Like Section 8(a)(1), Section 8(b)(1)(A) is violated by conduct that independently restrains or coerces employees in the exercise of their Section 7 rights regardless of whether the conduct also violates other provisions of Section 8(b). But whereas employer violations of Section 8(a) (2), (3), (4), and (5) are held to be violations of Section 8(a)(1) too, the Board has held, based on the intent of Congress when Section 8(b)(1)(A) was written, that violations of Section 8(b)(2) through (7) do not also "derivatively" violate Section 8(b)(1)(A). The Board does hold, however, that making or enforcing illegal union-security agreements or hiring agreements that condition employment on union membership not only violates Section 8(b)(2) but also Section 8(b)(1)(A), since such action restrains or coerces employees in their Section 7 rights.

Union conduct which is reasonably calculated to restrain or coerce employees in their Section 7 rights violates Section 8(b)(1)(A) whether or not it succeeds in actually restraining or coercing employees.

### What violates Section 8(b)(1)(A)

A union may violate Section 8(b)(1)(A) by coercive conduct of its officers or agents, of pickets on a picket line endorsed by the union, or of strikers who engage in coercion in the presence of union representatives who do not repudiate the conduct.

Unlawful coercion may consist of acts specifically directed at an employee such as physical assaults, threats of violence, and threats to affect an employee's job status. Coercion also includes other forms of pressure against employees such as acts of a union while representing employees as their exclusive bargaining agent (see Sec. 9(a), p. 10). A union which is a statutory bargaining representative owes a duty of fair representation to all the employees it represents. It may exercise a wide range of reasonable discretion in carrying out the representative function, but it violates Section 8(b)(1)(A) if, while acting as the employees' statutory bargaining representative, it takes or withholds action in connection with their employment because of their union activities or for any irrelevant or arbitrary reason such as an employee's race or sex.

Section 8(b)(1)(A) recognizes the right of unions to establish and enforce rules of membership and to control their internal affairs. This right is limited to union rules and discipline which affect the

Addendum 1    215

*Examples of violations of Section 8(b)(1)(A)*

rights of employees as union members and which are not enforced by action affecting an employee's employment. Also, rules to be protected must be aimed at matters of legitimate concern to unions such as the encouragement of members to support a lawful strike or participation in union meetings. Rules which conflict with public policy, such as rules which limit a member's right to file unfair labor practice charges, are not protected. And a union may not fine a member for filing a decertification petition although it may expel that individual for doing so.

Examples of restraint or coercion that violate Section 8(b)(1)(A) when done by a union or its agents include the following:

- Mass picketing in such numbers that nonstriking employees are physically barred from entering the plant.
- Acts of force or violence on the picket line, or in connection with a strike.
- Threats to do bodily injury to nonstriking employees.
- Threats to employees that they will lose their jobs unless they support the union's activities.
- Statement to employees who oppose the union that the employees will lose their jobs if the union wins a majority in the plant.
- Entering into an agreement with an employer which recognizes the union as exclusive bargaining representative when it has not been chosen by a majority of the employees.
- Fining or expelling members for crossing a picket line which is unlawful under the Act or which violates a no-strike agreement.
- Fining employees for conduct in which they engaged after resigning from the union.
- Fining or expelling members for filing unfair labor practice charges with the Board or for participating in an investigation conducted by the Board.

The following are examples of restraint or coercion that violate Section 8(b)(1)(A) when done by a union which is the exclusive bargaining representative:

- Refusing to process a grievance in retaliation against an employee's criticism of union officers.

## Section 8(b)(1)(B)—Restraint and Coercion of Employers

- Maintaining a seniority arrangement with an employer under which seniority is based on the employee's prior representation by the union elsewhere.
- Rejecting an application for referral to a job in a unit represented by the union based on the applicant's race or union activities.

Section 8(b)(1)(B) prohibits a labor organization from restraining or coercing an employer in the selection of a bargaining representative. The prohibition applies regardless of whether the labor organization is the majority representative of the employees in the bargaining unit. The prohibition extends to coercion applied by a union to a union member who is a representative of the employer in the adjustment of grievances. This section is violated by such conduct as the following:

- Insisting on meeting only with a company's owners and refusing to meet with the attorney the company has engaged to represent the company in contract negotiations, and threatening to strike to force the company to accept its demands.
- Striking against several members of an employer association that had bargained with the union as the representative of the employers with resulting individual contracts being signed by the struck employers.
- Insisting during contract negotiations that the employer agree to accept working conditions which will be established by a bargaining group to which it does not belong.
- Fining or expelling supervisors for the way they apply the bargaining contract while carrying out their supervisory functions.

*Examples of violations of Section 8(b)(1)(B)*

## Section 8(b)(2)—Causing or Attempting To Cause Discrimination

Section 8(b)(2) makes it an unfair labor practice for a labor organization to cause an employer to discriminate against an employee in violation of Section 8(a)(3). As discussed earlier, Section 8(a)(3) prohibits an employer from discriminating against an employee in regard to wages, hours, and other conditions of employment for the purpose of encouraging or discouraging membership in a labor organization. It does allow, however, the making of union-security agreements under certain specified conditions.

## What violates Section 8(b)(2)

A union violates Section 8(b)(2), for example, by demanding that an employer discriminate against employees because of their lack of union membership where there is no valid union-shop agreement in effect. The section can also be violated by agreements or arrangements with employers that unlawfully condition employment or job benefits on union membership, on the performance of union membership obligations, or on arbitrary grounds. Union conduct affecting an employee's employment in a way which is contrary to provisions of the bargaining contract may likewise be violative of the section. But union action which causes detriment to an individual employee in that individual's employment does not violate Section 8(b)(2) if it is consistent with nondiscriminatory provisions of a bargaining contract negotiated for the benefit of the total bargaining unit or if it is for some other legitimate purpose.

To find that a union caused an employer to discriminate, it is not necessary to show that any express demand was spoken. A union's conduct, accompanied by statements advising or suggesting that action is expected of an employer, may be enough to find a violation of this section if the union's action can be shown to be a causal factor in the employer's discrimination.

## Illegal hiring-hall agreements and practices

Contracts or informal arrangements with a union under which an employer gives preferential treatment to union members are violations of Section 8(b)(2). It is not unlawful for an employer and a union to enter an agreement whereby the employer agrees to hire new employees exclusively through the union hiring hall so long as there is neither a provision in the agreement nor a practice in effect that discriminates against nonunion members in favor of union members or otherwise discriminates on the basis of union membership obligations. Both the agreement and the actual operation of the hiring hall must be nondiscriminatory; referrals must be made without reference to union membership or irrelevant or arbitrary considerations such as race. Referral standards or procedures, even if nondiscriminatory on their face, are unlawful when they continue previously discriminatory conditions of referral. However, a union may in setting referral standards consider legitimate aims such as sharing available work and easing the impact of local unemployment. It may also charge referral fees if the amount of the fee is reasonably related to the cost of operating the referral service.

*Illegal union-security agreements*

Union-security agreements that require employees to become members of the union after they are hired are permitted by this section as previously discussed. Union-security agreements that do not meet all the requirements listed on page 3 will not support a discharge. A union that attempts to force an employer to enter an illegal union-security agreement, or that enters and keeps in effect such an agreement, violates Section 8(b)(2), as does a union that attempts to enforce such an illegal agreement by bringing about an employee's discharge. Even when a union-security provision of a bargaining contract meets all statutory requirements so that it is permitted by Section 8(a)(3), a union may not lawfully require the discharge of employees under the provision unless the employees had been informed of the union-security agreement and of their specific obligation under it. And a union violates Section 8(b)(2) if it tries to use the union-security provisions of a contract to collect payments other than periodic dues and initiation fees uniformly required of members. Assessments, fines, and penalties may not be enforced by application of a union-security contract.

Examples of violations of Section 8(b)(2) are:

- Causing an employer to discharge employees because they circulated a petition urging a change in the union's method of selecting shop stewards.
- Causing an employer to discharge employees because they made speeches against a contract proposed by the union.
- Making a contract that requires an employer to hire only members of the union or employees "satisfactory" to the union.
- Causing an employer to reduce employees' seniority because they engaged in antiunion acts.
- Refusing referral or giving preference on the basis of race or union activities in making job referrals to units represented by the union.
- Seeking the discharge of an employee under a union-security agreement for failure to pay a fine levied by the union.

*Examples of violations of Section 8(b)(2)*

## Section 8(b)(3)—Refusal To Bargain in Good Faith

Section 8(b)(3) makes it illegal for a labor organization to refuse to bargain in good faith with an employer about wages, hours, and other conditions of employment if it is the representative of that employer's employees. This section imposes on labor organizations the same duty to bargain in good faith that is imposed on employers by Section 8(a)(5). Both the labor organization and the employer are required to follow the procedure set out in Section 8(d) before terminating or changing an existing contract (see pages 7 and 8).

A labor organization that is the employees' representative must meet at reasonable times with the employer or his designated representative, must confer in good faith on matters pertaining to wages, hours, or other conditions of employment, or the negotiation of an agreement, or any question arising under an agreement, and must sign a written agreement if requested and if one is reached. The obligation does not require the labor organization or the employer to agree to a proposal by the other party or make a concession to the other party, but it does require bargaining with an open mind in an attempt to reach agreement. So, while a union may try in contract negotiations to establish wages and benefits comparable to those contained in other bargaining agreements in the area, it may not insist on such terms without giving the employer an opportunity to bargain about the terms. Likewise, a union may seek *voluntary* bargaining on nonmandatory subjects of bargaining (p. 26), such as a provision for an industry promotion fund, but may not *insist* on bargaining about such subjects or condition execution of a contract on the reaching of agreement on a nonmandatory subject.

Where a union has been bargaining with a group of employers in a multiemployer bargaining unit, it may withdraw at any time from bargaining upon that basis and bargain with one of the employers individually if the individual employer and the multiemployer group agree to the union's withdrawal. And even in the absence of employer consent a union may withdraw from multiemployer bargaining by giving the employers unequivocal notice of its withdrawal near the expiration of the agreement but before bargaining on a new contract had begun. In some circumstances a union may withdraw after a breakdown in the multiemployer bargaining.

Section 8(b)(3) not only requires that a union representative bargain in good faith with employers, but also requires that the union carry out its bargaining duty fairly with respect to the employees it represents. A union, therefore, violates Section 8(b)(3) if it negotiates a contract which conflicts with that duty, such as a contract with racially discriminatory provisions, or if it refuses to handle grievances under the contract for irrelevant or arbitrary reasons.

Section 8(b)(3) is violated by any of the following:

- Insisting on the inclusion of illegal provisions in a contract, such as a closed shop or a discriminatory hiring hall.
- Refusing to negotiate on a proposal for a written contract.
- Striking against an employer who has bargained, and continues to bargain, on a multi-employer basis to compel it to bargain separately.
- Refusing to meet with the attorney designated by the employer as its representative in negotiations.
- Terminating an existing contract and striking for a new one without notifying the employer, the Federal Mediation and Conciliation Service, and the state mediation service, if any.
- Conditioning the execution of an agreement upon inclusion of a nonmandatory provision such as a performance bond.
- Refusing to process a grievance because of the race, sex, or union activities of an employee for whom the union is the statutory bargaining representative.

Section 8(b)(4) prohibits a labor organization from engaging in strikes or boycotts or taking other specified actions to accomplish certain purposes or "objects" as they are called in the Act. The proscribed action is listed in clauses (i) and (ii), the objects are described in subparagraphs (A) through (D). A union commits an unfair labor practice if it takes any of the kinds of action listed in clauses (i) and (ii) as a means of accomplishing any of the objects listed in the four subparagraphs.

Clause (i) forbids a union to engage in a strike, or to induce or encourage a strike, work stoppage, or a refusal to perform services by "any individual employed by any person engaged in commerce or in an industry affecting commerce" for one of the objects listed in subparagraphs (A) through (D). The words "induce and encourage" are considered by the U.S. Supreme Court to be broad enough to include every form of influence or persuasion. For example, it has been held by the NLRB that a work stoppage on a picketed construction project was "induced" by a union through its business agents who, when they learned about the picketing, told the job stewards that they (the business agents) would not work behind the picket line. It was considered that this advice not only induced

*Examples of violations of Section 8(b)(3)*

## Section 8(b)(4)—Prohibited Strikes and Boycotts

*Proscribed action: Inducing or encouraging a strike, work stoppage, or boycott*

the stewards to leave the job, but caused them to pass the information on to their fellow employees, and that such conduct informed the other employees that they were expected not to work behind the picket line. The word "person" is defined in Section 2(1) as including "one or more individuals, labor organizations, partnerships, associations, corporations," and other legal persons. As so defined, the word "person" is broader than the word "employer." For example, a railroad company, although covered by the Railway Labor Act, is excluded from the definition of "employer" in the National Labor Relations Act and, therefore, neither the railroad company nor its employees are covered by the National Labor Relations Act. But a railroad company is a "person engaged in commerce" as defined above and, therefore, a labor organization is forbidden to "induce or encourage" individuals employed by a railroad company to engage in a strike, work stoppage, or boycott for any of the objects in subparagraphs (A) through (D).

Clause (ii) makes it an unfair labor practice for a union to "threaten, coerce, or restrain any person engaged in commerce or in an industry affecting commerce" for any of the proscribed objects. Even though no direct threat is voiced by the union, there may nevertheless be coercion and restraint that violates this clause. For example, where a union picketed a construction job to bring about the removal of a nonunion subcontractor in violation of Section 8(b)(4)(B), the picketing induced employees of several other subcontractors to stop work. When the general contractor asked what could be done to stop the picketing, the union's business agent replied that the picketing would stop only if the nonunion subcontractor were removed from the job. The NLRB held this to be "coercion and restraint" within the meaning of clause (ii).

*Proscribed action: Threats, coercion, and restraint*

Section 8(b)(4)(A) prohibits unions from engaging in clause (i) or (ii) action to compel an employer or self-employed person to join any labor or employer organization; or to force an employer to enter a hot cargo agreement prohibited by Section 8(e). Examples of violations of this section are:

*Subparagraph (A)—Prohibited object: Compelling membership in an employer or labor organization or compelling a hot cargo agreement*

*Examples of violations of Section 8(b)(4)(A)*

- In an attempt to compel a beer distributor to join a union, the union prevents the distributor from obtaining beer at a brewery by inducing the brewery's employees to refuse to fill the distributor's orders.

- In an attempt to secure for its members certain stevedoring work required at an employer's unloading operation, the union pickets to force the employer either to join an employer association with which the union has a contract or to hire a stevedoring firm that is a member of the association.
- A union pickets an employer (one not in the construction industry), or threatens to picket it, to compel that employer to enter into an agreement whereby the employer will only do business with persons who have an agreement with a union.

Section 8(b)(4)(B) contains the Act's secondary boycott provision. A secondary boycott occurs if a union has a dispute with Company A and in furtherance of that dispute causes the employees of Company B to stop handling the products of Company A, or otherwise forces Company B to stop doing business with Company A. The dispute is with Company A, called the "primary" employer, the union's action is against Company B, called the "secondary" employer, hence the term "secondary boycott." In many cases the secondary employer is a customer or supplier of the primary employer with whom the union has the dispute. In general, the Act prohibits both the secondary boycott and the threat of it. Examples of prohibited secondary boycotts are:

- Picketing an employer to force it to stop doing business with another employer who has refused to recognize the union.
- Asking the employees of a plumbing contractor not to work on connecting up air-conditioning equipment manufactured by a nonunion employer whom the union is attempting to organize.
- Urging employees of a building contractor not to install doors which were made by a manufacturer which is nonunion or which employs members of a rival union.
- Telling an employer that its plant will be picketed if that employer continues to do business with an employer the union has designated as "unfair."

The prohibitions of Section 8(b)(4)(B) do not protect a secondary employer from the incidental effects of union action that is taken directly against the primary employer. Thus, it is lawful for a union to urge employees of a secondary supplier at the primary employer's plant not to cross

*Subparagraph (B)—Prohibited object: Compelling a boycott or work stoppage*

*Examples of violations of Section 8(b)(4)(B)*

a picket line there. Section 8(b)(4)(B) also does not proscribe union action to prevent an employer from contracting out work customarily performed by its employees, even though an incidental effect of such conduct might be to compel that employer to cease doing business with the subcontractor.

In order to be protected against the union action that is prohibited under this subparagraph the secondary employer has to be a neutral as concerns the dispute between the union and the primary employer. For secondary boycott purposes an employer is considered an "ally" of the primary employer and, therefore, not protected from union action in certain situations. One is based on the ownership and operational relationship between the primary and secondary employers. Here, a number of factors are considered, particularly the following: Are the primary and secondary employers owned and controlled by the same person or persons? Are they engaged in "closely integrated operations"? May they be treated as a single employer under the Act? Another test of the "ally" relationship is based on the conduct of the secondary employer. If an employer, despite its claim of neutrality in the dispute, acts in a way that indicates that it has abandoned its "neutral" position, the employer opens itself up to primary action by the union. An example of this would be an employer who, claiming to be a neutral, enters into an arrangement with a struck employer whereby it accepts and performs farmed-out work of that employer who would normally do the work itself, but who cannot perform the work because its plant is closed by a strike.

*When an employer is not protected from secondary strikes and boycotts*

When employees of a primary employer and those of a secondary employer work on the same premises, a special situation is involved and the usual rules do not apply. A typical example of the shared site or "common situs" situation is where a subcontractor with whom a union has a dispute is engaged at work on a construction site alongside other subcontractors, with whom the union has no dispute. Picketing at a common situs is permissible if directed solely against the primary employer. But it is prohibited if directed against secondary employers regularly engaged at that site. To assist in determining whether picketing at a common site is restricted to the primary employer and therefore permissible, or directed at a secondary employer and therefore violative of the statute, the NLRB and the courts have suggested various guidelines for evaluating the object of the picketing, including the following:

*When a union may picket an employer who shares a site with another employer*

Subject to the qualification noted below, the picketing would appear to be primary picketing, if the picketing is:

1. Limited to times when the employees of the primary employer are working on the premises.
2. Limited to times when the primary employer is carrying on its normal business there.
3. Confined to places reasonably close to where the employees of the primary employer are working.
4. Conducted so that the picket signs, the banners, and the conduct of the pickets indicate clearly that the dispute is with the primary employer and not with the secondary employer.

These guidelines are known as the *Moore Dry Dock* standards from the case in which they were first formulated by the NLRB. However, the NLRB has held that picketing at a common situs may be unlawful notwithstanding compliance with the *Moore Dry Dock* standards if a union's statements or actions otherwise indicate that the picketing has an unlawful objective.

In some situations a company may set aside, or reserve, a certain plant gate, or entrance to its premises, for the exclusive use of a contractor. If a union has a labor dispute with the company and pickets the company's premises, including the gate so reserved, the union may be held to have violated Section 8(b)(4)(B). The U.S. Supreme Court has stated the circumstances under which such a violation may be found as follows:

There must be a separate gate, marked and set apart from other gates; the work done by the men who use the gate must be unrelated to the normal operations of the employer, and the work must be of a kind that would not, if done when the plant were engaged in its regular operations, necessitate curtailing those operations.

However, if the reserved gate is used by employees of both the company and the contractor, the picketing would be considered primary and not a violation of Section 8(b)(4)(B).

Section 8(b)(4)(B) also prohibits secondary action to compel an employer to recognize or bargain with a union that is not the certified representative of its employees. If a union takes action described in clause (i) or (ii) against a secondary employer, and the union's object is recognition by the primary employer, the union commits an unfair labor practice under this section. To establish

*Picketing contractors' gates*

*Subparagraph (B)—Prohibited object: Compelling recognition of an uncertified union*

Addendum 1   225

*Subparagraph (C)—Prohibited object: Compelling recognition of a union if another union has been certified*

*Subparagraph (D)—Prohibited object: Compelling assignment of certain work to certain employees*

*Publicity such as handbilling allowed by Section 8(b)(4)*

## Section 8(b)(5)—Excessive or Discriminatory Membership Fees

that the union has an object of recognition, a specific demand by the union for recognition need not be shown; a demand for a contract, which implies recognition or at least bargaining, is enough to establish an 8(b)(4)(B) object.

Section 8(b)(4)(C) forbids a labor organization from using clause (i) or (ii) conduct to force an employer to recognize or bargain with a labor organization other than the one that is currently certified as the representative of its employees. Section 8(b)(4)(C) has been held not to apply where the picketing union is merely protesting working conditions which are substandard for the area.

Section 8(b)(4)(D) forbids a labor organization from engaging in action described in clauses (i) and (ii) for the purpose of forcing any employer to assign certain work to "employees in a particular labor organization or in a particular trade, craft, or class rather than to employees in another labor organization or in another trade, craft, or class." The Act sets up a special procedure for handling disputes over work assignments that will be discussed later in this material (see page 53).

The final provision in Section 8(b)(4) provides that nothing in Section 8(b)(4) shall be construed "to prohibit publicity, other than picketing, for the purpose of truthfully advising the public, including consumers and members of a labor organization, that a product or products are produced by an employer with whom the labor organization has a primary dispute and are distributed by another employer." Such publicity is not protected if it has "an effect of inducing any individual employed by any person other than the primary employer" to refuse to handle any goods or not to perform services. The Supreme Court has held that this provision permitted a union to distribute handbills at the stores of neutral food chains asking the public not to buy certain items distributed by a wholesaler with whom the union had a primary dispute. Moreover, it has also held that peaceful picketing at the stores of a neutral food chain to persuade customers not to buy the products of a struck employer when they traded in these stores was not prohibited by Section 8(b)(4).

Section 8(b)(5) makes it illegal for a union to charge employees who are covered by an authorized union-security agreement a membership fee "in an amount which the Board finds excessive or discriminatory under all the circumstances." The section also provides that the Board in making its finding must consider among other factors "the practices and customs of labor organizations in the particular industry, and the wages currently paid to the employees affected."

Examples of violations of this section include:

- Charging old employees who do not join the union until after a union-security agreement goes into effect an initiation fee of $15 while charging new employees only $5.
- Increasing the initiation fee from $75 to $250 and thus charging new members an amount equal to about 4 weeks' wages when other unions in the area charge a fee equal to about one-half the employee's first week's pay.

*Examples of violations of Section 8(b)(5)*

### Section 8(b)(6)—"Featherbedding"

Section 8(b)(6) forbids a labor organization "to cause or attempt to cause an employer to pay or deliver or agree to pay or deliver any money or other thing of value, in the nature of an exaction, for services which are not performed or not to be performed."

### Section 8(b)(7)—Organizational and Recognitional Picketing by Noncertified Unions

Section 8(b)(7) prohibits a labor organization that is not currently certified as the employees' representative from picketing or threatening to picket with an object of obtaining recognition by the employer (recognitional picketing) or acceptance by his employees as their representative (organizational picketing). The object of picketing is ascertained from all the surrounding facts including the message on the picket signs and any communications between the union and the employer. "Recognitional" picketing as used in Section 8(b)(7) refers to picketing to obtain an employer's initial recognition of the union as bargaining representative of its employees or to force the employer, without formal recognition of the union, to maintain a specific and detailed set of working conditions. It does not include picketing by an incumbent union for continued recognition or for a new contract. Neither does it include picketing which seeks to prevent the employer from undermining area standards of working conditions by operating at less than the labor costs which prevail under bargaining contracts in the area.

Recognitional and organizational picketing are prohibited in three specific instances:

A. When the employer has lawfully recognized another union and a representation election would be barred by either the provisions of the Act or the Board's Rules, as in the case of a valid contract between the employer and the other union (8(b)(7)(A)). (A union is considered lawfully recognized when the employer's recognition of the union cannot be attacked under the unfair labor practice provisions of Section 8 of the Act.)

B. When a valid NLRB representation election has been held within the previous 12 months (8(b)(7)(B)).

C. When a representation petition is not filed "within a reasonable period of time not to exceed thirty days from the commencement of such picketing" (8(b)(7)(C)).

*Publicity picketing*

Subparagraph (C) is subject to an exception, called a proviso, which permits picketing "for the purpose of truthfully advising the public (including consumers)" that an employer does not employ union members or have a contract with a labor organization. However, such picketing loses the protection of this proviso if it has a substantial effect on the employer's business because it induces "any individual employed by any other person" to refuse to pick up or deliver goods or to perform other services.

*Expedited elections under Section 8(b)(7)(C)*

If an 8(b)(7)(C) charge is filed against the picketing union and a representation petition is filed within a reasonable time after the picketing starts, subparagraph (C) provides for an election to be held forthwith. This election requires neither a hearing nor a showing of interest among the employees. As a consequence the election can be held and the results obtained faster than in a regular election under Section 9(c), and for this reason it is called an "expedited" election. Petitions filed more than a reasonable time after picketing begins and petitions filed during picketing protected by the 8(b)(7)(C) proviso, discussed above, are processed under normal election procedures and the election will not be expedited. The reasonable period in which to file a petition cannot exceed 30 days and may be shorter, when, for instance, picketing is accompanied by violence.

Examples of violations of Section 8(b)(7) are as follows:

*Examples of violations of Section 8(b)(7)*

- Picketing by a union for organizational purposes shortly after the employer has entered a lawful contract with another union. (8(b)(7)(A))
- Picketing by a union for organizational purposes within 12 months after a valid NLRB election in which a majority of the employees in the unit voted to have no union. (8(b)(7)(B))
- Picketing by a union for recognition continuing for more than 30 days without the filing

## 228 WHEN HEALTH CARE EMPLOYEES STRIKE

of a representation petition where the picketing stops all deliveries by employees of another employer. (8(b)(7)(C))

### Section 8(e)—Entering a Hot Cargo Agreement

Section 8(e) makes it an unfair labor practice for an employer or a labor organization to enter a hot cargo agreement. This section applies equally to unions and to employers. The discussion of this section as an unfair labor practice of employers has been treated as a discussion of an unfair labor practice of unions as well. (See pages 28 and 29.)

### Section 8(g)—Striking or Picketing a Health Care Institution Without Notice

Section 8(g) prohibits a labor organization from engaging in a strike, picketing, or other concerted refusal to work at any health care institution without first giving at least 10 days' notice in writing to the institution and the Federal Mediation and Conciliation Service.

## How the Act Is Enforced

The rights of employees declared by Congress in the National Labor Relations Act are not self-enforcing. To ensure that employees may exercise these rights, and to protect them and the public from unfair labor practices, Congress established the NLRB to administer and enforce the Act.

### Organization of the NLRB

*The Board*

The NLRB includes the Board, which is composed of five members with their respective staffs, the General Counsel and staff, and the Regional, Subregional, and Resident Offices. The General Counsel has final authority on behalf of the Board, in respect to the investigation of charges and issuance of complaints. Members of the Board are appointed by the President, with consent of the Senate, for 5-year terms. The General Counsel is also appointed by the President, with consent of the Senate, for a 4-year term. Offices of the Board and the General Counsel are in Washington, D.C. To assist in administering and enforcing the law, the NLRB has established 33 Regional and a number of other field offices. These offices, located in major cities in various States and Puerto Rico are under the general supervision of the General Counsel.

*The General Counsel*

*The Regional Offices*

*Functions of the NLRB*

The Agency has two main functions: to conduct representation elections and certify the results, and to prevent employers and unions from engaging in unfair labor practices. In both kinds of cases the processes of the NLRB are begun only when requested. Requests for such action must be made in writing on forms provided by the NLRB and filed with the proper Regional office. The form used to request an election is called a "petition," and the form for unfair labor practices is called

Addendum 1   229

a "charge." The filing of a petition or a charge sets in motion the machinery of the NLRB under the Act. Before discussing the machinery established by the Act, it would be well to understand the nature and extent of the authority of the NLRB.

## Authority of the NLRB

The NLRB gets its authority from Congress by way of the National Labor Relations Act. The power of Congress to regulate labor-management relations is limited by the commerce clause of the United States Constitution. Although it can declare generally what the rights of employees are or should be, Congress can make its declaration of rights effective only in respect to enterprises whose operations "affect commerce," and labor disputes that "affect commerce." The NLRB, therefore, can direct elections and certify the results only in the case of an employer whose operations affect commerce. Similarly, it can act to prevent unfair labor practices only in cases involving labor disputes that affect, or would affect, commerce.

*Enterprises whose operations affect commerce*

"Commerce" includes trade, traffic, transportation, or communication within the District of Columbia or any Territory of the United States; or between any State or Territory and any other State, Territory, or the District of Columbia; or between two points in the same State, but through any other State, Territory, the District of Columbia, or a foreign country. Examples of enterprises engaged in commerce are:

*What is commerce*

- A manufacturing company in California that sells and ships its product to buyers in Oregon.
- A company in Georgia that buys supplies in Louisiana.
- A trucking company that transports goods from one point in New York State through Pennsylvania to another point in New York State.
- A radio station in Minnesota that has listeners in Wisconsin.

Although a company may not have any direct dealings with enterprises in any other State, its operations may nevertheless affect commerce. The operations of a Massachusetts manufacturing company that sells all of its goods to Massachusetts wholesalers affect commerce if the wholesalers ship to buyers in other States. The effects of a labor dispute involving the Massachusetts manufacturing concern would be felt in other States and the labor dispute would, therefore, "affect" commerce. Using this test, it can be seen that the operations of almost any employer can be said to affect commerce. As a result, the authority of the NLRB could extend to all but purely local enterprises.

*When the operations of an employer affect commerce*

Although the National Labor Relations Board could exercise its powers to enforce the Act in all cases involving enterprises whose operations affect commerce, the Board does not act in all such cases. In its discretion it limits the exercise of its power to cases involving enterprises whose effect on commerce is substantial. The Board's requirements for exercising its power or jurisdiction are called "jurisdictional standards." These standards are based on the yearly amount of business done by the enterprise, or on the yearly amount of its sales or of its purchases. They are stated in terms of total dollar volume of business and are different for different kinds of enterprises. The Board's standards in effect on July 1, 1976, are as follows:

1. *Nonretail business:* Direct sales of goods to consumers in other States, or indirect sales through others (called outflow), of at least $50,000 a year; or direct purchases of goods from suppliers in other States, or indirect purchases through others (called inflow), of at least $50,000 a year.
2. *Office buildings:* Total annual revenue of $100,000 of which $25,000 or more is derived from organizations which meet any of the standards except the indirect outflow and indirect inflow standards established for nonretail enterprises.
3. *Retail enterprises:* At least $500,000 total annual volume of business.
4. *Public utilities:* At least $250,000 total annual volume of business, or $50,000 direct or indirect outflow or inflow.
5. *Newspapers:* At least $200,000 total annual volume of business.
6. *Radio, telegraph, television, and telephone enterprises:* At least $100,000 total annual volume of business.
7. *Hotels, motels, and residential apartment houses:* At least $500,000 total annual volume of business.
8. *Privately operated health care institutions:* At least $250,000 total annual volume of business for hospitals; at least $100,000 for nursing homes, visiting nurses associations, and related facilities; at least $250,000 for all other types of private health care institutions defined in the 1974 amendments to the Act. The statutory definition includes: "any hospital, convalescent hospital, health maintenance organization, health clinic, nursing home, extended care facility,

Addendum 1    231

or other institution devoted to the care of the sick, infirm, or aged person." Public hospitals are excluded from NLRB jurisdiction by Section 2(2) of the Act.

9. *Transportation enterprises, links and channels of interstate commerce:* At least $50,000 total annual income from furnishing interstate passenger and freight transportation services; also performing services valued at $50,000 or more for businesses which meet any of the jurisdictional standards except the indirect outflow and indirect inflow standards established for nonretail enterprises.

10. *Transit systems:* At least $250,000 total annual volume of business.

11. *Taxicab companies:* At least $500,000 total annual volume of business.

12. *Associations:* These are regarded as a single employer in that the annual business of all association members is totaled to determine whether any of the standards apply.

13. *Enterprises in the Territories and the District of Columbia:* The jurisdictional standards apply in the Territories; all businesses in the District of Columbia come under NLRB jurisdiction.

14. *National defense:* Jurisdiction is asserted over all enterprises affecting commerce when their operations have a substantial impact on national defense, whether or not the enterprises satisfy any other standard.

15. *Private universities and colleges:* At least $1 million gross annual revenue from all sources (excluding contributions not available for operating expenses because of limitations imposed by the grantor).

16. *Symphony orchestras:* At least $1 million gross annual revenue from all sources (excluding contributions not available for operating expenses because of limitations imposed by the grantor).

Through enactment of the 1970 Postal Reorganization Act, jurisdiction of the NLRB was extended to the United States Postal Service, effective July 1, 1971.

In addition to the above-listed standards, the Board asserts jurisdiction over gambling casinos in

Nevada and Puerto Rico, where these enterprises are legally operated, when their total annual revenue from gambling is at least $500,000.

Ordinarily if an enterprise does the total annual volume of business listed in the standard, it will necessarily be engaged in activities that "affect" commerce. The Board must find, however, based on evidence, that the enterprise does in fact "affect" commerce.

The Board has established the policy that where an employer whose operations "affect" commerce refuses to supply the Board with information concerning total annual business, etc., the Board may dispense with this requirement and exercise jurisdiction.

Finally, Section 14(c)(1) authorizes the Board, in its discretion, to decline to exercise jurisdiction over any class or category of employers where a labor dispute involving such employees is not sufficiently substantial to warrant the exercise of jurisdiction, provided that it cannot refuse to exercise jurisdiction over any labor dispute over which it would have asserted jurisdiction under the standards it had in effect on August 1, 1959. In accordance with this provision the Board has determined that it will not exercise jurisdiction over racetracks, owners, breeders, and trainers of racehorses, and real estate brokers.

In addition to the foregoing limitations the Act states that the term "employee" shall include any employee *except* the following:

- Agricultural laborers.
- Domestic servants.
- Any individual employed by his parent or spouse.
- Independent contractors.
- Supervisors.
- Individuals employed by an employer subject to the Railway Labor Act.
- Government employees, including those employed by the U.S. Government, any Government corporation or Federal Reserve Bank, or any State or political subdivision such as a city, town, or school district.

*The Act does not cover certain individuals*

Supervisors are excluded from the definition of "employee" and, therefore, not covered by the Act. Whether an individual is a supervisor for purposes of the Act depends on that individual's authority

*Supervisor defined*

over employees and not merely a title. A supervisor is defined by the Act as any individual who has the authority, acting in the interest of an employer, to cause another employee to be hired, transferred, suspended, laid off, recalled, promoted, discharged, assigned, rewarded, or disciplined, either by taking such action or by recommending it to a superior; or who has the authority responsibly to direct other employees or adjust their grievances; provided, in all cases, that the exercise of authority is not of a merely routine or clerical nature, but requires the exercise of independent judgment. For example, a foreman who determined which employees would be laid off after being directed by the job superintendent to lay off four employees would be considered a supervisor and would, therefore, not be covered by the Act; a "strawboss" who, after someone else determined which employees would be laid off, merely informed the employees of the layoff and who neither directed other employees nor adjusted their grievances would not be considered a supervisor and would be covered by the Act.

All employees properly classified as "managerial," not just those in positions susceptible to conflicts of interest in labor relations, are excluded from the protection of the Act. This was the thrust of a decision of the Supreme Court in 1974.

The term "employer" includes any person who acts as an agent of an employer, but it does *not* include the following:

*The Act does not cover certain employers*

- The United States or any State Government, or any political subdivision of either, or any Government corporation or Federal Reserve Bank.
- Any employer subject to the Railway Labor Act.

**NLRB Procedure**

*Procedure in representation cases*

The authority of the NLRB can be brought to bear in a representation proceeding only by the filing of a petition. Forms for petitions must be signed, sworn to or affirmed under oath, and filed with the Regional Office in the area where the unit of employees is located. If employees in the unit regularly work in more than one regional area, the petition may be filed with the Regional Office of any of such regions. Section 9(c)(1) provides that when a petition is filed, "the Board shall investigate such petition and if it has reasonable cause to believe that a question of representation affecting commerce exists shall provide for an appropriate hearing upon due notice." If the Board finds from the evidence presented at the hearing that "such a question of representation exists, it shall direct an election by secret ballot and shall certify the results thereof." Where there are three or more choices on the ballot and none receives a majority, Section 9(c)(3) provides for a runoff between the choice that received the largest and the choice that received the second largest number of valid votes in the election. After the election, if a union receives a majority of the votes cast, it is certified; if no union gets a majority, that result is certified. A union that has been certified is entitled to be recognized by the employer as the exclusive bargaining agent for the employees in the unit. If the employer fails to bargain with the union, it commits an unfair labor practice.

The procedure in an unfair labor practice case is begun by the filing of a charge. A charge may be filed by an employee, an employer, a labor organization, or any other person. Like petitions, charge forms, which are also available at Regional Offices, must be signed, sworn to or affirmed under oath, and filed with the appropriate Regional Office—that is, the Regional Office in the area where the alleged unfair labor practice was committed. Section 10 provides for the issuance of a complaint stating the charges and notifying the charged party of a hearing to be held concerning the charges. Such a complaint will issue only after investigation of the charges through the Regional Office indicates that an unfair labor practice has in fact occurred.

In certain limited circumstances where an employer and union have an agreed-upon grievance arbitration procedure which will resolve the dispute, the Board will defer processing an unfair labor practice case and await resolution of the issues through that grievance arbitration procedure. If the grievance arbitration process meets the Board's standards, the Board may accept the final resolution and defer to that decision. If the procedure fails to meet all of the Board standards for deferral, the Board may then resume processing of the unfair labor practice issues.

An unfair labor practice hearing is conducted before an NLRB administrative law judge in accordance with the rules of evidence and procedure that apply in the U.S. District Courts. Based on the hearing record, the administrative law judge makes findings and recommendations to the Board. All parties to the hearing may appeal the administrative law judge's decision to the Board. If the Board considers that the party named in the complaint has engaged in or is engaging in the unfair labor practices charged, the Board is authorized to issue an order requiring such person to cease and desist from such practices and to take appropriate affirmative action.

*Procedure in unfair labor practice cases*

Section 10(b) provides that "no complaint shall issue based upon any unfair labor practice occurring more than six months prior to the filing of the charge with the Board and the service of a copy thereof upon the person against whom such charge is made." An exception is made if the charging party "was prevented from filing such charge by reason of service in the armed forces, in which event the six-month period shall be computed from the day of his discharge." It should be noted that the charging party must, within 6 months after the unfair labor practice occurs, file the charge with the Regional Office *and* serve copies of the charge on each person against whom the charge is made. Normally service is made by sending the charge by registered mail, return receipt requested.

*The 6-month rule limiting issuance of complaint*

If the Regional Director refuses to issue a complaint in any case, the person who filed the charge may appeal the decision to the General Counsel in Washington. Section 3(d) places in the General Counsel "final authority, on behalf of the Board, in respect of the investigation of charges and issuance of complaints." If the General Counsel reverses the Regional Director's decision, a complaint will be issued. If the General Counsel approves the decision not to issue a complaint, there is no further appeal.

*Appeal to the General Counsel if complaint is not issued*

To enable the NLRB to perform its duties under the Act, Congress delegated to the Agency certain powers that can be used in all cases. These are principally powers having to do with investigations and hearings.

**Powers of the NLRB**

As previously indicated, all charges that are filed with the Regional Offices are investigated, as are petitions for representation elections. Section 11 establishes the powers of the Board and the Regional Offices in respect to hearings and investigations. The provisions of Section 11(1) authorize the Board or its agents to

*Powers concerning investigations*

- Examine and copy "any evidence of any person being investigated or proceeded against that relates to any matter under investigation or in question."
- Issue subpenas, on the application of any party to the proceeding, requiring the attendance and testimony of witnesses or the production of any evidence.
- Administer oaths and affirmations, examine witnesses, and receive evidence.
- Obtain a court order to compel the production of evidence or the giving of testimony.

The National Labor Relations Act is not a criminal statute. It is entirely remedial. It is intended to prevent and remedy unfair labor practices, not to punish the person responsible for them. The Board is authorized by Section 10(c) not only to issue a cease-and-desist order, but "to take such affirmative action including reinstatement of employees with or without back pay, as will effectuate the policies of this Act."

The object of the Board's order in any case is twofold: to eliminate the unfair labor practice and to undo the effects of the violation as much as possible. In determining what the remedy will be in any given case, the Board has considerable discretion. Ordinarily its order in regard to any particular unfair labor practice will follow a standard form that is designed to remedy that unfair labor practice, but the Board can, and often does, change the standard order to meet the needs of the case. Typical affirmative action of the Board may include orders to an employer who has engaged in unfair labor practices to:

- Disestablish an employer-dominated union.
- Offer certain named individuals immediate and full reinstatement to their former positions or, if those positions no longer exist, to substantially equivalent positions without prejudice to their seniority and other rights and privileges, and with backpay, including interest.
- Upon request, bargain collectively with a certain union as the exclusive representative of the employees in a certain described unit and sign a written agreement if an understanding is reached.

Examples of affirmative action that may be required of a union which has engaged in unfair labor practices include orders to:

- Notify the employer and the employee that it has no objection to reinstatement of certain employees, or employment of certain applicants, whose discriminatory discharge, or denial of employment, was caused by the union.
- Refund dues or fees illegally collected, plus interest.

*The Act is remedial, not criminal*

*Affirmative action may be ordered by the Board*

*Examples of affirmative action directed to employers*

*Examples of affirmative action directed to unions*

- Upon request, bargain collectively with a certain employer and sign a written agreement if one is reached.

The Board's order usually includes a direction to the employer or the union or both requiring them to post notices in the employer's plant or the union's office notifying the employees that they will cease the unfair labor practices and informing them of any affirmative action being undertaken to remedy the violation. Special care is taken to be sure that these notices are readily understandable by the employees to whom they are addressed.

## Special Proceedings in Certain Cases

Special proceedings are required by the Act in certain kinds of cases. These include the determination of jurisdictional disputes under Section 10(k) and injunction proceedings under Section 10(l) and (j).

*Proceedings in jurisdictional disputes*

Whenever it is charged that any person has engaged in an unfair labor practice in violation of Section 8(b)(4)(D), the Board must hear and determine the dispute out of which the unfair labor practice arises. Section 8(b)(4)(D) prohibits unions from striking or inducing a strike to compel an employer to assign particular work to employees in one union, or in one trade or craft, rather than another. For a jurisdictional dispute to exist, there must be real competition between unions or between groups of employees for certain work. In effect, Section 10(k) provides an opportunity for the parties to adjust the dispute during a 10-day period after notice of the 8(b)(4)(D) charge has been served. At the end of this period if the parties have not submitted to the Board satisfactory evidence that they have adjusted, or agreed on a method of adjusting, the dispute, the Board is "empowered and directed" to determine which of the competing groups is entitled to have the work.

*The investigation of certain charges must be given priority*

Section 10(l) provides that whenever a charge is filed alleging a violation of certain sections of the Act relating to boycotts, picketing, and work stoppages, the preliminary investigation of the charge must be given priority over all other types of cases in the Regional Office where it is filed. The unfair labor practices subject to this priority concerning the investigation are those defined in Section 8(b)(4)(A), (B), or (C), all three subparagraphs of Section 8(b)(7), and Section 8(e). Section 10(m) requires that second priority be given to charges alleging violations of Section 8(a)(3), the prohibition against employer discrimination to encourage or discourage membership in a union, and Section 8(b)(2), which forbids unions to cause or attempt to cause such discrimination.

If the preliminary investigation of any of the first priority cases shows that there is reasonable cause to believe that the charge is true and that a complaint should issue, Section 10(l) further requires that the U.S. District Court be petitioned to grant an injunction pending the final determination of the Board. The section authorizes the court to grant "such injunctive relief or temporary restraining order as it deems just and proper." Another provision of the section prohibits the application for an injunction based on a charge of violation of Section 8(b)(7) (the prohibition on organizational or recognitional picketing in certain situations) if a charge against an employer alleging violation of Section 8(a)(2) has been filed and the preliminary investigation establishes reasonable cause to believe that such charge is true.

*Injunction proceedings under Section 10(l)*

*Injunction relief may be sought in other cases*

Section 10(j) allows the Board to petition for an injunction in connection with any unfair labor practice after a complaint has been issued. This section does not require that injunctive relief be sought, but only makes it possible for the Board to do so in cases where it is considered appropriate.

**Court Enforcement of Board Orders**

If an employer or a union fails to comply with a Board order, Section 10(e) empowers the Board to petition the U.S. Court of Appeals for a court decree enforcing the order of the Board. Section 10(f) provides that any person aggrieved by a final order of the Board granting or denying in whole or in part the relief sought may obtain a review of such order in any appropriate circuit court of appeals. When the court of appeals hears a petition concerning a Board order, it may enforce the order, remand it to the Board for reconsideration, change it, or set it aside entirely. If the court of appeals issues a judgment enforcing the Board order, failure to comply may be punishable by fine or imprisonment for contempt of court.

*In the U.S. Court of Appeals*

*Review by the U.S. Supreme Court*

In some cases the U.S. Supreme Court may be asked to review the decision of a circuit court of appeals particularly where there is a conflict in the views of different courts on the same important problem.

## Conclusion

In this material the entire Act has been covered, but, of necessity, the coverage has been brief. No attempt has been made to state the law in detail or to supply you with a textbook on labor law. We have tried to explain the Act in a manner intended to make it easier to understand what the basic provisions of the Act are and how they may concern you. If it helps you to recognize and know your rights and obligations under the Act, and aids in determining whether you need expert assistance when a problem arises, its purpose will have been satisfied. More than that: the objective of the Act will have been furthered.

The objective of the National Labor Relations Act, to avoid or reduce industrial strife and protect the public health, safety, and interest, can best be achieved by the parties or those who may become parties to an industrial dispute. Voluntary adjustment of differences at the community and local level is almost invariably the speediest, most satisfactory, and longest lasting way of carrying out the objective of the Act.

Efforts are being made in all our Regional Offices to increase the understanding of all parties as to what the law requires of them. Long experience has taught us that when the parties fully understand their rights and obligations, they are more ready and able to adjust their differences voluntarily. Seldom do individuals go into a courtroom, a hearing, or any other avoidable contest, knowing that they are in the wrong and that they can expect to lose the decision. No one really likes to be publicly recorded as a law violator (and a loser too). Similarly, it is seldom that individuals refuse to accept an informal adjustment of differences that is reasonable, knowing that they can obtain no better result from the formal proceeding, even if they prevail.

The consequences of ignorance in these matters—formal proceedings that can be time-consuming and costly, and which are often followed by bitterness and antagonism—are economically wasteful, and usually it is accurate to say that neither party really wins. It is in an attempt to bring about more widespread awareness of the basic law and thus help the parties avoid these consequences that this material has been prepared and presented as a part of a continuing program to increase understanding of the National Labor Relations Act.

240   When Health Care Employees Strike

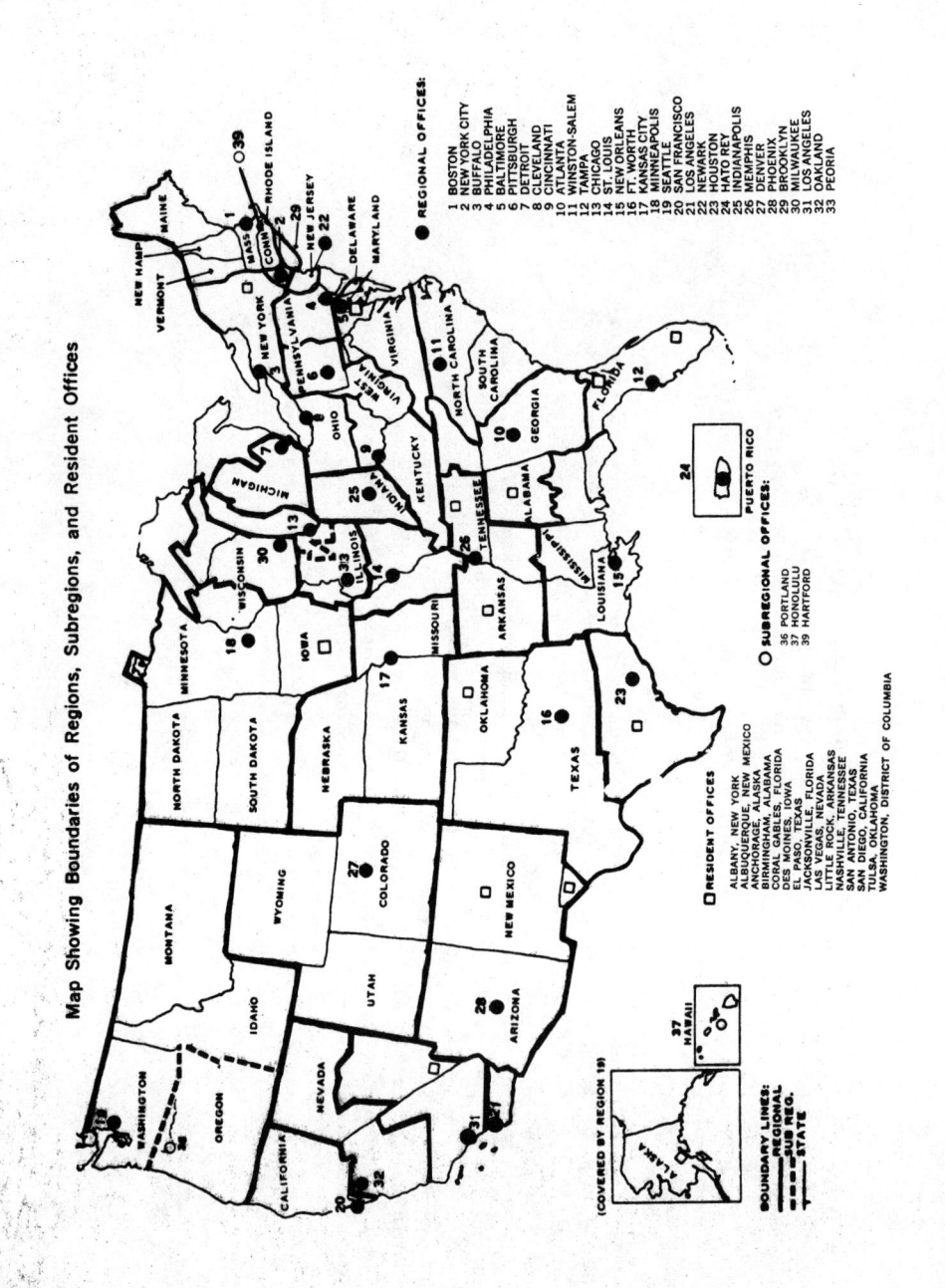

## National Labor Relations Board Regional Directory

1. Boston, Mass. 02110, 12th Floor, Keystone Bldg., 99 High St.; *Telephone:* 617-223-3300. *Director:* Robert S. Fuchs; *Regional Attorney:* Michael F. Walsh.

39. (Subregion) Hartford, Conn. 06103, 750 Main St., Suite 1200; *Telephone:* 202-727-2154. *Officer-in-Charge:* Peter B. Hoffman.

2. New York, N.Y. 10278, 3614 Federal Bldg., 26 Federal Plaza; *Telephone:* 212-264-0300. *Director:* Vacancy; *Regional Attorney:* Alvin P. Blyer.

3. Buffalo, N.Y. 14202, 901 Federal Bldg., 111 W. Huron St.; *Telephone:* 716-846-4931. *Director:* Thomas W. Seeler; *Regional Attorney:* Richard L. De Prospero.

4. Philadelphia, Pa. 19106, 4400 William J. Green Jr. Federal Bldg., 600 Arch St.; *Telephone:* 215-597-7601. *Director:* Peter W. Hirsch; *Regional Attorney:* Leonard Leventhal.

5. Baltimore, Md. 21201, Edward A. Garmatz Fed. Bldg. and Court House, 101 W. Lombard St.; *Telephone:* 301-962-2822. *Director:* Vacancy; *Regional Attorney:* Louis J. D'Amico.

6. Pittsburgh, Pa. 15219, 10th Floor, Porter Bldg., 601 Grant St.; *Telephone:* 412-644-2977. *Director:* Henry Shore; *Regional Attorney:* Edward A. Grupp.

7. Detroit, Mich. 48226, 300 Patrick V. McNamara Federal Bldg., 477 Michigan Ave.; *Telephone:* 313-226-3200. *Director:* Bernard Gottfried; *Regional Attorney:* Harry D. Camp.

8. Cleveland, Ohio 44199, 1695 Anthony J. Celebrezze Federal Bldg., 1240 E. 9th St.; *Telephone:* 216-522-3715. *Director:* Bernard Levine; *Regional Attorney:* John Kollar.

9. Cincinnati, Ohio 45202, 3003 Federal Office Bldg., 550 Main St.; *Telephone:* 513-684-3686. *Director:* Emil C. Farkas; *Regional Attorney:* Thomas M. Sheeran.

10. Atlanta, Ga. 30303, Marietta Tower, Suite 2400, 101 Marietta Street, N.W.; *Telephone:* 404-221-2896. *Director:* Curtis L. Mack; *Regional Attorney:* William E. Caldwell.

11. Winston-Salem, N.C. 27101, 447 U.S. Courthouse, Fed. Bldg., 215 N. Main Street; *Telephone:* 919-761-3201. *Director:* Reed Johnston; *Regional Attorney:* Hugh F. Malone.

12. Tampa, Fla. 33602, 706 Robert L. Timberlake Jr. Federal Office Bldg., 500 Zack St.; *Telephone:* 813-228-2641. *Director:* Harold A. Boire; *Regional Attorney:* Charles E. Deal.

13. Chicago, Ill. 60604, 881 Everett McKinley Dirksen Bldg., 219 S. Dearborn St.; *Telephone:* 312-353-7570. *Director:* Vacancy; *Regional Attorney:* Donald D. Crawford.

14. St. Louis, Mo. 63101, Room 448, 210 N. 12th Blvd.; *Telephone:* 314-425-4167. *Director:* Joseph H. Solien; *Regional Attorney:* Vacancy.

15. New Orleans, La. 70113, 2700 Plaza Tower, 1001 Howard Ave.; *Telephone:* 504-589-6361. *Director:* Vacancy; *Regional Attorney:* Fallon W. Bentz.

16. Fort Worth, Tex. 76102, 8A24 Federal Office Bldg., 819 Taylor St.; *Telephone:* 817-334-2921. *Director:* Michael M. Dunn; *Regional Attorney:* Jerome L. Avedon.

17. Kansas City, Kans. 66101, 616 Two Gateway Center, Fourth at State; *Telephone:* 816-374-4518. *Director:* Thomas C. Hendrix; *Regional Attorney:* Harold E. Jahn.

Addendum I 241

18 Minneapolis, Minn. 55401, 316 Federal Bldg., 110 S. 4th St.; *Telephone*: 612–725–2611.

*Director*: Robert J. Wilson; *Regional Attorney*: Herbert S. Dawidoff.

19 Seattle, Wash. 98174, 2948 Federal Bldg., 915 2d Ave.; *Telephone*: 206–442–4532.

*Director*: Vacancy; *Regional Attorney*: Walter J. Mercer.

36 (Subregion) Portland, Oreg. 97205, 825 Pittock Block, 921 SW Washington St.; *Telephone*: 503–221–3085.

*Officer-in-Charge*: Elwood G. Strumpf.

20 San Francisco, Calif. 94102, 13018 Federal Bldg., Box 36047, 450 Golden Gate Ave.; *Telephone*: 415–556–3197.

*Director*: Vacancy; *Regional Attorney*: Robert H. Miller.

37 (Subregion) Honolulu, Hawaii 96850, 300 Ala Moana Blvd., Room 7318; *Telephone*: 808–546–5100.

*Officer-in-Charge*: Dennis R. MacCarthy.

21 Los Angeles, Calif. 90014, 24th Floor, City National Bank Building, 606 S. Olive Street; *Telephone*: 213–688–5200.

*Director*: Wilford W. Johansen; *Regional Attorney*: Michael Fogerty.

22 Newark, N.J. 07102, 1600 Peter D. Rodino Jr. Federal Bldg., 970 Broad St.; *Telephone*: 201–645–2100.

*Director*: Arthur Eisenberg; *Regional Attorney*: William A. Pascarell.

23 Houston, Tex. 77002, 920 One Allen Center, 500 Dallas Ave.; *Telephone*: 713–226–4296.

*Director*: Louis V. Baldwin, Jr.; *Regional Attorney*: Arthur Safos.

24 Hato Rey, P.R. 00918, 591 Federico Degatau Fed. Bldg., U.S. Courthouse, Carlos E. Chardon Avenue; *Telephone*: 809–753–4347.

*Director*: Martin Arlook; *Regional Attorney*: Michael S. Maram.

25 Indianapolis, Ind. 46204, 232 Federal Office Bldg., 575 N. Pennsylvania St.; *Telephone*: 317–269–7430.

*Director*: William T. Little; *Regional Attorney*: George M. Dick.

26 Memphis, Tenn. 38104, 8th Floor, Mid-Memphis Tower, 1407 Union Avenue; *Telephone*: 901–222–2725.

*Director*: Gerald P. Fleischut; *Regional Attorney*: John F. Harrington.

27 Denver, Colo. 80202, 260 U.S. Custom House, 721 19th St.; *Telephone*: 303–837–3555.

*Director*: W. Bruce Gillis, Jr.; *Regional Attorney*: Albert A. Metz.

28 Phoenix, Ariz. 85067, 2d Floor, 3030 North Central Ave.; *Telephone*: 602–241–2350.

*Director*: Milo V. Price; *Regional Attorney*: Peter N. Maydanis.

29 Brooklyn, N.Y. 11241, 4th Floor, 16 Court St.; *Telephone*: 212–330–7713.

*Director*: Samuel M. Kaynard; *Regional Attorney*: Harold L. Richman.

30 Milwaukee, Wis. 53203, 230 Commerce Bldg., 744 N. 4th St.; *Telephone*: 414–291–3861.

*Director*: George S. Squillacote; *Regional Attorney*: Joseph A. Szabo.

31 Los Angeles, Calif. 90024, 12100 Federal Bldg., 11000 Wilshire Blvd.; *Telephone*: 213–824–7352.

*Director*: Roger W. Goubeaux; *Regional Attorney*: Bryon B. Kohn.

32 Oakland, Calif. 94604, Breuner Bldg, 2201 Broadway, 2d floor; *Telephone*: 415–273–7200.

*Director*: James S. Scott; *Regional Attorney*: Alan R. Berkowitz.

33 Peoria, Ill. 61602, 16th Floor, Savings Center Tower, 411 Hamilton Avenue; *Telephone*: 309–671–7080.

*Director*: Glenn A. Zipp; *Regional Attorney*: Michael B. Ryan.

Addendum 1   243

RESIDENT OFFICES:

Albany, N.Y. 12207
Leo W. O'Brien Federal Bldg.; Clinton Ave. at N. Pearl St.; *Telephone*: 518-472-2215.
*Resident Officer*: Thomas J. Sheridan.

Albuquerque, N. Mex. 87110
Patio Plaza Bldg., Upper Level, 5000 Marble Ave., NE.; *Telephone*: 505-766-2508.
*Resident Officer*: Robert A. Reisinger.

Anchorage, Alaska 99513
510 Anchorage Fed. Office Bldg., 701 C St.; *Telephone*: 907-271-5015.
*Resident Officer*: Delano D. Eyer.

Birmingham, Ala. 35203
2102 City Federal Bldg., 2026 2d Ave. North; *Telephone*: 205-254-1492.
*Resident Officer*: C. Douglas Marshall.

Coral Gables, Fla. 33146
410 Madruga Bldg., 1570 Madruga Ave.; *Telephone*: 305-350-5391.
*Resident Officer*: James L. Jeffers.

Des Moines, Iowa 50309
Federal Home Loan Bank Bldg., 907 Walnut St.; *Telephone*: 515-243-4391.
*Resident Officer*: Richard Anderson.

El Paso, Tex. 79902
307 Pershing Bldg., 4100 Rio Bravo St.; *Telephone*: 915-543-7737.
*Resident Officer*: Laureano A. Medrano.

Jacksonville, Fla. 32202
278 Federal Bldg., 400 W. Bay St.; *Telephone*: 904-791-3768.
*Resident Officer*: John C. Wooten.

Las Vegas, Nev. 89101
Room 3402, 300 Las Vegas Blvd. S.; *Telephone*: 702-385-6416.
*Resident Officer*: Kenneth A. Rose.

Little Rock, Ark. 72201
Suite 1120, 1 Union National Plaza; *Telephone*: 501-378-6311.
*Resident Officer*: Ronald M. Sharp.

Nashville, Tenn. 37203
Estes Kefauver Fed. Bldg., U.S. Courthouse, 801 Broadway; *Telephone*: 615-749-5921.
*Resident Officer*: Alton W. Barksdale.

San Antonio, Tex. 78206
Rm. A509, Fed. Office Bldg., 727 E. Durango Blvd.; *Telephone*: 512-229-6140.
*Resident Officer*: John C. Crawford.

San Diego, Calif. 92189
U.S. Courthouse, Rm. 2-N-20, 940 Front Street; *Telephone*: 714-293-6184.
*Resident Officer*: Claude R. Marston.

Tulsa, Okla. 74135
Skyline East Bldg., First Floor, South Tower, 6128 E. 38th St.; *Telephone*: 918-664-1420.
*Resident Officer*: Francis A. Molenda.

Washington, D.C. 20037
100 Gelman Bldg., 2120 L St., NW., *Telephone*: 202-254-7612.
*Resident Officer*: Angela S. Anderson.

# Addendum 2

# Federal Mediation and Conciliation Service Offices

**NATIONAL OFFICE***

**Administrative Offices**

The address and telephone number of the Administrative Offices of the National Office are as follows: 2100 K Street, N.W., Washington, D.C. 20427. 202–653–5290.

| Region | State | Region | State |
|---|---|---|---|
| South | Alabama | West | Kansas |
| West | Alaska | South | Kentucky |
| West | Arizona | South | Louisiana |
| South | Arkansas | East | Maine |
| West | California | South | Maryland |
| West | Colorado | East | Massachusetts |
| East | Connecticut | Central | Michigan |
| East | Delaware | Central | Minnesota |
| South | District of Columbia | South | Mississippi |
| South | Florida | South | Missouri |
| South | Georgia | West | Montana |
| West | Hawaii | West | Nebraska |
| West | Idaho | West | Nevada |
| Central | Illinois | East | New Hampshire |
| Central | Indiana | East | New Jersey |
| West | Iowa | West | New Mexico |

*National Office covers District of Columbia; Montgomery and Prince George's Counties in Maryland; Arlington and Fairfax Counties and City of Alexandria in Virginia.

| Region | State | Region | State |
|---|---|---|---|
| East | New York | East | Vermont |
| South | North Carolina | South | Virginia |
| Central | Ohio | West | Washington |
| South | Oklahoma | South | West Virginia |
| West | Oregon | Central | Wisconsin |
| East | Pennsylvania | West | Wyoming |
| East | Rhode Island | | |
| South | South Carolina | Territories and Possessions | |
| Central | South Dakota | | |
| South | Tennessee | South | Guam |
| South | Texas | South | Puerto Rico |
| West | Utah | South | Virgin Islands |

## REGIONAL, DISTRICT, AND FIELD OFFICES

**Eastern Region**

*Regional Office*

Jacob K. Javitz Federal Building
Room 2937
26 Federal Plaza
New York, NY 10278
Tel.: 212-264-1000

*District Offices*

Park Square Building
Room 207
31 St. James Avenue
Boston, MA 02116
Tel.: 617-223-7345

Jacob K. Javitz Federal Building
Room 2937
26 Federal Plaza
New York, NY 10278
Tel.: 212-264-1000

Mall Building
Room 401

Fourth and Chestnut Streets
Philadelphia, PA 19106
Tel.: 215-597-7690

*Field Offices*

Connecticut
　Federal Building & Courthouse
　Room 793
　450 Main Street
　Hartford, CT 06103
　Tel.: 203-244-2551

Maine
　Federal Office Building
　Room 305
　Portland, ME 04101
　Tel.: 207-833-3549

Massachusetts
　Federal Building & Courthouse
　Room 32
　595 Main Street
　(For Mail: P.O. Box 1348)
　Worcester, MA 01601
　Tel.: 617-793-0291

New Jersey
　Station Plaza 1
　20 Evergreen Place
　East Orange, NJ 07018
　Tel.: 201-645-2202

　Federal Building
　Room 514
　402 East State Street
　Trenton, NJ 08608
　Tel.: 609-394-7195

New York
　U.S. Post Office & Courthouse
　Room 306
　495 Broadway
　(For Mail: P.O. Box 870)
　Albany, NY 12201
　Tel.: 518-472-4223

　New Federal Building
　Room 1105
　111 West Huron Street
　Buffalo, NY 14202
　Tel.: 716-846-4501

　Imperial Square Building
　Room 404
　175 Fulton Avenue
　Hempstead, Long Island
　NY 11550
　Tel.: 516-538-3232

　U.S. Courthouse & Federal Building
　Room 1041
　100 South Clinton Street
　Syracuse, NY 13202
　Tel.: 315-423-5316

Pennsylvania
　Professional Building
　Suite 123
　1503 N. Cedar Crest Boulevard
　Allentown, PA 18104
　Tel.: 215-776-4235

　Commerce Building
　Room 420
　12th and State Streets
　Erie, PA 16501
　Tel.: 814-455-4914

　100 Chestnut Office Building
　Suite 300
　Front and Chestnut Streets
　Harrisburg, PA 17101
　Tel.: 717-782-2220

　William S. Moorehead
　Federal Building
　Room 2017
　1000 Liberty Avenue
　Pittsburgh, PA 15222
　Tel.: 412-644-2992

Rhode Island
　Boying Building
　80 Quaker Lane
　Providence, RI 02893
　Tel.: 401-528-4441

**Southern Region**

*Regional Office*

Suite 400
1422 West Peachtree Street, N.W.
Atlanta, GA 30309
Tel.: 404-881-2473

*District Offices*

Suite 400
1422 West Peachtree Street, N.W.
Atlanta, GA 30309
Tel.: 404-881-2473

Suite 325
12140 Woodcrest Executive Drive
St. Louis (Creve Coeur), MO 63141
Tel.: 314-425-3291

FMCS Building
2nd Floor
2100 K Street, N.W.
Washington, DC 20427
Tel.: 202-653-5390

*Field Offices*

Alabama
  South Twentieth Building
  Room 428
  908 South 20th Street
  Birmingham, AL 35205
  Tel.: 205-254-1445

  Federal Building & Courthouse
  Room 45
  113 Saint Joseph Street
  Mobile, AL 36602
  Tel.: 205-690-2141

Arkansas
  Federal Office Building
  Room 2530
  700 West Capital
  Little Rock, AR 72201
  Tel.: 501-378-6193

Florida
  Federal Office Building
  Suite 309-E
  299 East Broward Boulevard
  Ft. Lauderdale, FL 33301
  Tel.: 305-527-7294

  Suite 8
  2747 Art Museum Drive
  Jacksonville, FL 32207
  Tel.: 904-791-2630

  Federal Office Building
  Room 731
  500 Zack Street
  Tampa, FL 33602
  Tel.: 813-228-2591

Indiana
  Riverside One
  Suite 211
  101 Court Street
  Evansville, IN 47708
  Tel.: 812-423-4271

Kentucky
  Building Two
  Suite 222
  200 Executive Park
  Louisville, KY 40207
  Tel.: 502-582-5205

Louisiana
  F. Edward Hebert Federal
  Building
  Room 924
  600 South Street
  New Orleans, LA 70130
  Tel.: 504-589-6112

Maryland
  Federal Office Building
  Room 1011
  31 Hopkins Plaza
  Baltimore, MD 21201
  Tel.: 301-837-2429

Missouri
  Bank of Springfield Office Center
  Suite 313
  300 South Jefferson Street
  Springfield, MO 65806
  Tel.: 417-865-2793

North Carolina
  First Union National Bank
  Building
  Room 1115
  307 South Tryon Street
  Charlotte, NC 28282
  Tel.: 704-371-6629

Ohio
  Federal Office Building
  Room 9504
  550 Main Street
  Cincinnati, OH 45202
  Tel.: 513-684-2951

Oklahoma
  U.S. Post Office & Courthouse
  Room 513
  Third and Robinson Streets
  Oklahoma City, OK 73102
  Tel.: 402-221-4984

Tennessee
  Tennessee Bank Building
  Room 622
  701 Market Street
  Chattanooga, TN 37402
  Tel.: 615-266-4470

  Northshore Building 1
  Suite 209
  1111 Northshore Drive
  Knoxville, TN 37919
  Tel.: 615-588-1315

  Clifford Davis Federal Building
  Room 475
  167 North Main Street
  Memphis, TN 38103
  Tel.: 901-521-3276

  West End Building
  Suite 401
  1808 West End Avenue
  Nashville, TN 37203
  Tel.: 615-251-5935

Texas
  Room 812
  1114 Commerce Street
  Dallas, TX 75242
  Tel.: 214-767-2917

  Bob Casey Federal Building
  Room 6016
  515 Rusk Avenue
  Houston, TX 77002
  Tel.: 713-226-4257

  Suite B 404
  727 East Durango Street
  San Antonio, TX 78206
  Tel.: 512-229-5170

Virginia
  Federal Office Building
  Room 8225
  400 North Eighth Street
  (For Mail: P.O. Box 10027)
  Richmond, VA 23240
  Tel.: 804-771-2841

West Virginia
  Federal Office Building
  Room 2040
  425 Juliana Street
  (For Mail: P.O. Box 1945)
  Parkersburg, W. VA 26101
  Tel.: 304-485-6329

**Central Region**

*Regional Office*

Insurance Exchange Building
Room 1641
175 West Jackson Boulevard
Chicago, IL 60604
Tel.: 312-353-7350

*District Offices*

Insurance Exchange Building
Room 1641
175 West Jackson Boulevard
Chicago, IL 60604
Tel.: 312-353-7351

Federal Building & Courthouse
Room 432
231 West Lafayette Street
Detroit, MI 48226
Tel.: 313-226-7765

*Field Offices*

Illinois
Nucli Building
Room 770
3024 West Lake Street
Peoria, IL 61615
Tel.: 309-671-7062

U.S. Courthouse & Federal Building
Room 214
211 South Court Street
Rockford, IL 61101
Tel.: 815-987-4251

Indiana
Airport Executive Courts
Suite B-105
2346 South Lynhurst Drive
Indianapolis, IN 46241
Tel.: 317-269-7233

JMS Building
Suite 523
108 North Main Street
South Bend, IN 46601
Tel.: 219-232-9961

Michigan
Federal Building & Courthouse
Room 250
110 Michigan Street, N.W.
Grand Rapids, MI 49503
Tel.: 616-456-2401

Kalamazoo Building
Suite 307
107 West Michigan Avenue
Kalamazoo, MI 49007
Tel.: 616-345-2409

New Federal Building
Box 626
100 South Warren Avenue
Saginaw, MI 48606
Tel.: 517-753-5171

Minnesota
Suite 250
17 Washington Avenue, North
Minneapolis, MN 55401
Tel.: 612-725-6151

Ohio
Federal Building & Courthouse
Room 410
2 South Main Street
Akron, OH 44308
Tel.: 216-375-5720

Suite 202
2242 South Hamilton Road
Columbus, OH 43227
Tel.: 614-469-5575

Federal Building & Courthouse
Room 603
200 West Second Street
Dayton, OH 45402
Tel.: 513-225-2891

Federal Building
Room 709
234 Summitt Street
Toledo, OH 43604
Tel.: 419-259-6400

Wisconsin
Vainisi Building
Suite A
1841 South Ridge Road
Green Bay, WI 54304
Tel.: 414-433-3866

Lewis Center
Room 401
615 East Michigan Avenue
Milwaukee, WI 53202
Tel.: 414-291-3296

**Western Region**

*Regional Office*

Francisco Bay Building
Suite 235
50 Francisco Street
San Francisco, CA 94133
Tel.: 415-556-4670

*District Offices*

Wilsher Hobart Building
Suite 700
3660 Wilshire Boulevard
Los Angeles, CA 90010
Tel.: 213-688-7183

Francisco Bay Building
Suite 235
50 Francisco Street
San Francisco, CA 94133
Tel.: 415-556-4670

Traders Bank Building
Suite 600
1125 Grand Avenue
Kansas City, MO 64106
Tel.: 816-374-3026

Fourth and Vine Building
Room 440
2615 Fourth Avenue
Seattle, WA 98121
Tel.: 206-442-5800

*Field Offices*

Alaska
  Federal Building & U.S. Courthouse
  P.O. Box 8
  701 C Street
  Anchorage, AK 99513
  Tel.: 907-271-5023

Arizona
  Valley Center Building
  Suite 2980
  201 North Central Avenue
  Phoenix, AZ 85073
  Tel.: 602-261-3647

California
  New Federal Building
  Room 2330 W
  2800 Cottage Way
  Sacramento, CA 95825
  Tel.: 916-484-4534

  Federal Building & Courthouse
  Room 6-S-19
  880 Front Street
  San Diego, CA 92188
  Tel.: 714-293-6260

  Suite 230
  1600 North Broadway
  Santa Ana, CA 92706
  Tel.: 714-836-2624

Colorado
  Federal Building & Courthouse
  Room 1708
  1961 Stout Street
  Denver, CO 80294
  Tel.: 303-837-3186

Hawaii
  New Federal Building
  Room 4113
  300 Ala Moana Boulevard
  (For Mail: P.O. Box 50022)
  Honolulu, HI 96850
  Tel.: 808-546-7525

Iowa
  Executive Plaza Building
  Suite 305
  4403 First Avenue, S.E.
  Cedar Rapids, IA 52402
  Tel.: 319-399-2426

  Federal Building
  Room 595
  210 Walnut Street
  Des Moines, IA 50309
  Tel.: 515-284-4110

Kansas
  Century Plaza
  Room 612
  111 West Douglas
  Wichita, KS 67202
  Tel.: 316-267-6173

Montana
  Central Plaza
  Suite 310
  600 Central Avenue
  Great Falls, MT 59401
  Tel.: 406-452-0180

Nebraska
  Hirschfield Building
  Room 303
  6818 Grover Street
  Omaha, NE 68106
  Tel.: 402-221-9401

New Mexico
  Federal Building
  Room 3002
  517 Gold Avenue, S.W.
  Albuquerque, NM 87101
  Tel.: 505-766-2459

Oregon
  Commerce Plaza
  Suite 126
  7100 S.W. Hampton Street
  Portland, OR 97223
  Tel.: 503-221-2176

Utah
  Federal Office Building
  Room 8402
  125 South State Street
  Salt Lake City, UT 84138
  Tel.: 801-524-5250

Washington
  U.S. Courthouse
  Room 791
  920 West Riverside Avenue
  Spokane, WA 99201
  Tel.: 509-456-2508

## STATE AND TERRITORIAL MEDIATION AND CONCILIATION AGENCIES

Alabama
  Department of Labor
  State Administrative Building
  Suite 600
  Montgomery 36130

Alaska
  Department of Labor
  Post Office Box 1149
  Juneau 99811

Arizona
  Industrial Commission
  Labor Department
  1601 West Jefferson Street
  Phoenix 85007

Arkansas
  Department of Labor
  Capitol Hill Building
  Little Rock 72201

Addendum 2    253

California
  Department of Industrial Relations
  State Conciliation Service
  State Building Annex
  455 Golden Gate Ave.
  San Francisco 94102
  *Mailing Address:*
  Post Office Box 603
  San Francisco 94101

Colorado
  Department of labor and Employment
  Division of Labor
  251 E. 12th Ave.
  Denver 80203

Connecticut
  Labor Department
  Board of Mediation & Arbitration
  200 Folly Brook Boulevard
  Wethersfield 06109

Delaware
  Department of Labor
  State Mediation Service
  801 West St.
  Wilmington 19899

District of Columbia
  Federal Mediation and Conciliation Service
  2100 K St., N.W.
  Washington, D.C. 20001
  *Public Employees:*
  District of Columbia Board of Labor Relations
  Suite 821
  1010 Vermont Ave., N.W.
  Washington, D.C. 20005

Florida
  Mediation & Conciliation Service
  1321 Executive Center Drive, East
  Tallahassee 32301

Georgia
  Department of Labor
  State Labor Building
  54 Washington St.
  Atlanta 30334

Hawaii
  Department of Labor & Industrial Relations
  825 Mililani St.
  Honolulu 96813

Idaho
  Department of Labor & Industrial Services
  Employer & Employee Relations Division
  Room 400, State House
  317 Main St.
  Boise 83720

Illinois
  Department of Labor
  Conciliation & Mediation Service
  910 South Michigan Ave.
  Chicago 60605
  *Public Employees:*
  Office of Collective Bargaining
  Room 200
  525 West Jefferson St.
  Springfield 62702

Indiana
  Division of Labor
  Department of Mediation & Conciliation Service
  Indiana State Office Building
  Room 1013, 100 North Senate Ave.
  Indianapolis 46204

*Public Employees:*
Education Employment Board
9247 N. Meridian
Indianapolis 46260

Iowa
Bureau of Labor
State House, 4th Floor
East 7th Street and Court Ave.
Des Moines 50319

Kansas
Department of Human Resources
Division of Labor-Management &
Employment Standards
610 W. 10th St.
Topeka 66612

Kentucky
Department of Labor
U.S. 127 South
Frankfort 40601

Louisiana
Department of Labor
1015 State Land & Natural
Resources Bldg.
Post Office Box 44094
Baton Rouge 70804

Maine
Board of Arbitration &
Conciliation
State Office Bldg.
Augusta 04333

Maryland
Division of Labor & Industry
Mediation & Conciliation Service
203 East Baltimore Street
Baltimore 21202

Massachusetts
Department of Labor &
Industries
Board of Conciliation &
Arbitration
Saltonstall Office Building
Government Center
100 Cambridge Street
Boston 02202

Michigan
Department of Labor
Employment Relations
Commission
Leonard Plaza Building
309 N. Washington Square
Lansing 48909

Minnesota
Bureau of Mediation Services
Veterans Service Building
First Floor
20 W. 12th St.
St. Paul 55155

Mississippi
Has no authorized agency to mediate labor dispute

Missouri
Department of Labor &
Industrial Relations
State Board of Mediation
421 E. Dunklin
Jefferson City 65101

Montana
Department of Labor & Industry
Capitol Station
Helena 59601

Nebraska
Department of Labor
P.O. Box 94600
550 S. 16th St.
Lincoln 68509

Nevada
Department of Labor

Room 601, 505 East King St.
Carson City 89701
*Mailing Address:*
Capitol Complex
Carson City 89701

New Hampshire
Board of Conciliation &
Arbitration
62 Congress St.
Portsmouth 03801

*Public Employees:*
Public Employee Labor
Relations Board
Pine Inn Plaza
117 Manchester St.
Concord 03301

New Jersey
Department of Labor & Industry
State Board of Mediation
Room 306, 1100 Raymond Blvd.
Newark 07102

New Mexico
No state agency has been authorized to mediate and conciliate labor disputes; however, the Labor and Industrial Commission assumes responsibility in assisting parties in settlement of controversies.

Labor and Industrial Bureau
Kennedy Hall
College of Santa Fe
Santa Fe 87501

New York
Mediation Board
2 World Trade Center
34th Floor
New York 10007

*Public Employees:*
Office of Collective Bargaining
250 Broadway
New York 10047

North Carolina
Department of Labor
Conciliation & Arbitration
Division
4 W. Edenton St.
Raleigh 27611

North Dakota
Department of Labor
State Capitol
Bismarck 58501

Ohio
Department of Industrial
Relations
2323 West 5th Ave.
Columbus 43216

Oklahoma
Department of Labor
State Capitol
Oklahoma City 73105

*Public Employees:*
Public Employees Relations Board
3000 City National Bank Tower
Post Office Box 25715
Oklahoma City 73102

Oregon
Employment Relations Board
Conciliation Service Division
402 Capitol Tower Building
388 State St.
Salem 97310

Pennsylvania
Department of Labor and
Industry
Bureau of Mediation

Labor & Industry Building
Harrisburg 17120

Puerto Rico
Department of Labor and Human Resources
Bureau of Conciliation & Arbitrations
Munoz Rivera Ave., Corner Domenech St.
Hato Rey 00917

Rhode Island
Department of Labor
220 Elmwood Ave.
Providence 02907

South Carolina
Department of Labor
Division of Conciliation
3600 Forest Drive
Post Office Box 11329
Columbia 29211

South Dakota
Department of Labor
Division of Labor & Management Relations
Foss Building
Pierre 57501

Tennessee
Although no agency has been authorized to mediate labor disputes, the Commissioner of Labor, under general duties of his office, assists disputing parties in settlement of controversies.

Department of Labor
501 Union Building
Nashville 37219

Texas
Although no agency has been authorized by statute to mediate labor disputes, the Department of Labor and Standards will assist disputing parties in settlement of controversies.

Department of Labor & Standards
Box 12157
Capitol Station
Austin 78711

Utah
Industrial Commission
Labor Relations Commission
350 East 500 South
Salt Lake City 84111

Vermont
Department of Labor & Industry
State Office Building
Montpelier 05602

Virginia
Department of Labor & Industry
Post Office Box 12064
4th Street Office Building
Richmond 23241

Virgin Islands
Department of Labor
Post Office Box 708
Christiansted, St. Croix 00820

Washington
Department of Labor & Industries
General Administration Building
Olympia 98504
*Public Employees:*
State Personnel Board
600 South Franklin Ave.
Olympia 98504

West Virginia
Department of Labor

Capitol Complex
1900 Washington St.
East Charleston 25305

Wisconsin
Department of Industry, Labor & Human Relations
201 East Washington Ave.
Post Office Box 2209
Madison 53702

Wisconsin Employment Relations Commission
Room 906, 30 West Mifflin St.
Madison 53703

Wyoming
Although no state agency has been authorized by statute to mediate and conciliate labor disputes, the Department of Labor and Statistics does assist disputing parties in the settlement of controversies.

Department of Labor and Statistics
Barrett Building
Fourth Floor
Cheyenne 82002

# Part II
# Strike Manual

## ABOUT THE MANUAL

Designed for use in times of employee strike or similar labor/management conflict, this manual is written generically and, as such, refers to no specific union or hospital. Instead, the terms "union" and "hospital" are used whenever reference is made to the parties in conflict. Similarly, employees are referred to only as "striking" or "nonstriking." Nonstriking employees include employees who belong to unions not party to the conflict and nonunion employees.

It is the sincere wish of the authors that the need will never arise to implement the plan embodied in the pages that follow. If you do, however, find yourself at loggerheads with a union and a ten-day strike notice has been filed, this manual will provide you with the basic elements necessary to develop your own tailor-made, comprehensive, and workable strike plan. No one plan can fit all facilities, but this manual can serve as a guide. You can substitute, add, or delete plan specifics to fit your needs.

Functions listed in this manual may not be available at your institution; some of these, such as *Resident Manager for Housing,* may need to be established during the work stoppage on an *ad hoc* basis.

## EMPLOYEE STRIKE CONTINGENCY PLAN

Key to the survival of any health care facility during a strike that affects a significant portion of its employee population is a carefully and systematically developed strike contingency plan. An employee strike contingency plan is an intelligent alternative to surrendering to your adversary, under duress and out of lack of preparedness, what you believe to be a fair and honest last position. Paramount to the strike plan's effectiveness are the key objectives on which it is based and on which it must serve. Specifically, the plan must strive to:

1. minimize the disruption of patient care;
2. maximize the quality of patient care; and
3. minimize the negative economic effects of the strike.

Essential measures to consider at the onset of plan development are:

1. stockpiling essential supplies;
2. categorizing patients into three classes:
    (a) those able to be sent home;
    (b) those who probably could be sent home; and
    (c) those who definitely require care;

3. consolidating patients into fewer wards;
4. assigning to supervisors, professionals, and volunteers remaining on the job all functions normally performed by striking workers.[1]

Effective organization of the employee strike contingency plan begins with the assignment of a strike plan administrator, who will in turn establish committees that will be responsible for the development of major plan subdivisions. Appropriate committee staffing is obviously essential to the plan's success; thus careful consideration must be given to who will chair and staff each committee. Selections should be made based on knowledge, experience, and ability in that area of the plan for which the committee is responsible. At a minimum, the plan should address:

- institutional policy;
- manpower or personnel plan;
- services to nonstriking employees;
- patient services;
- operational equipment, supplies, and services;
- security; and
- communication.

The Strike Plan Administrator will coordinate the efforts of the various committees, monitor committee meetings, provide intercommittee communication to avoid confusion and duplication of effort, and ultimately compile the written plan.

When developing the manpower plan in hospitals where some employees are represented by unions other than that which is on strike, plan developers must consider the threshold issue of the reaction of these other unions to the conflict. Will they pull their workers out in sympathy and support? Will the employee members of these other unions slow down their activities or engage in other conflict-related job actions at the site? The status and availability of *all employees not directly involved in the actual conflict* (and this includes employees of other unions) must be known before meaningful personnel or manpower planning can take place. Important to this determination is whether the other unions' collective bargaining agreements include no-sympathy strike provisions as part of their no-strike, no-lockout clauses.

As discussed in Chapter 2, a no-sympathy strike clause does not guarantee that a union will not go out in sympathy, but it is a deterrent.

As highlighted in the medical services section of this plan and in Chapter 4, essential to the effective development of the strike contingency plan is the basic premise that jobs and functions abandoned by the striking work force can be effectively handled by nonstriking workers and strike volunteers. If this is not the case, there can be no manpower plan to speak of, and the institution determines how it can safely and efficiently transfer and discharge its patient population for the duration of the conflict (or until acceptable strike replacements can be installed) and in-house rebuilding thereafter. To consider patient transfer, arrangements must be made with neighboring hospitals not affected by the strike and able to accommodate significant patient load increases, to allow temporary medical staff privileges to physicians at the struck facility to admit and care for their patients.

With specific regard to communications, the hospital should notify customers and suppliers, government authorities (where a hospital is working under government grants or contracts), and the U.S. Postal Service. Additionally, a spokesperson should be assigned to report timely and accurate information to the news media. Finally, a communication network with both striking and nonstriking workers should be established to report status of negotiations and other strike-related information.

The labor relations function during the conflict is twofold. Primarily, labor relations negotiators will try to bring about a settlement with the union through meaningful collective bargaining, employing the assistance of a mediator. The labor relations staff will be a conduit for communications between negotiators, hospital management, and the picket line. The staff will communicate developments in negotiations to management as well as to striking employees, arranging, to the extent possible, emergency services to the institution necessary to effect critical patient care, providing management with picket line developments, and supplying mediators with required resource information.

The role of the institution's legal office during the conflict includes responsibility for all legal matters arising in connection with the work stoppage, and advising management as to which legislation and legal mechanisms are available and best suited for use in effectively managing the conflict.

---

**NOTE**

1. D. Bird, "Hospitals Girding for Strike Today," *The New York Times* (January 7, 1976), p. 1.

## STRIKE PLAN ADMINISTRATION AND COMMITTEES

COMMAND GROUP—KEY SENIOR MANAGERS
Spokespersons for the Hospital—Chief Executive Officer
                                     Department Head of
                                     Public Relations
  Strike Plan Administrator(s)    —Key Senior Administrator(s)
COMMITTEES

1. Personnel Policies.
   Chair:           Department Head of Human Resources
   Staff:           Representatives of Human Resources and Personnel Services, Labor Relations and Nursing
2. Financial Operations.
   Chair:           Department Head of Finance
   Staff:           Representatives of Financial Division
3. Personnel/Manpower Planning.
   (a) Nonstriking Hospital Personnel
   (b) Volunteers
   (c) Medical Staff
   Chair:           Department Head of Support Services
   Staff:           Representatives of Support Services Departments, Nursing, Volunteer Service, Human Resources and Personnel Services, and Labor Relations
4. Communications.
   Chair:           Department Head of Public Relations
   Staff:           Representatives of Administration, Human Resources and Personnel Services, Labor Relations, and Legal Department
5. Medical Services.
   Nursing Services
   Unit Management
   Medical Services
   Chair:           Department Head of Nursing/Chief Medical Officer
   Staff:           Representatives of Nursing, Social Services, Admitting, Medical Attending Staff, House Staff, Engineering and Plant Operations, as well as chair of Supplies and Services Strike Contingency Plan Committee

6. Accommodations.
   Chair: Department Head of Real Estate
   Staff: Representatives of Real Estate and Building Service
7. Ancillary Services.
   Chair: Department Head of Clinical Services
   Staff: Designated Clinical Services' Administrators
8. Engineering and Plant Operations.
   Chair: Department Head of Engineering
   Staff: Representatives of Engineering
9. Supplies and Services.
   Chair: A Support Services administrator
   Staff: Designated Support Services Department representatives, and representatives of Nursing, Clinical Service, and Engineering Departments
10. Security.
    Chair: Department Head of Security
    Staff: Representatives of Security, Labor Relations, and Public Relations
11. Labor/Employee Relations.
    Chair: Department Head of Labor Relations
    Staff: Representatives of Labor Relations and Legal Department
12. Legal.
    Chair: Department Head of Legal Department
    Staff: Representatives of Administration, Legal Department, Labor Relations, with possible outside law firm support
13. Post-Strike "House" Rebuilding.
    Chair: Top administrative level employee, familiar with the total hospital operation

## PERSONNEL POLICIES

During the strike the hospital will be operating under a unique set of conditions, far removed from the norm, and the hospital will have to develop tailor-made policies to fit the period of conflict. These policies should address, among other things, compensation for both striking (money earned prior to the strike) and nonstriking employees, time recording, time off, and out-of-pocket expenses for nonstriking workers and volunteers.

**STAFFING**

All nonstriking employees will be expected to work during the strike. They may be assigned to a specific department, or asked to report to the Manpower Planning Committee. Nurses will be expected to work normal schedules within assigned areas.

**COMPENSATION**

1. Time Records.
   To be paid, employees must submit time records. These time records, reflecting hours worked up to and beyond regular full-time work week, must be authorized by the home department and head of department to which employee is assigned during the work stoppage. This time record will determine the amount of compensation employee is to receive.
2. Pay for Additional Time Worked.
   (a) Employees exempt from premium pay for overtime hours worked in accordance with federal law and earning less than $ *(to be determined)* will be paid straight time for all overtime hours worked.
   (b) Employees exempt from premium pay for overtime hours worked in accordance with federal law and earning more than $ *(to be determined)* will not be eligible for pay for overtime hours worked.
   (c) Non-exempt employees, for whom premium pay for overtime hours worked is mandated by federal law, will submit timesheets in lieu of time cards and will be paid time-and-one-half for overtime worked regardless of salary.
3. Compensatory Time.
   Employees exempt from premium pay for overtime hours worked in accordance with federal law and earning in excess of $ *(to be determined)* will be eligible for compensatory time at the rate of one hour

compensatory time for each hour worked in excess of regular payable hours. Compensatory time will be scheduled, monitored, and controlled by department heads after the strike.
4. Review of Extraordinary Strike Expenses.
There will be no automatic strike expense stipends. However, a committee will be established to set guidelines for payment of extraordinary strike-related expenses incurred by employees during the strike. This committee will review requests by employees for reimbursement in accordance with its guidelines. The recommendation of this committee will be sent for final approval to the appropriate senior administrators.
5. House Staff.
House Staff will receive regular pay; thus, they will not be required to submit time records.
6. Faculty (if teaching facility).
    (a) Faculty members earning in excess of $ *(to be determined)* will not be eligible for additional pay for overtime worked nor will they be eligible for compensatory time off. Thus, they will not be required to submit timesheets.
    (b) Faculty members earning less than $ *(to be determined)* who work overtime hours will be eligible for pay at straight time rates for overtime hours worked, if they submit timesheets reflecting hours worked and authorized by the head of their department and the head of the department to which they are assigned.
7. Medical and other students (if teaching facility).
Medical and other students are available for assignment during the strike as needed, and will be paid a stipend to be determined in advance by Personnel Policies Committee.

## SICK PAY

1. Striking employees will not be eligible for sick pay during the strike. Nonstriking employees will be eligible for such pay in accordance with established policy. *Proof of illness will be required.*
2. All employees who are eligible for Workers' Compensation or disability benefits during the strike period will receive payments.

## VACATION

1. Moratorium on vacation begins with receipt of strike notice. From that time until end of strike no vacation time should be granted.

Exceptions to this provision will require the approval of the hospital administrator or designee.
2. Employees on vacation may be called back to work before or during the strike. Such decisions should be carefully reviewed by the Personnel/Manpower Planning Committee.

## MEAL POLICY

Employees will be issued three free meal tickets daily (appropriately labeled for breakfast, lunch, and dinner) by department head to which employee is assigned. Tickets will entitle holder to meals served in cafeteria. The tickets will be dated and are nonrefundable.

## TRANSITION PERIOD FOLLOWING STRIKE

The goal of the hospital is to return to a normal operational schedule as quickly as possible after the strike. Employees may be asked to work overtime, recalled from vacations, or temporarily reassigned during the transition period. The order of reinstatement of striking employees, after the strike ends, will be determined by the appropriate department head and the Financial Operations Committee.

## FINANCIAL DIVISION OPERATIONS

During a strike, the Financial Division should function with a reduced table of organization to accommodate scaled-down hospital operations as well as financial management of the strike itself.

## FUNCTIONAL RESPONSIBILITIES OF DEPARTMENTS WITHIN THE FINANCIAL DIVISION

1. Payroll.
    (a) Utilization
        (1) Nonstriking employees (both exempt and nonexempt from premium overtime compensation) exclusive of House Staff will be required to submit timesheets (time records).
        (2) House Staff employees will not be required to submit time records and will receive regular pay during the strike regardless of hours worked or services rendered.
    (b) Distribution
        (1) The Personnel/Manpower Planning Committee will generate departmental manpower assignment time sheets (Exhibit 1), which assignee department heads must submit to Payroll weekly. These timesheets will be used for identification of employees, hours worked, charge/recharge reporting and allocation, and as a reconciliation tool against individual employee time records.
        (2) Payroll will generate individual employee timesheets (Exhibit 2) and instructions and distribute them to all department heads for issuance to their employees. These timesheets will be used by the employee to track his or her time according to assignment in the institution, and will be reconciled with the departmental manpower assignment timesheets on a weekly basis. During the strike, additional individual timesheets will be available in the Payroll Department at time of check distribution and at other times.
    (c) Collection
        (1) Employees will submit individual employee timesheets on the last day worked in a given week to the department head in the area where the employee last worked.
        (2) Department heads are responsible for depositing both the individual employee timesheets and the departmental manpower assignment timesheets in the slot marked "Payroll

**Exhibit 1** Departmental Manpower Assignment Timesheet

Assigned Department No.: _____  Location: _____  Date: _____
Approved by: _____  Supervisor: _____

| EMPLOYEE NAME | | (Date) | | (Date) | | (Date) | | (Date) | | (Date) | | (Date) | | (Date) | | Week Total Hours Worked |
|---|---|---|---|---|---|---|---|---|---|---|---|---|---|---|---|---|
| | | Time | Total Hours Worked | Time | Total Hours Worked | Time | Total Hours Worked | Time | Total Hours Worked | Time | Total Hours Worked | Time | Total Hours Worked | Time | Total Hours Worked | |
| | In Out | | | | | | | | | | | | | | | |
| | In Out | | | | | | | | | | | | | | | |
| | In Out | | | | | | | | | | | | | | | |
| | In Out | | | | | | | | | | | | | | | |
| | In Out | | | | | | | | | | | | | | | |
| | In Out | | | | | | | | | | | | | | | |
| | In Out | | | | | | | | | | | | | | | |

If additions are to be made to this sheet, write in name, department, employee number, and weekly or biweekly.

**Exhibit 2** Individual Employee Timesheet

Employee's Name _____
Week Ending _____

Employee Number _____
"Home" Department Number _____
"Home" Department Name _____

Check Appropriate Box
☐ Biweekly Employee Payroll
☐ Weekly Employee Payroll

Department You Worked in
(Use separate line for each department)

Total Hours Worked in Department

Verified by Dept. Head
(Signature)
_____

| Name | Number | Sun | Mon | Tues | Wed | Thu | Fri | Sat | Total for Week |
|------|--------|-----|-----|------|-----|-----|-----|-----|----------------|
|      |        |     |     |      |     |     |     |     |                |
|      |        |     |     |      |     |     |     |     |                |
|      |        |     |     |      |     |     |     |     |                |
|      |        |     |     |      |     |     |     |     |                |
|      |        |     |     |      |     |     |     |     |                |
| Totals |      |     |     |      |     |     |     |     | Total Hours    |

| Regular Hours | Overtime Hours | Sick Hours | Holiday Hours | Free Hours | Other Hours | Vacation Hours |
|---------------|----------------|------------|---------------|------------|-------------|----------------|
|               |                |            |               |            |             |                |

Please complete this form accurately and completely to avoid delays in verification and processing. Submit timesheets on last day worked in a given work week to the department head in the area where you last worked. Department heads are responsible for depositing timesheets in the slot marked *"PAYROLL DEPARTMENT—TIME CARDS ONLY"* at the Mailroom by *12:00 noon on Monday.*

Employee Signature _____

Department—Time Records Only" in the mailroom by noon on Monday following the close of the work week.
(3) If the strike occurs in the middle of a work week, department heads should observe the following procedures:
- For weekly paid nonexempt employees (employees who normally use time cards), complete and sign each employee's time card for the number of days worked up to the strike. Time worked after the strike begins is to be entered on the individual employee timesheet. Give each employee his or her completed time card and instruct the employee to attach this card to the first timesheet to be submitted.
- For biweekly paid exempt employees (employees who do not normally use time cards):
  (a) Submit to Payroll in the normal fashion the standard biweekly attendance registers for days worked *prior* to the strike.
  (b) Salary Accounting*:
    - All hours worked by an employee (both regular and overtime) will be charged to the employee's "home" department.
    - After the fact, the departmental manpower assignment timesheets will be used to report in which departments actual strike hours were worked and by whom worked.
  (c) Check Distribution:
    - Payroll of striking workers (for hours worked prior to strike). Checks will be distributed by Payroll staff. Adequate security will be provided during distribution (location should be far from patient areas and with direct access to street).
    - All Other Payroll. Check distribution by Payroll staff. Security to provide coverage during distribution.
    - Employees must present identification to get paid.

---

*Payroll consideration should include the basis on which and method of how nonstriking salaries will be expensed institutionally for services rendered during the stoppage. That is, will a department closed during the strike be charged with the salaries of its nonstriking workers who are servicing other departments? Should a department, predominantly composed of union workers and closed during the stoppage, not be charged with "normal" salary expenditures? Will a department functioning during the strike be made to absorb the additional salary expense of higher paid nonstriking workers?

- A special phone service will be provided and announced for information regarding payroll check distribution during the strike.
2. Accounts Payable.
    (a) Skeleton staff will process the following for payment, in order of priority:
    - strike-related expenses
    - emergency rush checks
    - utilities
    - patient refunds
    (b) All checks will be issued manually. Any other processing will be handled on an individual review basis as time and staff permit.
3. Patients Accounts/Ambulatory Accounts.
    (a) Work in Patients Accounts will depend on computer support. On day three of the strike, all bills will be held in order to accumulate charges. For the first three days of the strike, bills will be processed. After that, emphasis will switch to credit and collection.
    (b) Cashiering function will continue as close to normal as possible.
4. Fund Accounting (where applicable).
    (a) Requests for normal processing (i.e., purchase orders, check requests, etc.) will be limited to emergencies only. They will not be reviewed on an individual basis. Because deliveries will be curtailed during the strike, fund administrators should be prepared and plan their purchasing accordingly.
5. Other Finance Areas.
    (a) Budget and Reimbursement Departments will be nonoperational during the strike.
    (b) Technical Accounting. All checks and cash received will be deposited.
    - "Swing" staff will work on financial statements when not in payroll or Accounts Payable.
    (c) Operational Accounting. Checks already generated will be released in the usual manner.

## PERSONNEL/MANPOWER PLANNING

The heart of an Employee Strike Contingency Plan is unquestionably its Personnel/Manpower Planning section. The manpower plan matches skills, special knowledge, and working preference of nonstriking workers with the needs of the institution during the stoppage. If the hospital is so equipped, these matching programs should be computerized because manual matching, while possible, is an extremely cumbersome and time-consuming task. As will be discussed in the Medical Services section, the Nursing Department should not be included in the Manpower Plan as a resource for striking worker replacements.

### PLAN OVERVIEW

1. Additional Personnel.
   Departments will deploy all available (excess) nonstriking personnel from within their own departments as well as volunteers from other departments (who are known to them) for needed hospital coverage. If a shortfall still occurs, additional personnel shall be requested by departments from the Personnel/Manpower Planning Committee.
2. Specific Requests.
   Requests for additional personnel are to be as specific as possible, i.e., day shift, evening shift, or night shift; Monday–Friday only; special skills necessary; specialty license required; bachelor's degree preferred; heavy lifting; patient care experience; etc.
3. Training.
   Additional personnel supplied by Personnel/Manpower Planning Committee will be trained by requesting departments. The Personnel/Manpower Planning Committee will schedule individuals as much in advance as possible, so that training can be effected.

### PLAN OUTLINE

1. Prior to Strike.
   (a) Twelve weeks prior to expiration of contract, the Committee solicits an *Available Personnel Inventory* and a *Personnel Needs Survey* under an introductory cover memorandum by the Hospital Administrator (Exhibit 3).
   
   Included with the request is a roster of nonstriking departmental employees. Department heads are asked to verify this roster, to correct as necessary, and to designate employee as either A,

**Exhibit 3** Memorandum

To: Senior Managers  Date: _____
       Department Heads

From: Hospital Administrator  Subject: Strike Plan

The hospital's contract with the union expires on _____ . Preparation for negotiations between the union and the hospital have begun.

Both the hospital and the union have expressed their interest in negotiating a satisfactory settlement before the agreement expires. However, we must develop contingency plans now in case a strike occurs.

_____(name)_____ , _____(title)_____ , has been named Strike Plan Coordinator. He will have a number of committee chairpersons working with him. We request at this time that you read the attached memorandum and submit, as requested, necessary information relative to the development and organization of a strike personnel manpower contingent that will be employed in the event of a strike.

We look forward to your cooperation in this important planning effort.

To: Senior Managers  Date: _____
       Department Heads

From: Chairperson  Subject: Strike Plan
       Strike Personnel/Manpower
       Planning Committee

The first step in our planning effort is to develop a *Personnel Needs Survey* and an *Available Personnel Inventory*. This will establish the basic information necessary for the formation of a centralized personnel pool.

*Personnel Needs Survey*

If your department must be operational during a work stoppage, you will need to assess your overall staffing requirements. Department heads should make their own arrangements for coverage by using:
1. nonstriking employees in *their own* departments; and
2. nonstriking employees in *other* departments.

We encourage department heads to proceed with identifying these employees and scheduling them accordingly for strike duty. In the case of employees whose skills are desired but who do not currently work in your unit, please contact the appropriate department head for clearance.

In the event you have exhausted these available alternatives, but find that you still have a personnel shortfall, then proceed with developing a detailed Personnel Needs Survey that would show the additional staff you would require from a central personnel pool. For each job, please include the qualifications needed and the hours and days of the week that coverage should be provided. Use the examples below as a guide:
   a) Heavy lifting, on feet most of the time—12:00 a.m. to 8:00 a.m. (7 days per week);
   b) Patient transport—wheelchair/stretcher—7:30 a.m. to 3:30 p.m. (M–F);
   c) Desk job clerical—typing a must—9:00 a.m. to 5:00 p.m. (M–F);
   d) Admitting Clerk—light typing preferred—8:30 a.m. to 4:30 p.m. (7 days per week); and
   e) Lab Technician—____(specialty)____ license required—8:00 a.m. to 4:00 p.m. (M–F).

## Exhibit 3 continued

When completed, the Personnel Needs Survey will represent the number of positions required from the centralized personnel pool.

*Available Personnel Inventory*

Attached please find a roster of employees in your department. All employees are nonstriking employees and as such will be available for work assignments within the hospital.

Delete the names of all personnel no longer in your department (please indicate whether terminated or transferred, and if transferred name of the new department); correct names and classification of those employees who have recently been reclassified; and add the names of all new employees inadvertently omitted (if newly transferred into your department, indicate department from which transferred).

If you wish the nonstriking employees in your department to be assigned to your department, please indicate by placing "A" next to their names. You may do this for all or part of your staff, depending on your overall staffing requirements.

Place a "B" next to the names of those employees who will be reassigned by agreement (between department heads) to another department. Indicate the departments to which these employees will be assigned.

Finally, the remaining employees who can be reassigned by the Central Personnel Pool should be designated with a "C" next to their names. For those employees designated with a "C," list in the space provided to the right any special skills or licenses that the individual may have.

When completed, all employees listed on the Available Personnel Inventory should have an "A," "B," or "C" next to their names. Please return both documents—the Personnel Needs Survey and the Available Personnel Inventory—to my office no later than _____.

The process of deploying personnel to those areas requiring additional staff will be computerized. The program will select employees for assignment, first by skill, and then randomly if skill is not a factor.

We will forward to you no later than _____ two listings:

1. *Listing #1*—will indicate the nonstriking employees in your department who, by your direction, will be assigned to your department in full or partial satisfaction of your requested personnel needs.
2. *Listing #2*—will indicate the assignment of all your nonstriking employees throughout the hospital.

If you have any questions, do not hesitate to call me.

Thank you.

**Exhibit 3** continued

## Personnel Needs Survey

Date: _____

Department Name: _____
Department No.: _____ Location: _____ Supervisor: _____

| Job Classification To Be Filled | Brief Job Description | Days of the Week | Hours To Be Worked | Special Job Requirements/Skills Needed |
|---|---|---|---|---|
| | | | | |
| | | | | |
| | | | | |
| | | | | |
| | | | | |
| | | | | |
| | | | | |
| | | | | |

## Available Personnel Inventory

Date: _____

Department Name: _____
Department No.: _____ Location: _____ Supervisor: _____

| Nonstriking Employee Name | Employee Number | PD* | JCL**# | Employee Grade | Special Skill | Designate As Either A, B, or C |
|---|---|---|---|---|---|---|
| | | | | | | |
| | | | | | | |
| | | | | | | |
| | | | | | | |
| | | | | | | |
| | | | | | | |
| | | | | | | |
| | | | | | | |
| | | | | | | |

\* PD = Paid (weekly or biweekly)
\*\*JCL = Job Classification

B, or C. An *A* is to be placed by name of employees needed by the department in the event of a strike. A *B* is to be placed by names of employees who will be working in other departments per agreement of department heads. A *C* should be placed by names of remaining employees to denote their availability for the Central Personnel Pool. Special skills should be noted. These *C* employees will comprise the *Available Personnel Inventory*.

If staffing requirements cannot be met by other departments, a *Personnel Needs Survey* is required. Department heads are asked to list each job opening, description of work, days of week and hours that coverage is needed. This list will represent the number of positions required from the centralized personnel pool.

(b) Personnel from *Available Personnel Inventory* listing are manually assigned to needs, first on a voluntary basis and then on a forced-assigned basis. Listings of assignments are distributed to departments for adjustments and questions three weeks before the strike begins. Departments completing the *Personnel Needs Survey* are advised of personnel assigned to their areas, as well as the name and phone number of the contact person with whom training sessions should be planned.

(c) Several days prior to the strike, final listings of personnel assignments complete with updates and corrections (Exhibit 4) are distributed to Home and Receiving departments along with departmental manpower assignment time sheets (Exhibit 1). The departmental manpower assignment time sheets (accompanied by a complete set of instructions) are to be completed by the department to which personnel are assigned and then forwarded to Finance.

2. Operations.
    (a) The Personnel Assignment Station is located in the Main Hospital Conference Room and commences operations at 6:00 a.m. on the strike day and thereafter should be open 24 hours a day. Maps of the institution, time sheets, parking information, beeper information, etc., will be available to Personnel Assignment staff.
    (b) Coverage of Personnel Assignment phones begins 24 hours prior to strike and thereafter operates on a 24-hour basis throughout the strike. Phone extensions are ____ , ____ , and ____ .
    (c) All personnel assignments are made in advance; thus phone coverage is necessary only to answer questions and fill openings as they occur or to replace "no-show" assignments. As employees and other volunteers offer their time, either in person at the

station or by phone, lists of volunteers are compiled. Volunteers are contacted as needs are identified.
   (d) Personnel Assignment staff will contact departments to inquire if assigned volunteers have arrived and if additional personnel is needed or available.
3. Post-Strike.
   Personnel Assignment phones will be covered to facilitate a smooth "emergency" to "normal" staffing transition.

## Exhibit 4  Memorandum

| To: | Senior Managers<br>Department Heads | Date: _____ |
|---|---|---|
| From: | Chairman<br>Strike Personnel/Manpower<br>Planning Committee | Subject:  Strike Plan |

 Attached are updated staff assignments for your department during the strike. The first list (Manpower Assignment—Home Department) contains all of your nonstriking employees and their assignments. If you requested additional staff, a second list (Manpower Assignment—Receiving Department) is attached, naming those people specifically assigned to your department.

Please observe the following regarding staff assignments:

1. Inform your staff of these assignments.
2. If there are any discrepancies or questions regarding these revised and updated lists, please call me at extension _____ .
3. Only accept for work the staff listed on the attached lists. If a staff member who is not on the list reports for work, call the Personnel Assignment Desk for confirmation of the assignment.
4. Also call the Personnel Assignment Desk if:
   (a) You can spare any staff to be assigned to critical areas of need.
   (b) You wish to have a staff member transferred.
   (c) You need additional staff.
5. In addition, attached are three sets of Departmental Manpower Assignment timesheets for all employees working in your department in the event of a strike. Please note the following instructions:
   (a) Complete all information as required for time worked in *your* department *only*.
   (b) Add names of employees at work in your department that do not appear on the list.
   (c) Sign and deposit timesheets in the Payroll mail slot in the Mailroom located at _____ by noon on the Monday following week worked.

Finally, attached is an example of how the Manpower Assignment mechanism works.

Manpower Assignment—Home Department

Date: _____

Home Department Name: _____ Location: _____ Supervisor: _____
Home Department Number: _____

**Exhibit 4** continued

| Employee Name | Employee Number | Grade | Assigned Department ||| Skill | Receiving Supervisor |
|---|---|---|---|---|---|---|---|
| | | | Name | Shift | Number | | |
| | | | | | | | |
| | | | | | | | |
| | | | | | | | |
| | | | | | | | |
| | | | | | | | |
| | | | | | | | |
| | | | | | | | |

Manpower Assignment—Receiving Department

Date: _____
Receiving Department Name: _____ Location: _____ Supervisor: _____
Receiving Department Number: _____

| Employee Name | Employee Number | Grade | Home Department ||| Skill | Home Supervisor |
|---|---|---|---|---|---|---|---|
| | | | Name | Shift | Number | | |
| | | | | | | | |
| | | | | | | | |
| | | | | | | | |

**Exhibit 4** continued

### Example of How Manpower Assignment Mechanism Actually Works

You are the supervisor of the Print Shop. Reporting to you are three printers (nonstriking employees). Of course, all three employees are skilled printers. In addition, one of them (Mr. Beta) has telephone switchboard skills. Mr. Alpha is the most senior and most experienced printer. Mr. Gamma is the least senior and least experienced printer.

You receive your departmental roster and are instructed to designate assignments for all three during the strike period. You have determined that to operate the print shop, which will be necessary for communication purposes during the strike, you will require, in addition to yourself, one employee.

What You Do:

1. You select Mr. Alpha, the most experienced printer, to remain in the shop. Per instruction sheet, you place an "A" next to his name on the roster.
2. You agree with the Telephone Switchboard supervisor and with Mr. Beta that during the strike Mr. Beta will assist with incoming hospital calls. Accordingly, you place a "B" next to Mr. Beta's name indicating that he will be reassigned by agreement. You indicate the Telephone Room as the site of reassignment.
3. Mr. Gamma, unskilled for purposes of reassignment outside the Print Shop, is designated with a "C" indicating that he is available to the Central Personnel Pool for institutional assignment as needed.
4. You return the roster with your response as to what your operational needs will be (Personnel Needs Survey).

The product of 1 through 4 above is a two-document set indicating the strike assignments of your employees as follows:

List No. 1:—Print shop employees assigned to Print Shop:
       Mr. Alpha
List No. 2:—Print Shop employees assigned to areas other than the Print Shop:
    Mr. Beta:  Department assignment _____
    Mr. Gamma: Department assignment _____

## SUPPLIES AND SERVICES

The hospital must have adequate supplies during the strike. This will require some stockpiling, based upon information gathered through the use of institutional surveys. In addition, a level of services to be provided during the strike must be outlined and communicated prior to the actual strike.

This section contains the text of typical institutional survey results, as well as an example of an operational schedule for a Support Services department in a struck hospital. Exhibits 5 to 8 are forms that may facilitate preparation of these materials.

**Exhibit 5** Supplies

A two-week to four-week supply of goods should be available in the hospital on the day prior to scheduled start of strike.

| Area Surveyed | Comments |
|---|---|
| Anesthesia | |
| Building Services | |
| Clinical Services | |
| Central Sterile Supply | |
| Engineering | |
| Food Service | |

**Exhibit 5** continued

Laundry

Nursing Department

Pharmacy

Purchasing

Radiology and Radiotherapy

Respiratory Therapy

Miscellaneous Supplies

## Exhibit 5 continued
## SAMPLE SURVEY: SUPPLIES

A two-week to four-week supply of goods should be available in the hospital on the day prior to scheduled start of strike.

| Area Surveyed | Comments |
|---|---|
| Anesthesia | Gases and supplies will be available. No problems identified. |
| Building Services | Full four-week supply. No problems identified. |
| Clinical Services | a) Pathology: Those items that have an expiration date will be hand-carried by Security into the hospital.<br>b) Blood Center drivers are members of the striking union. The Blood Bank shall keep in close touch with administration at the Blood Center to determine what plans they are making to have blood delivered to the hospital in the event of a work stoppage. If necessary, the Security Department will pick up and deliver the blood. |
| Central Sterile Supply | a) Disposable O.R. linens and instruments have been chosen and are being placed on order. The company will allow the return of the merchandise, but a restocking charge of 10–15 percent will be levied.<br>b) Arrangements are being made with Engineering to care for the equipment. |
| Engineering | a) Fuel oil will not be a problem because we can use either oil or gas.<br>b) Garbage will be picked up by outside firms. Problems are not anticipated.<br>c) Engineering will maintain regular contact with departments it services. |
| Food Service | Freezer goods will be overstocked. Perishables will be stocked according to useful life. Bakery and dairy products will be delivered in the early a.m. every other day. If the deliveries cannot be made, powdered milk will be used and baked goods eliminated. Security will secure the receiving area for food storage. |
| Laundry | Disposables, on consignment, have been purchased with approval of representatives from Central Sterile Supply, Operating Rooms, and OBS/GYN. |
| Nursing Department | Baby formula vendor will be contacted to see whether they will cross the picket line. If necessary, supplies will be picked up by Security. |
| Pharmacy | Sufficient supplies. No problems foreseen. |
| Purchasing | a) General Stores currently increasing inventory on those items regularly used.<br>b) Stock orders should be in the Department of Purchasing not later than six weeks prior to the announced start of the strike.<br>c) Vendors shall be queried as to which goods are and |

## Exhibit 5 continued

| | |
|---|---|
| | are not returnable in the event of the announced strike.<br>d) During the last week prior to the announced start of the strike, a large order of dry ice will be available. |
| Radiology and Radiotherapy | No problems identified. |
| Respiratory Therapy | a) All necessary gas supplies will be in-house one week prior to announced start of strike.<br>b) Engineering will top off all liquid oxygen and nitrous oxide tanks.<br>c) An additional tank truck will be brought into the Engineering yard prior to announced start of strike. |
| Miscellaneous Supplies | In addition to above, a two-week to four-week shipment of supplies will be secured in the following areas:<br>a) General Stores<br>b) I.V. |

## Exhibit 6 Services

| *Department* | *Comments* |
|---|---|
| Communications | |
| Food Service | |
| Housekeeping | |
| Traffic and Information | |
| Laundry | |

**Exhibit 6** continued

Mailroom _____
_____
_____
_____
_____

Print Shop _____
_____
_____
_____
_____

Purchasing _____
_____
_____
_____
_____

General Stores _____
_____
_____
_____
_____

Receiving _____
_____
_____
_____
_____

## SAMPLE SURVEY: SERVICES

Departments surveyed and their comments:

1. *Communications*
   The department will be open seven days a week, twenty-four hours a day. All usual services such as paging, voice and beeper, patient information, sending telegrams, and answering switchboard calls and transfers will be provided.
   See attached list of Personnel who will be carrying beepers during the strike.
   It is possible some delays may be encountered in placing of long-distance phone calls, depending upon available staffing.
2. *Food Service*
   All normally scheduled operations for cafeteria and patient meals will be retained, seven days per week. The following services will be canceled: Catering, Executive Dining Room, and Snack Bar. Vending will be provided as long as the supplies last (two weeks), unless more deliveries can be received. A seven-day, non-selective cycle menu consisting of four categories including regular, clear, full liquid, and modified will be maintained. All dietary restrictions will be adhered to. Menus will

**Exhibit 6** continued

be reviewed by the dietitian staff, and patients with special food requirements will be offered a limited variety of substitutes. No selective menus will be circulated.

Cold production (salads, etc.) will be very limited after three days due to the short shelf life of produce items.

Disposable dishes and utensils will be used on patient trays.

3. *Housekeeping*

All usual housekeeping operations will be provided, including checkouts and Operating Room case cleaning, on a seven-day, two-shifts-per-day schedule. Priority will be given to all open inpatient units, the Emergency Room, and outpatient areas.

No coverage will be provided to closed offices or O P D Clinics. Limited coverage will be provided to ancillary areas for basic cleaning functions. As much effort as possible will be given to public access areas. All special, cycle, or project work will be curtailed.

4. *Traffic and Information*

All usual duties will be performed, including patient escort, elevator, and messenger operations. A reduced level of service is planned for the evening and night shifts. Routine Specimen pick-up and delivery will be provided. The department will be open seven days a week, twenty-four hours a day. Due to limited manpower, the department probably will not be able to provide a full cadre of elevator operators.

5. *Laundry*

All basic laundering services will be provided with a limited work force working an eight- to twelve-hour shift or longer if necessary, seven days per week.

It is anticipated that a reduction in workload will occur, as a result of bed-unit closings and reduced changes in bed linen.

Limited services to those OPD and Emergency Room areas open will be provided.

6. *Mailroom*

The Mailroom will remain open with a supervisory crew to perform the following services:

- Sorting/Delivering Mail (principally to patients and to vital department operations). Mail delivery will be curtailed to nonpatient departments.
- Packages/Flowers will be delivered to patients.
- Pneumatic Tube Systems will be serviced to keep the system operational.

The department will be open Monday through Friday from 8:00 a.m. to 8:00 p.m. and on Saturday from 8:00 a.m. to 4:00 p.m.

It is expected that departments will be picking up and delivering their own mail where possible. A daily delivery and pick-up will be made to a location to be announced.

7. *Print Shop*

The Print Shop will be open to service the hospital with necessary printing work and to support any strike communication reports. The work includes grants, emergency jobs, and forms pertinent to patient care. No routine work will be performed. The department will be staffed by only supervisory personnel.

The Print Shop will deliver all bulletins to the hospital if conditions permit.

8. *Purchasing*

The department will be closed; however, supervisory personnel will be available in General Stores to assist with expediting any emergency orders.

**Exhibit 6** continued

        All unused consignment orders will be returned within 60 days for a 15 percent handling fee.
9. *General Stores*
   The following services will be available:
   - Par Stocks IV Solutions, Sets, Sterile Dressings, Paks—6 days/week
   - IV Solutions/Sets to Operating Rooms—3 days/week
   - Exchange Carts—7 days/week
   - Weekly Orders—Nursing, Operating Rooms, Support Services—5 days/week
   - Orders—CSS, Building Service, Dietary, Laundry—5 days/week
   - Labs, Offices—As required
   - Emergency Orders—As required
   
   Where possible, emergency orders will be handled by Stores' personnel who are part-stocking floors. Otherwise, volunteer messengers will be asked to pick up and deliver.
10. *Receiving*
    Receiving will be secured and closed. Two supervisory personnel will be on call to respond to any emergency truck deliveries that get through and transport any dry ice and gas cylinders as required. One trailer that can be hooked up to electrical power has been rented, to house freezer food stuffs.

**Exhibit 7** Hours of Scheduled Operations

Sample
Support Services
Hours of Scheduled Operations

| Area | Monday through Friday | Saturday and Sunday | Comments |
|---|---|---|---|
| Communications | Round the clock | Round the clock | |
| Cafeteria | Breakfast—6:30 a.m.–9:00 a.m.<br>Coffee—9:15 a.m.–10:00 a.m.<br>Lunch—11:00 a.m.–2:00 p.m.<br>Cold Sandwich—2:00 p.m.–4:00 p.m.<br>Dinner—4:30 p.m.–9:00 p.m. | Same as Monday thru Friday | |
| Catering | Closed | Closed | |
| Patient Meals Distribution | Breakfast—7:00 a.m.–9:00 a.m.<br>Lunch—11:00 a.m.–1:00 p.m.<br>Dinner—4:00 p.m.–6:00 p.m. | Same as Monday thru Friday | |
| Dietetics (Request Changes) | Breakfast—6:00 a.m.–7:00 a.m.<br>Lunch—9:30 a.m.–10:00 a.m.<br>Dinner—2:00 p.m.–2:30 p.m. | Same as Monday thru Friday | Special diets will be handled by staff |
| Executive Dining Room | Closed | Closed | |
| Housekeeping | 7:00 a.m.–11:00 p.m. | 7:00 a.m.–11:00 p.m. | Inpatient-high priority<br>Open-OPD<br>Offices/Lab-limited services |
| Traffic and Information | Round the clock<br>Skeleton staff after 4:00 p.m. | Round the clock<br>Skeleton staff after 4:00 p.m. | 1 pick-up/delivery location |

| | | |
|---|---|---|
| Laundry | 7:00 a.m.–7:00 p.m. | Hours as required |
| Mail | 8:00 a.m.–4:00 p.m.<br>4:00 p.m.–8:00 p.m. | Patient mail—high priority<br>STAT only |
| Print Shop | 8:00 a.m.–4:00 p.m. | Skeleton staff for grants/bulletins, etc. |
| Purchasing | Closed | Emergency orders can be placed by calling General Stores |
| General Stores | 7:00 a.m.–11:00 p.m. | |
| Receiving | Closed | Backup people in Stores available for accepting deliveries |

**Exhibit 8** Page Identification—Key Personnel

---

The following hospital personnel will be carrying beepers during the strike—to communicate with these employees, simply call the page operator.

*Name*                                                                                *Title*




*Note:* Four (4) additional beepers will be assigned on a daily basis and passed from shift to shift. These "ad hoc" assignments will be communicated daily.

# ENGINEERING AND PLANT OPERATIONS

As long as the facility is in operation, there is a need for Engineering and Plant Operations to provide, among other services, heating, cooling, utilities, and emergency services.

**RESPONSIBILITIES**

1. Director of Engineering, Planning and Real Estate—will plan, direct, supervise, and coordinate all Engineering Department activities in the broad areas outlined below:
   - Operations of all heating, air conditioning, and ventilation plants
   - Provision of utilities and emergency power
   - Maintenance and repair of structures and equipment
   - Fire protection and prevention
   - Recovery from damage to facilities from any cause
   - Management of emergency repair forces
2. Associate Director of Engineering—will assist the Director of Engineering and act for the Director in the Director's absence.
3. Senior Maintenance Engineer—will maintain and repair buildings, structures, utility systems, equipment, and facilities of the hospital.
4. Director of Fire Safety—will plan, organize, and direct the fire prevention, safety and fire fighting programs of the hospital.
5. Plant Assistant Director—will supervise personnel engaged in the operation, maintenance, and repair of high- and low-pressure steam plants, central air conditioning systems, emergency power generating systems, gas and oxygen distribution systems, heating systems, incinerators, refrigeration, and waste disposal.
6. Senior Biomedical Electronics Engineer—Will supervise personnel engaged in maintenance, repair, and checking of biomedical and electronics equipment.

**FUNCTIONS**

1. Engineer Subcommand Post.
   (a) Shall be established in the Office of the Director of Engineering.
   (b) Shall be manned 24 hours a day, with two 12-hour shifts per day. Shifts to be 6:00 a.m. to 6:00 p.m., and 6:00 p.m. to 6:00 a.m. First shift to commence at designated date and time.
   (c) Responsibility for the direction of the Subcommand Post will rotate.

(d) The Director of the Subcommand Post shall report to the Hospital Command Post every three hours as to the status of the Engineering Department.

(e) Upon change of shift, each director will brief the oncoming director as to the status of all ongoing activities.

2. Administrative Personnel.
   (a) The following personnel shall perform their regular administrative/personnel and reporting functions from 6:00 a.m. to 6:00 p.m.

   _____
   _____
   _____
   _____
   _____

3. Maintenance Engineering.
   (a) Machine Shop—will answer all emergency calls for repair of equipment and machinery. Routine service calls or repairs shall be accomplished if time and conditions permit.

   *Personnel Assigned*

   | 6:00 a.m. to 6:00 p.m. | 6:00 p.m. to 6:00 a.m. |
   | --- | --- |
   | _____ | _____ |
   | _____ | _____ |
   | _____ | _____ |
   | _____ | _____ |

   (b) Plumbing Shop—will answer all emergency calls, such as stopped drains, broken lines, leaking pipes, etc. Routine service calls or repairs will be handled only if time and conditions permit.

   *Personnel Assigned*

   | 6:00 a.m. to 6:00 p.m. | 6:00 p.m. to 6:00 a.m. |
   | --- | --- |
   | _____ | _____ |
   | _____ | _____ |
   | _____ | _____ |
   | _____ | _____ |

(c) Electrical Shop—will answer all emergency calls, such as blown fuses, tripped circuit breakers, existence of an electrical hazard, broken outlets, etc. Routine service calls and repairs will be handled only if time and conditions permit.

*Personnel Assigned*

| 6:00 a.m. to 6:00 p.m. | 6:00 p.m. to 6:00 a.m. |
|---|---|
| _____ | _____ |
| _____ | _____ |
| _____ | _____ |
| _____ | _____ |

(d) Elevator Shop—will answer all emergency calls relative to elevator malfunctions.

*Personnel Assigned*

| 6:00 a.m. to 6:00 p.m. | 6:00 p.m. to 6:00 a.m. |
|---|---|
| _____ | _____ |
| _____ | _____ |
| _____ | _____ |
| _____ | _____ |

(e) Carpentry Shop—will answer all emergency calls such as broken windows, doors, damaged medical equipment, etc. Shall install window and door preventive devices upon orders of higher authority. Routine service calls and repairs shall only be accomplished if time and conditions permit.

*Personnel Assigned*

| 6:00 a.m. to 6:00 p.m. | 6:00 p.m. to 6:00 a.m. |
|---|---|
| _____ | _____ |
| _____ | _____ |
| _____ | _____ |
| _____ | _____ |

(f) Paint Shop—generally will be closed until further notice. Non-striking personnel of the Paint Shop will be assigned to other duties within the Engineering Department.

(g) Preventive Maintenance Shop—same explanation as item (f) above.
(h) Biomedical Electronics Shop—will respond to all calls requiring repairs to electronic equipment.

*Personnel Assigned—6:00 a.m. to 6:00 p.m.*

| Bio-Medical | Electronics |
|---|---|
| _____ | _____ |
| _____ | _____ |
| _____ | _____ |
| _____ | _____ |
| _____ | _____ |

4. Chemical Safety.
Personnel assigned will perform normal, routine services, i.e., storage, treatment, and disposal of chemicals.

*Personnel Assigned—6:00 a.m. to 6:00 p.m.*

_____
_____
_____
_____
_____

5. Fire and Safety.
Personnel assigned will answer all calls pertaining to fire protection, prevention, and safety; will answer calls pertaining to smell of smoke, gas, or fumes of any type; will conduct inspections concerning bomb warnings; will ensure that liquid oxygen tank is topped off, no later than the day prior to scheduled start of strike.

*Personnel Assigned*

| 6:00 a.m. to 6:00 p.m. | 6:00 p.m. to 6:00 a.m. |
|---|---|
| _____ | _____ |
| _____ | _____ |
| _____ | _____ |
| _____ | _____ |

6. Plant Engineering.
(a) All Plants—will operate and be maintained in usual efficient manner. Will ensure that the oil tanks are topped off no later than the day prior to scheduled start of strike.

*Personnel Assigned*
6:00 a.m. to 6:00 p.m.    6:00 p.m. to 6:00 a.m.

_____    _____
_____    _____
_____    _____
_____    _____

(b) Incinerators and Bulk Reduction—will operate and maintain the incinerators and compactors in their usual efficient manner; provide flatbed trucks at strategic points.

*Personnel Assigned*
6:00 a.m. to 6:00 p.m.    6:00 p.m. to 6:00 a.m.

_____    _____
_____    _____
_____    _____
_____    _____

7. Patrols and Emergency Assignments—Specific assignments to be announced.

*Personnel Assigned*
6:00 a.m. to 6:00 p.m.    6:00 p.m. to 6:00 a.m.

_____    _____
_____    _____
_____    _____
_____    _____

(a) Patrols will be made at various intervals, so as not to establish a pattern, and will be so scheduled by personnel comprising each patrol.
(b) Two engineers will make rounds together; they will carry a Multitone Page Unit. Under no conditions will one engineer patrol alone.
(c) The engineers will check all gates to make sure they are secure and check all engine room doors.

(d) They will immediately report any unauthorized personnel or damage in these areas to the Engineer Subcommand who will notify Security.
8. Sleeping Accommodations.
Shall be available for hospital general labor pool. (See Staff Accommodations.)

## STAFF ACCOMMODATIONS

Many nonstriking employees are concerned about crossing picket lines. The hospital should, to the extent possible, provide temporary housing and/or sleeping accommodations to working staff to allay these concerns. Working departments might establish mini-dorms in office space, utilizing cots and hospital linens, pillows, and blankets. These departmental accommodations could supplement that which the institution could provide through its Housing Department.

### HOUSING

Housing accommodations will be available during the course of the strike. To receive an accommodation, an employee *must* bring his or her validated hospital identification card to the Resident Manager's office. This office will be open between the hours of 8:00 p.m. and 8:00 a.m., seven days per week. Each employee must leave his or her I.D., at which point he or she will be issued a key for a room chosen from a bank of available rooms.

In order to have an I.D. returned, the employee must return the key by 8:00 a.m. the following morning. A wake-up call service will be provided at 7:00 a.m.

### COTS

In addition, folding cots (to be obtained from Building Services) will be issued from the Resident Manager's office during the same hours. These can be taken back to the departments or used to add to the occupancy in the above-mentioned dormitory rooms.

### ADDITIONAL SPACE

In case of an expanded need, cots will be set up in the hospital gymnasium, auditorium, or other adaptable space.

## SECURITY

During the strike the institution must take protective measures to reduce, if not eliminate, incidents of vandalism and theft. To this end, local police should be contacted and arrangements made to cover the area being picketed, in an attempt to discourage violence and to ensure critical deliveries are made. Hospital windows in the area of the picket line should be boarded up to protect against damage. All but main entrances to the hospital complex should be locked to avoid entry by those seeking to damage or steal property. In essence, only limited access to the hospital should be maintained. In addition, local fire department authorities should be contacted and fire patrol arrangements made. Insurance carriers should be notified of the strike. Incidents of damage should be immediately reported to Engineering and Plant Operations.

In the event of a strike the Security Department should be fully operational.

**MAJOR RESPONSIBILITIES**

1. Safeguarding employees and hospital property
2. Screening admission to the hospital complex
3. Coordinating deliveries of supplies

**PROCEDURE**

1. At the onset of a strike, security guards, uniformed supervisors, and management personnel will be placed on two shifts of 12-hour duration. Days off will be canceled, except for emergencies.
2. Need for additional manpower is not anticipated.
3. Assignments will be updated daily to reflect changing conditions, e.g., deliveries, concentration of pickets, acts of vandalism or violence, etc.
4. The parking lot will be closed. The close proximity of the lot to the strike picketers makes it unwise to continue this service during the strike. (Exception to this decision can be made where the parking facility is well protected and situated.)
5. Hospital bus service will be discontinued for safety reasons, as in 4 above.
6. Notification to the local police department precinct has been effected. Security has requested police coverage of the hospital periphery, including nearby public transportation.

## SCREENING ADMISSION TO THE HOSPITAL COMPLEX

1. In the event of a strike only main entrances to the complex will be open.
2. Security has available identifying buttons for all nonstriking workers and volunteers, which will be issued during the strike.
   (a) Department heads are to submit to Security the number of buttons needed as soon as the required ten-day strike notice is received by the institution.
   (b) For security reasons the buttons will be available for pick-up only by a supervisory department representative two days prior to the strike deadline given by the union.
3. Screening of visitors will be effected at the main hospital entrances. Visitors will be issued stick-on passes that will be clearly visible to all working staff.

## COORDINATION OF EMERGENCY DELIVERIES

1. The Security Department will coordinate emergency supply deliveries with the vendor, police department, and receiving personnel.
2. All vendors must contact the Security Department prior to transport so that details and timing of delivery can be arranged. It is imperative that they be so informed.
3. The Security Department will be available to assist in the delivery of blood, if the occasion arises.
4. Special coverage will be given to oxygen tank storage areas.

## AUXILIARY SERVICES

1. Locksmithing. The locksmith supervisor will be reassigned to the Security Department for supervisory responsibilities, but will be available for emergency locksmithing functions. An outside locksmith will also be available for emergencies.
2. Investigations. Follow-up investigations to reported incidents will be handled on a priority basis as evaluated by Security and as circumstances permit.
3. Security Clerical Staff. The staff will prepare assignment sheets, index lost and found items, and/or be assigned to the manpower pool.

## MEDICAL SERVICES

The institution's primary objective is to maximize the delivery of effective patient care. During a work stoppage, the hospital will endeavor to maintain as many of the essential patient services as possible.

The institution's ability to operate at normal or near normal levels of service and, in fact, for it to survive at all during a strike is directly related to the maintenance of patient census. Census maintenance is not possible without adequate, direct, hands-on patient care. The importance, then, of the role of the nurse and of the Nursing Department during such a crisis is obvious. For this reason, nonstriking nurse employees, and for that matter, nonstriking, non-nurse employees as well, should not be included as "personnel available for reassignment" in your Employee Strike Contingency Plan. Nurses probably will be called upon, as will Attendings and House Staff physicians, to function outside of their established job descriptions, but for the most part will perform their normal tasks.

The sections included in the Medical Services Plan are as follows:

1. Nursing Services
2. Unit Management
3. Medical Services
   - Medicine
   - MSCU
   - Neurology
   - Orthopaedics
   - Oncology
   - Surgery
   - Vascular
   - Cardiothoracics
   - Otolaryngology
   - Ophthalmology
   - Neurosurgery
   - Urology
   - CICU, Ames, Rose
   - FICU
   - Pediatrics
   - K-9 Nursery
   - OB/GYN
   - Private
   - Renal Treatment
   - Emergency Room

- Psychiatry
- Clinical Research Center
4. Social Work Services
5. Patient Representative Services

## DEPARTMENT OF NURSING EMPLOYEE STRIKE CONTINGENCY PLAN

1. Manpower Command Post (24-hour coverage).
   Location:
   Manned by: _____  8:00 a.m.– 4:00 p.m.
   _____  4:00 p.m.–12:00 a.m.
   _____  12:00 a.m.– 8:00 a.m.
   Function:
   - To provide nursing, aide, and clerical personnel to clinical areas.
   - To provide ongoing training to assigned volunteers as needed (Exhibit 9).
2. Clinic Areas in Service
   - Emergency Room (including Employee Health Service)
   - Psychiatry
   - GYN (Cancer)
   - Anti-Coagulation
   - Neoplastic Diseases Clinic (Hematology)
   - Prenatal
   - Dental Emergencies
   - Medication Refill
   - Pediatric Hematology
   - Communications Disorders Center
   - Dialysis
   - Pediatric Acute Care
   - Abortion Clinic
   (a) Operating Room Scheduling
       Daily assessment by: Director of Nursing
                            Director of Surgery
                            Director of Anesthesiology
                            Assistant Director of Nursing for OR
                            Assistant Director of Nursing for RR
   (b) Prescription Renewals
       Location: _____
       Manned by: _____ 8:00 a.m.–5:00 p.m.

**Exhibit 9** Outline—Volunteer Training

---
Hospital Name
Department of Nursing

Tasks to be included in Volunteer Training Sessions:
Pass Trays—Feed patients—Pass water
Charts—New patients
Telephone
Intercom
Emergency Calls—Who to call and what
Addressograph imprinter
What to do in transferring patient
Traffic Control—especially when units are closing/closed. Creating good relationships in times of stress.
Bed Making

---

## NURSING SERVICE ADMINISTRATION AGREEMENTS

1. Nursing administrative staff will work primarily in their own areas to coordinate staff and patient care over a 24-hour period.
2. Central Nursing administrative support to areas will be provided as follows:
    (a) Day Shift
       - Assigned Associate Directors
       - Secretarial staff
       - Weekends—a minimum of two senior nursing personnel plus a secretary
    (b) Evening Shift (including weekends)
       - Assigned evening Assistant Director, Coordinators, Administrative Supervisors
    (c) Night Shift
       - Assigned Night Assistant Director, Administrative Supervisor, Coordinator
3. Clinical Resource Division—core staff necessary to train volunteers.
    - Otherwise staff will be assigned to regular clinical areas
    - New hires of one month or less assigned to clinical areas to provide patient care with supervision by CRN
4. Private Duty Nursing Officer.
    - Coverage by Associate or Assistant Directors of Nursing
    - Two secretarial staff for each shift

5. Administrative Support Services.
   - Office Systems
   - Payroll
6. Central Listing.
   - One Nursing Administrative Staff per day

**UNIT MANAGEMENT**

1. Closing and Opening of Units.
   (a) Aim.
   Maintain census as high as possible—adjustment made daily based on patient needs and available resources. Return to budgeted census within 48 hours after strike is over.
   Major Variables
   - Manpower available
   - Type of Operating Room Schedule
   - Coordination of admitting process with available resources
2. Closing of Units/Patient Care Areas.
   (a) Outpatient Department will be closed with the *exception* of the following clinics and departments:
   - ER and PAC including Psych ER
   - Methadone Clinic
   - Neoplastic Clinic—general and peds
   - Neoplastic—GYN
   - Anticoagulant
   - Prenatal
   - Dental Emergency
   - Abortion Unit
   - Dialysis Unit
   Prescription Triage Area Located in _____
   Employee Health Service will be located in Emergency Room.
3. Closing Inpatient Areas.
   (a) Aim.
   Consolidate patients and staff when necessary to best utilize resources (see Exhibit 10, an example of a survey of available bed space).
   (b) Variables.
   - OR Schedule—humber of surgical beds required must be closely monitored.
   - Ability to consolidate medical patients to Hospital's Clinical Center.

**Exhibit 10** Bed Space Survey

| Inpatient Units | Total Beds | Inpatient Units | Total Beds |
|---|---|---|---|
| *Medicine* | | *Maternal Child Health* | |
| Unit #1 | 42 | Unit #1 | 22 |
| Unit #2 | 42 | Unit #2 | 22 |
| Unit #3 | 40 | Unit #3 | 26 |
| Unit #4 | 42 | Unit #4 | 15 |
| Unit #5 | 34 | Unit #5 | 30 |
| Unit #6 | 37 | Unit #6 | — |
| Unit #7 | 42 | Unit #7 | 32 |
| Unit #8 | 42 | Unit #8 | 22 |
| Unit #9 | 19 | Unit #9 | 24 |
| Unit #10 | 8 | Unit #10 | 35 |
| | | Unit #11 | 3 |
| | | Unit #12 | 32 |
| *Psychiatry* | | Unit #13 | 24 |
| Unit #1 | 15 | | |
| Unit #2 | 22 | | |
| Unit #3 | 22 | *Private/Renal Dialysis* | |
| Unit #4 | 22 | Unit #1 | 29 |
| Unit #5 | 22 | Unit #2 | 29 |
| | | Unit #3 | 44 |
| | | Unit #4 | 26 |
| *CTC/Surgical Division* | | Unit #5 | 27 |
| Unit #1 | 27 | Unit #6 | 39 |
| Unit #2 | 27 | Unit #7 | 31 |
| Unit #3 | 23 | Unit #8 | 8 |
| Unit #4 | 30 | | |
| Unit #5 | 22 | | |
| Unit #6 | 31 | *Clinical Research Center* | |
| Unit #7 | 31 | Unit #1 | 12 |
| Unit #8 | 27 | | |
| Unit #9 | 27 | | |
| Unit #10 | 16 | | |
| ICU #1 | 6 | | |
| CCU #1 | 8 | | |
| ICU #2 | 17 | | |

- Ability to consolidate surgical patients to Surgical Pavilion; as Medical Surgical units close in Private, consolidate to Clinical Center and Surgical Pavilion.
- Ability to maintain ICUs for concentration of critically ill patients.
- ER remaining open.
- Consolidate Pediatric patients.

4. Coordination of Closing.
   - Recommendations will be made to Director of Nursing after consultation with Admitting and Nursing.
   - Coordination of mechanics of closings will be the responsibility of the Associate Director of Nursing.
   - Each Medical Service will make available a senior physician to work in the closing process as required.
   - The following departments will be involved in the closing of each unit:

| Department | Function |
| --- | --- |
| Admitting/Central Listing | Discharge and relocation of patients. |
| Pharmacy | Securing and returning of narcotics and controlled drugs. |
| Social Service | Coordinate with volunteer service to assist in providing information to families and in supporting families and patients. |
| Security | Secure units with Nursing and make rounds of closed areas. |
| Support Services: | |
| —Laundry | Cancel laundry delivery to the unit. Any unused linen will be returned to the Laundry. |
| —Traffic/Information and Telephone/Communication | Must be notified of closing of unit. |
| —Central Supply | Central Sterile Supply items should be secured on units. |
| —Store Room | Must be notified of closing of unit. |
| —Dietary | Must be notified of nursing unit closing. Trays for patients transferred will be rerouted. |
| —Building Service | Must be notified of closing of units. Reroute supplies and deliveries. |
| —Engineering | Must be notified of closing of units. |
| —Security | Frequent daily rounds will be made to ensure security of nursing units. |

5. Opening of Units.
   (a) Recommendation to open units will be made to Director of Nursing, after consultation by Admitting and designated physician.

(b) Relocation of "misplaced" patients will be kept to a minimum in consultation with designated physician after considering anticipated length of stay.
(c) Adequate physician coverage for work-up of patients will be arranged through each chairperson (see Exhibits 11 and 12).

6. Coordination of Openings (Units).
   (a) Building Service: Will open Nursing/Unit beds: schedule cleaning activities.
   (b) Laundry: Will deliver clean linens to the unit.
   (c) Pharmacy: Must obtain narcotic and controlled-drug cabinet keys from divisional office. Will return narcotic and controlled drugs to Nursing Unit. Joint count will be required.
   (d) Central Sterile Supply: Must be notified of opening.
   (e) Store Room: Must be notified of opening.
   (f) Dietary: Must be notified of opening.
   (g) Traffic/Information: Must be notified of opening.
   (h) Telephone/Communication: Must be notified of opening.
   (i) Engineering: Must be notified of opening.
   (j) Security: Must be notified of opening.

**Exhibit 11** Physician Activities on Unit

Hospital Name
Physicians' Activities on Nursing Units

1. Vital signs, i.e., TRP—BP and CVP
2. Trays—feeding patients
3. Personal care—lift patients, turn, ambulate, transport to X-Ray, etc.
4. Dressings—change sterile
5. Soaks—hot, wet, irrigation
6. Irrigating catheters
7. Intravenous therapy—administer, monitor, and record
8. Venipuncture
9. Suction trach
10. Levine tube and other drainages
11. Respirator care—respirators—MA 1—Bennett—Emerson—Bird
12. Intake and output
13. Administering medications
14. Evening and night rounds reassuring the patients and ordering sedation
15. Transportation of patients
16. "Specialing" patients on respirators, etc.
17. Triage

**Exhibit 12** Unit Management Teams

| Service | The Hospital Unit Management Teams | | |
|---|---|---|---|
| | M.D. | Unit Managers | R.N. |
| *Medicine* | | | |
| Unit #1 | | | |
| Unit #2 | | | |
| Unit #3 | | | |
| Unit #4 | | | |
| Unit #5 | | | |
| Unit #6 | | | |
| | | | |
| CU #1 | | | |
| CU #2 | | | |
| CU #3 | | | |
| Dialysis | | | |
| | | | |
| *Pediatrics* | | | |
| Unit #1 | | | |
| Unit #2 | | | |
| Unit #3 | | | |
| Unit #4 | | | |
| | | | |
| Nursery #1 | | | |
| Nursery #2 | | | |
| Nursery #3 | | | |
| | | | |
| *Obs-Gyn* | | | |
| Unit #1 | | | |
| Unit #2 | | | |
| Unit #3 | | | |
| Unit #4 | | | |
| Unit #5 | | | |
| Unit #6 | | | |
| | | | |
| *Neurosurgery* | | | |
| Unit #1 | | | |
| | | | |
| *Neurology* | | | |
| Unit #1 | | | |
| | | | |
| *Orthopaedics* | | | |
| Unit #1 | | | |
| | | | |
| *Ent.* | | | |
| Unit #1 | | | |

**Exhibit 12** continued

*Ophthalmology*
  Unit #1

*Oncology*
  Unit #1
  Unit #2

*Psychiatry*
  Unit #1
  Unit #2
  Unit #3
  Unit #4
  Unit #5

*Surgery*
  Unit #1
  Unit #2
  Unit #3
  Unit #4
  Unit #5

*Transplant*
  Unit #1

*F.I.C.U.*
  Unit #1

*Private*
  Unit #1
  Unit #2
  Unit #3
  Unit #4
  Unit #5
  Unit #6
  Unit #7

7. Relocation of Patients in the Event of a Strike.
    (a) When a need to relocate patients becomes evident, every effort should be made to keep the anxiety levels of patients, families, and staff as low as possible. Communication should begin during the admitting process, and the patient thereafter should be kept informed of strike developments by unit personnel.
    (b) Patients should be encouraged to send clothing, etc., home with their families.

(c) A list of all patients on the floor, with their current locations and destinations, should be prepared (see Exhibit 13).
(d) If entire floor is to be relocated, elevator should be reserved for this purpose; wheelchairs and stretchers should be provided.
(e) Patients should be moved in the following order:
- Ambulatory
- Wheelchair patients
- Critical patients on stretchers
(f) A patient destination list should be made available to:
- Clinical Supervisor
- Senior Clinical Nurse
- Traffic and Information Supervisor
  (Central Listing will dispatch destination)
(g) New location I.D.s should be made by Admitting and sent to the patients' new locations.
(h) Dietary must make necessary meal changes (location, time) with Administration according to time of move.
(i) The evening prior to move, all patients should be given large brown paper bags marked with patients' names in large letters. If articles have not been sent home, families should be asked to do so during visiting hours. (Supervisors should coordinate and follow through on evenings.)
(j) Staff will attempt to organize patients' belongings in bags and prepare patients for moves.
(k) Nursing supervisor should coordinate moves on unit by directing T & I and checking each patient's I.D. band, chart and belongings. Name should be checked on list and destination noted as patient leaves floor.
(l) Upon completion of moves, narcotics are returned to Pharmacy, unit is inspected for security purposes, all supply closets *LOCKED*, and keys given to Supervisors. Building Service strips all beds and cleans unit.

## MEDICINE

Following is the Employer Strike Contingency Plan for the Department of Medicine.* It includes:

1. Plan
2. Floor Activities—Strike Resident

---

*The authors have selected the area of Medicine to be used as a sample service plan within the Medical Services section of the Strike Contingency Plan. Each individual service functioning during the strike would complete such a plan.

**Exhibit 13** Patient Transfer/Relocation

Hospital Name
Department of Nursing
Patient Transfer/Relocation Sheet

| Room No. | Name of Patient | Doctor/Service | Destination Room No. | Time Unit Notified | Time of Transfer | Date | Problems/Comments |
|---|---|---|---|---|---|---|---|
| | | | | | | | |

3. Identification of physicians responsible for triage functions in Admissions, should admissions be curtailed. (See Exhibit 14.)
4. Chart detailing strike coverage. (See Exhibit 15.)
5. Chart detailing post-strike unit coverage. (See Exhibit 16.)

1. Facilities
   (a) Semi-Private Facility
   Full occupancy can be maintained; hospital stay may be slightly prolonged.

   One extra resident/ward will be assigned Monday through Friday, 7:30 a.m. to 5:00 p.m., immediately after the strike begins. This "strike resident" will be available under the direction of the Department of Medicine and the ward resident, who performs and coordinates strike-related duties. In addition to being assigned to floors (where appropriate) medical students will be available for assorted duties to include:
   - Blood Drawing/IV
   - Lab Results Review
   - EKG s
   - Special Problems

   Weekend coverage will revert to the normal house staff schedule. During the strike, interns will be expected to review their patients daily, to provide essential services.

   This supplementary staff will be comprised of personnel relieved of normal duties during the strike to cover specially adjusted duties in the private services and in the Emergency Room freeing house staff to provide additional coverage in the semi-private pavilion.

   (b) Private Facility
   During the strike attending physicians admitting patients to the private facility will be responsible for the history, physical examination, and admitting orders of their patients. They may phone the Chief Medical Resident to convey admitting orders for the daytime covering physician, to ensure prompt attention for their patients. However, this does not relieve them of the responsibility to provide a note and appropriate orders either accompanying the patients or on the admission dates.

   Daytime problems will be the responsibility of the private attending physician (when possible) or the covering physician. After 5:00 p.m. (to 9:00 a.m.) problems will be the responsibility of the private attending physician (when possible) or the assigned house staff.

**Exhibit 14** Identification of Physicians' Triage Functions

---

Department _____Medicine_____

If a decision is made to curtail admissions, an attending physician will be needed to triage functions in the admissions office.

It is recommended that this be the same person each day.

If needed, others may be so designated. Please clearly identify arrangements.

*Attending*          *Beeper No.*          *Telephone No.*          *Comments*

---

Weekend coverage will revert to the normal house staff schedule, but private physicians will continue their increased responsibilities in the admitting process.

(c) Emergency Room

Coverage will be provided by house staff and supplemented by physicians. The PGY-3 schedule will remain unchanged; two residents will provide 12-hour shifts (8:00 a.m.–8:00 p.m. and 8:00 p.m.–8:00 a.m.). During daytime hours (9:00 a.m.–5:00 p.m.) this staff will be supplemented by physicians and walk-in house staff (Fellows). These supplementary physicians will be responsible for prescription triage, employee health patients, and OPD patients sent to ER.

(d) Admitting

The Cardiology Division will handle EKGs in Semiprivate admitting. Weekend coverage will revert to the normal house staff schedule. Excess loads during the week in the ER will be staffed by use of consultations from fellows, and return of the residents to the ER from the Semiprivate facility.

During the strike, private physicians will be asked to assume an increased supervisory role of their patients in the Semiprivate

**Exhibit 15** Physician Strike Change

Department of ___Medicine___
19___ Strike Plan-Unit ___

| *Day | Date | Physician In Charge | Housestaff | Beeper # | Telephone # | M.D. Responsible for Evening/Night Rounds ||||
|---|---|---|---|---|---|---|---|---|---|
| | | | | | | Evening | Night | Beeper # | Telephone # |
| Day 1 | | | | | | | | | |
| Day 2 | | | | | | | | | |
| Day 3 | | | | | | | | | |
| Day 4 | | | | | | | | | |
| Day 5 | | | | | | | | | |
| Day 6 | | | | | | | | | |
| Day 7 | | | | | | | | | |
| Day 8 | | | | | | | | | |
| Day 9 | | | | | | | | | |
| Day 10 | | | | | | | | | |
| Day 11 | | | | | | | | | |
| Day 12 | | | | | | | | | |
| Day 13 | | | | | | | | | |
| Day 14 | | | | | | | | | |

*If work stoppage exceeds 14 days, coverage cycle to begin again from Day 1.

**Exhibit 16**  Physician Post-strike Coverage

|  | Attending in Charge | Beeper No. | Telephone No. | Additional Personnel Requested | Comments |
|---|---|---|---|---|---|
| Post-Strike Day 1 | | | | | |
| Day 2 | | | | | |
| Day 3 | | | | | |
| Day 4 | | | | | |
| Day 5 | | | | | |
| Day 6 | | | | | |
| Day 7 | | | | | |

Department of Medicine
Bringing Hospital Back to Full Census Within 48 Hours after Strike
Unit _____

facility. This additional support, it is hoped, will allow the new medical house staff to provide continued excellent care despite the increased duties required by the strike-related changes in support services.

(e) Post-Strike

No special problems are expected as we bring medical services back to normal. Because of the supplementary personnel planned for during the strike, the house staff should be able to revert to a normal schedule immediately, providing that support services are available.

2. Floor Activities—Strike Resident
   (a) Blood Drawing/IV
      - Difficult patients—IV team
      - Ambulatory and routine patients—strike resident and medical students 7:30 a.m.–9:00 a.m. M–F
      - STAT and bedbound patients—appropriate interns

(b) EKGs
- Ambulatory and routine patients—strike resident and medical students in treatment room on each floor—9:30 a.m.–10:30 a.m.
- STAT and bedbound patients—appropriate interns.

(c) Administrative Duties
- Review: Recent lab review for abnormals; collate to patient file. Review slips (blood work) by volunteers.

(d) Special problems
- Nursing problems
- Special patients
- Call lab for STAT results

Note: In the semiprivate facility, the Department of Cardiology will perform EKGs.

## ANCILLARY SERVICES

There follow several sample schedules that may facilitate continuation of ancillary services during a hospital strike. (See Exhibits 17 through 19.)

**AVAILABLE DATA PROCESSING SERVICES**

**Operations**

12-hour shifts

Computer Room—6 operators                                   7 days
1st Shift 8:00 a.m.–8:00 p.m.
2nd Shift 8:00 p.m.–8:00 a.m.

Data Entry—10 operators                                     5 days
1st Shift 8:00 a.m.–8:00 p.m.

The following applications will be processed normally:

1. Admissions, discharges, transfers, and census reports
2. Inpatient Billing
3. Pharmacy
4. Outpatient Visit Registration
5. Payroll
6. Alcoholism Treatment
7. Outpatient Ancillary Statistics
8. Outpatient Billing
9. Drugs/Stores

All other processing will be suspended for the duration of the strike. The following transactions will be key recorded inhouse:

1. Payroll
2. Inpatient Billing
3. Alcoholism Treatment

All other transactions will be sent out of house to an outside vendor. The on-line system will be up for the normal 22 hours.
After the strike, all backlog key recording work will be sent to an outside vendor.

**Exhibit 17** Emergency Room/PAC, Personnel Assignments

| Assignment | Employee Assigned |
|---|---|
| *8:00 a.m.–4:00 p.m.* | |
| Supervisor | |
| Registration Terminal (Adult) | |
| Registration Terminal (Adult) | |
| Registration Terminal (PAC) | |
| Secretary (PAC/Adult Bloods & Abnormals) | |
| PAC Unit Clerk/Holding Area | |
| Adult Unit Clerk | |
| Patient Transport/Messenger | |
| Note: Holding Area will be covered from the Front Desk | |
| *4:00 a.m.–Midnight* | |
| Supervisor | |
| Unit Clerk (Adult) | |
| Unit Clerk/Cashier (PAC) | |
| Registration Terminal (Adult) | |
| Registration Terminal (Adult) | |
| Registration Terminal (PAC) | |
| Patient Transporter/Messenger | |
| *Midnight–8:00 a.m.* | |
| Supervisor | |
| Unit Clerk (PAC) | |
|   1) Holding Area | |
|   2) Cashiering | |
| Unit Clerk (Adult) | |
| Registration (Adult and PAC) | |
| Patient Transporter/Messenger | |

## Systems and Programming

Ten staff members will work in Operations, operating the computer and key recording.

The three systems programmers will be retained to handle system corrections.

Two programmers/analysts will be retained to make necessary modifications to the Payroll system.

The balance of the staff (5) has been made available to the general labor pool.

All project development will be suspended for the duration of the strike.

**Exhibit 18** Sample Schedule of Ancillary Services

| Department | Hours of Operation | Scope of Services (OPD will be closed) | Limitations Tests Not Performed | Help Required | Special Supplies or Outside Services Needed |
|---|---|---|---|---|---|
| Admitting —Central Listing | 24 hrs/day 7 days/wk | Normal volume of admissions. | N/A | 9 volunteers, as follows: *Central Listing* (2) 8:00 a.m.–4:00 p.m. (1) 4:00 p.m.–Midnight (telephones) (1) Midnight–8:00 a.m. (typist) (collect census) | |
| —Clinical Center | 8:00 a.m.–midnight 7 days/wk | Limit of 2 bookings per caller. Adjust reservation allocation to allow a floating reservation policy. | | *Clinical Center* (1) 9:00 a.m.–5:00 p.m. (1) Noon–8:00 a.m. | |
| —Maternity | 24 hrs/day 7 days/wk | | | *Maternity* (1) 8:00 a.m.–4:00 p.m. (typist) | |
| —Pre-Admitting | 7:00 a.m.–7:00 p.m. 7 days/wk | To meet demand where possible | | *Pre-Admitting* (1) 9:00 a.m.–5:00 p.m. | |

| | | | | |
|---|---|---|---|---|
| Ambulatory Care —E.R. & PAC | 24 hrs/day 7 days/wk | (See Attached Schedule) | | (1) 9:00 a.m.–5:00 p.m. (typist) 23 FTE to remain in department |
| Anesthesiology | 7:45 a.m.–4:00 p.m. Mon–Fri On Call 24 hrs/day 7 days/wk | Full O.R. Schedule | None | 7 volunteers in addition to 8 FTE to remain in department. 15-day inventory on order |
| Blood Bank | 24 hrs/day 7 days/wk | Maintain full surgical schedule for 7 days if no blood deliveries— longer if delivered. | Diagnostic immunohema- tology 1. Ham Test 2. Donath Landsteiner 3. Iosantibody titer 4. Cold agglutin titration. | 18 FTE to remain in department. 2 FTE to be reassigned from research area. Blood and compo- nents from local blood program |
| Central Sterile Supply | 7:30 a.m.–11:00 p.m. | Prepared for full surgi- cal schedule for 30 days. | None | In addition to 6 FTE to remain in department: 6 to clean, inspect and package O.R. trays. 2 to process CSS trays. Normal 45-day inventory increased to 60 days. |

**Exhibit 18** continued

| Department | Hours of Operation | Scope of Services (OPD will be closed) | Limitations Tests Not Performed | Help Required | Special Supplies or Outside Services Needed |
|---|---|---|---|---|---|
| Central Sterile Supply (cont.) | | | | 2 to pick up soiled equipment for reprocessing. | |
| Chemistry | 24 hrs/day 7 days/wk | 100% routine IP 100% Stat Service Lab #2 may close Lab #3 may close | All tests performed; potential delays in turnaround time. | 14.5 FTE to remain in department. (6–8 techs. request) (2) 4:00 p.m.–12 midnight (3) clerks 9:00 a.m.–5:00 p.m. (3) clerks 5:00 p.m.–1:00 a.m. (1) clerk 1:00 a.m.–9:00 a.m. | Some tests to be sent to commercial labs. |
| C.L.I.C. | 8:30 a.m.–6:30 p.m. 7 days/wk | 90% normal inpatient demand | Evening interim report at 6:00 p.m. rather than 11:00 p.m. | None | None |
| Clinical Mic/ Hematology —Main Lab | 6:00 a.m.–8:00 p.m. 7 days/wk | 90% normal inpatient demand | HGB electrophoresis Haptoglobin G6PD, Folic Acid, | 11 FTE to remain in department. Need clerical help at all times: 2 FTE. | Coulter service. |

| | | | |
|---|---|---|---|
| —ER Lab | 24 hrs/day 7 days/wk | | VB$_{12}$, Iron, UIBC |
| —Coag. | 6:00 a.m.–8:00 p.m. 5 days/wk | | 24 hr. protein, hemosiderin LE prep; reticulocyte |
| —OPD Lab | Closed | | Diff. unless necessary coag. profile |
| —Clinical Ctr. | No coverage | | Urine Microscopic (except for positive protein). |
| —Prenatal Lab | Closed | | |
| Infection Control | Service not available | — | 1 FTE RN to be reassigned. | — |
| Library | 9:15 a.m.–4:45 p.m. Monday–Friday | Circulation desk open Serials check in AV/CA center open | Operator photocopying. Interlibrary loans. Reference; hold or recalls. Notifies, reference, acquisitions, binding, cataloging. | 6 FTE to remain in department. | None. |
| Microbiology | 9:00 a.m.–5:00 p.m. 7 days/wk. | 50–75% normal inpt. demand; all bacteriology and antibiotic sensitivity. | Mycobacterium culture parasitology serology, and virology restricted to | 9 FTE to remain in department. | Media delivery, 2–3 week shelf life. |

**Exhibit 18** continued

| Department | Hours of Operation | Scope of Services (OPD will be closed) | Limitations Tests Not Performed | Help Required | Special Supplies or Outside Services Needed |
|---|---|---|---|---|---|
| | | | urgent cases. Gram stain and acid-fast stain—STAT only. | | |
| Nuclear Med. | 9:00 a.m.–5:00 p.m. Mon–Fri | 80–85% normal inpatient demand; no outpatients. All services available. | None | 19 FTE to remain in department. | Radiopharmaceutical deliveries; no problem anticipated. |
| Pathology | 9:00 a.m.–5:00 p.m. Mon–Fri all areas. 9:00 a.m.–noon on Saturday for Surg. Path. | Frozen section and rush cases handled normally. Other services may be delayed. | Nondiagnostic surgical path. & EM, routine Gyn, cytology, autopsy pathology materials will be processed for preservation but final processing will be delayed until after strike. | | Immunopathology kits containing radioisotopes. |
| Pharmacy | 24 hrs/day 7 days/wk. | Close OPD pharmacy on (location) . Full service to hospital. | None | 55 FTE to remain in department. Need (3) messengers: | |

| | 7 FTE To Be Reassigned | | | |
|---|---|---|---|---|
| Quality Assurance | | | | (2) 8:00 a.m.–4:00 p.m.<br>(1) 4:00 p.m.–Midnight | |
| Radiology | 24 hrs/day<br>7 days/wk. | No OPD Cases<br>40–50% routine cases assuming ⅓ reduction in OR cases | CT scan, special procedures and protables on STAT basis only. | *Transporters*<br>7 days/wk<br>(6) 8:00 a.m.–4:00 p.m.<br>(3) 4:00 p.m.–Midnight<br>*Fileroom Clerks*<br>7 days/wk<br>(2) 8:00 a.m.–4:00 p.m.<br>(1) 4:00 p.m.–Midnight<br>*Reception Clerks*<br>7 days/wk<br>(2) 8:00 a.m.–4:00 p.m.<br>(2) 4:00 p.m.–Midnight<br>*Transcribers—M/F*<br>(3) 8:00 a.m.–4:00 p.m. | X-O-mat and CT Scan Service |
| Radiotherapy | 8:00 a.m.–5:00 p.m.<br>Mon–Fri | 100% | None | 3 Transporters | Radioactive Isotopes |
| Rehab. Med. | 8:30 a.m.–4:30 p.m.<br>Mon–Fri | 80–100% of inpatient demand; bedside treatment when possible. | Procedures requiring specialized or nonmovable equip- | 3 Clerical<br>6 Transporters | None |

**Exhibit 18** continued

| Department | Hours of Operation | Scope of Services (OPD will be closed) | Limitations Tests Not Performed | Help Required | Special Supplies or Outside Services Needed |
|---|---|---|---|---|---|
| Rehab. Med. (cont.) | | | ment will be limited if transportation is not available. | | |
| Respiratory Therapy | 24 hrs/day 7 day/wk | 80% inpatient services. 100% STAT services. | Routine IPPB Treatment | 4 FTE to remain in department. | Two weeks of supplies to be on hand. |
| Surg. Clin. Labs. | 9:00 a.m.–5:00 p.m. Mon-Fri.; if not, 7:30 a.m.–6:30 p.m., Mon.–Fri. | 50% | All services available in turnaround time. | 1 FTE to remain in department. Need 2 FTE licensed lab. techs. | None |
| Therapeutic Activities | 9:00 a.m.–5:00 p.m. Mon-Fri | | | 9 FTE to remain in department to cover all activities | |

**Exhibit 19** Sample Schedule for Clinics

| Clinic | Days and Hours of Operation | Present Volume/Session | Proposed Location | Staffing Required and No. | Employee Assignment | Comments/Issues |
|---|---|---|---|---|---|---|
| Anti-Coagu. | T/Th/Fri 8:00 a.m.–Noon | 12 | | M.D. 1<br>R.N. 2<br>Clerical 1 | | Laboratory needs impact on operation. Pharmacy coverage needed for Drug Mixing. |
| Neo-Plast. | M/Th/Fri 8:00 a.m.–Noon | 12–17 | | M.D. 1<br>R.N. 2<br>Clerical 2 | | Patients are on protocol. |
| Ped. Hema. | M/W 9:00 a.m.–4:30 p.m.<br>Th 1:00 p.m.–4:00 p.m. | 20 | | M.D. 2<br>R.N. 1<br>Clerical 2 | | Patients are on protocol. |
| GYN Tumor | Th. 9:00 a.m.–1:00 p.m. | 15 | | M.D. 1<br>R.N. 1<br>Clerical 1 | | Patients are on protocol. |
| PNC/High Risk PIS | M/T/Th/F 8:00 a.m.–4:00 p.m. | 85 | | M.D. 4<br>R.N. 5<br>Clerical 3 | | Nonstress Testing must be available. |
| NRC | M–S 7:00 a.m.–7:00 p.m. | 150–300 | | Clerical 7 | | Possibility one employee will be available for the pool. |
| Dental Emerg. | As Needed | 6–8 | | D.D.S. 1<br>Clerical 1 | | |
| Psych Walk-In | M–F 9:00 a.m.–4:00 p.m. | Erratic | | M.D. 1<br>Clerical 1 | | |
| Communication Disorder | As needed | — | | Spec. Path. & Audio. | | Inpatient requests only. |
| Emerg. Rm. | 24 hours | — | | | | |

## THE MEDICAL RECORD DEPARTMENT OPERATIONAL STRIKE PLAN

**Overview**

1. The Inpatient Census will be maintained at normal levels.
2. Clinics will be closed for the duration of the strike.
3. The Emergency Room shall continue to operate seven (7) days per week, 24 hours per day.

**Available Manpower Resources**

Exhibit 20 lists personnel assigned to work in the Medical Records Department during the strike.

## OUTLINE OF THE MEDICAL RECORDS OPERATIONAL STRIKE PLAN

1. Areas of Medical Records whose operations shall cease or be significantly curtailed for the duration of the strike are the following:
   - Tumor Registry
   - Chart Retrieval for OPD Clinics (staff will pull and deliver charts for the next scheduled clinic visits as soon as notice of end of strike is received)
   - Microfilm Auditing
2. Priority shall be given to the following areas:
   - ADT—Chart Pickup
   - Chart Diagnostic Review
   - Coding/Abstracting
   - Patient Index
   - Chart Retrieval for Emergency Room and Patient Care Areas
   - Chart Receiving
   - Analyzing/Processing—on STAT basis
   - STAT Requests—Medical/Legal Information
3. STAT Medical/Legal Information requests shall be handled by the following personnel: _____
_____
4. There will be two 12-hour shifts (8:00 a.m. to 8:00 p.m., and 8:00 p.m. to 8:00 a.m.) for 24-hour coverage of the department. (Work schedule will be posted at the time of Strike Notice.)

**Exhibit 20** Manpower Allocation

| Employee Name | Adt P-Up | Cdr | C/A | A/P | Cht Comp. | Cht Recv. | Cht Retr. | Pt. Index | Micro-film | Call-backs | Med. Info. | Death Cert. | Sub-poena | Cht Prep. | Loose Filing | Tracking |
|---|---|---|---|---|---|---|---|---|---|---|---|---|---|---|---|---|
| | | | | | | | | | | | | | | | | |
| | | | | | | | | | | | | | | | | |
| | | | | | | | | | | | | | | | | |
| | | | | | | | | | | | | | | | | |
| | | | | | | | | | | | | | | | | |
| | | | | | | | | | | | | | | | | |
| | | | | | | | | | | | | | | | | |
| | | | | | | | | | | | | | | | | |
| | | | | | | | | | | | | | | | | |
| | | | | | | | | | | | | | | | | |

5. Patient Index responsibilities will be conducted from the Conservatrieve Area. The Emergency Room, Nursing Office, Hospital Communication Director, and Strike Command have been notified to call the Conservatrieve Area for all chart retrieval.
6. An alternating daily schedule will be set up for pickup of charts from the Nursing Units. (See schedule for pickup of charts from floors.)
7. Personnel responsible for Chart Diagnostic Review will take, on a rotating basis, the Yellow Sheets to the Patients Accounts Department.

## HINTS FOR POST-STRIKE HOUSE REBUILDING

Upon completion of the strike the following steps should be taken to return the facility to normal operation as quickly as possible:

1. Building Service.
   Management personnel, including supervisory staff, should remain available two to three days after cessation of the strike for assignment as required.
   "Teams" should be developed to follow a checklist procedure for restoring a patient room/unit to use. This will include floors, windows, bathrooms, beds, linen, furniture, etc. Project/cycle work should be deferred so that priority can be given to accelerating the process of reopening these patient areas.
2. General Stores.
   Daily par stocking should not be affected. Weekly orders should be estimated for each unit based on the orders normally received prior to the strike. These orders should be issued automatically within two days after the strike ends.
3. Laundry.
   A standard list should be developed indicating items/supplies necessary to ready the unit for full occupancy.
4. Traffic and Information.
   Staffing should be increased to accommodate the inevitable demand for increased services to patients during the post-strike surge in admissions and transfers.
5. Purchasing.
   Priority should be given to purchase orders for vital drugs and supplies over routine processing.

# AMERICAN HOSPITAL ASSOCIATION GUIDELINES

## Hospital In-Service Volunteer Activities during an Employee Work Stoppage

As a result of some of the problems faced by volunteers during a work stoppage by hospital employees, the American Hospital Association's Committee on Volunteers has developed these guidelines concerning the role of volunteers during a work stoppage. This document is intended as a guide for hospital administrators and managers and includes specific guidelines for the director of volunteer services and for volunteers. The guidelines were approved by the AHA House of Delegates on February 1, 1978.

When a hospital is struck by its employees, many important patient care services can only be provided through the generous services of volunteers. A hospital strike may result in substantial anxiety and fear on the part of patients. However, these can be minimized through the invaluable assistance of volunteers in calming patients and meeting many other patient needs. Such volunteer services provide needed continuity of patient care during a strike.

These guidelines are intended to assist hospital management in planning for the effective, proper, and safe use of volunteers during an employee work stoppage. Inasmuch as labor organization strategies vary depending on a number of factors, these guidelines should be modified in any given work stoppage in accordance with the recommendations of the institution's labor relations counsel.

### ADVANCE PLANNING

The National Labor Relations Act (Taft-Hartley Act) requires that a labor organization give a ten-day notice to a health care institution prior to a strike. Although a hospital has this ten-day period to prepare for a strike, it should not wait until this "eleventh hour." Rather, it should prepare a standby plan long before a work stoppage becomes imminent. Included in the plan should be a comprehensive educational program to inform in-service volunteers about union strike and picket line tactics, employee reactions and how to cope with them, and pertinent provisions of the Taft-Hartley Act.

An employee work stoppage is usually a traumatic experience for everyone involved—employees, patients, management, and those volunteers who offer their services during a strike in an effort to keep the hospital open and functioning for the benefit of its patients and to ensure essential continuity in patient care. This trauma can be minimized or reduced if management plans its course of action prior to a work stoppage. If such a plan includes the utilization of in-service volunteers, the details should be thoroughly reviewed jointly by the director of volunteer services, the hospital administrator, and the labor relations counsel. Likewise, if the plan includes utilization of volunteers from the community, the policy should state how they will be screened, in what areas they will be utilized, and in what capacity they will be utilized, and it should designate the responsible management person.

Because in-service volunteers often work side by side with employees, some of the hospital's core in-service volunteers who serve regularly in the hospital may find it difficult to remain untouched by the atmosphere created during an employee work stoppage. They may find it equally difficult to remain indifferent to the community's reaction of such labor-management disputes. Present-day labor relations has taken on a social as well as an economic character and therefore affects the institution's relationship to the community.

## PLAN OF ACTION

The following is designed to orient directors of volunteer services and volunteers to actions to be taken and precautions to be observed prior to, during, and following an employee work stoppage.

**Prior to Work Stoppage**

- The director of volunteer services should be familiar with the hospital's policy concerning the use of both regular in-service volunteers and/or volunteers recruited from the community during an employee work stoppage. Some administrators prefer not to use in-service volunteers. Others attempt to augment in-service volunteers with specially recruited volunteers from the community.
- If the policy dictates the use of volunteers, the director of volunteer services and the hospital administrator should meet with the institution's labor relations counsel for guidance in determining the role and activities of volunteers during the work stoppage.

- The director of volunteer services should conduct an audit of volunteer skills. The information obtained by means of this audit will assist in assigning volunteers to tasks they can perform most effectively.
- A poll of the volunteers should be conducted to compile a list of those willing to serve during a work stoppage. This decision may be affected by an individual volunteer's philosophy and the attitude of immediate relatives concerning the volunteer's serving during a work stoppage. The poll should determine what assignments the volunteers prefer, how long they are willing or able to serve (days, weeks), which days, the number of hours they are able to serve, and what shift they are willing to serve on daily.
- The administration should determine how many volunteers will be needed. This number may vary according to the number of employees involved in the work stoppage and the department(s) and skills involved.
- The minimum age of volunteers who will be permitted to serve should be established. Because of the highly emotional state of some strikers, it normally would not be a good idea to expect minors to cross a picket line.

**During a Work Stoppage**

The director of volunteers should:
- Arrange with management for volunteers to be escorted through the picket line when entering and leaving the hospital. Safe entry and exit can be provided in several ways.
  - Management personnel can personally escort the volunteers.
  - Local police officers assigned to the picket line can escort the volunteers.
  - Arrangements can be made to meet the volunteers for each shift at a predetermined location away from the hospital, bring them in at one time in a convoy of autos or a bus, and return them to the pickup point at the end of their shift.
- Arrange for volunteers to be escorted to and from public transportation, if such action is indicated.
- Arrange for the safekeeping of volunteers' personal cars that are parked on hospital premises.
- Instruct volunteers not to wear their uniforms. A distinctive uniform makes volunteers readily identifiable to pickets, and striking employees often resent the use of volunteers as what they call "strike breakers."

- Issue volunteers official entry passes. These passes will make an escort available to them and will keep unauthorized persons out of the hospital.

Volunteers should:

- Obtain instructions from the supervisor on safety rules and practices related to job performance prior to beginning an assigned task.
- Check with the supervisor before performing patient care tasks that could subject the volunteer or the hospital to a malpractice suit or that legally should be performed by a specially qualified person.
- Immediately report to the supervisor the presence of a stranger in the work area. Union representatives will sometimes try to enter the hospital to learn who is working or to publicize an alleged lack of adequate patient care.
- Not communicate in any way, either at home or at the hospital, with persons from the news media. Volunteers who work in a limited area often are not aware of the total picture and may give information that is incomplete or inaccurate. All such inquiries should be referred to a person who is designated in advance by management.
- Not discuss with patients their personal feelings about the work stoppage, the predicted outcome, and so forth. Such talk could have an adverse effect on patients and should be done only in reply to a direct question and then in a discreet manner.
- Inform relatives how they can be reached at the hospital by telephone, if necessary. Normally, it is difficult to reach a person directly by telephone during a work stoppage because the hospital switchboard is open only to urgent calls.

Whether a record of volunteer hours served during a work stoppage should be maintained for service record purposes is a matter for each volunteer to decide. For a number of reasons, some volunteers may not wish to have such service made a matter of official record.

**Following a Work Stoppage**

Depending on the length, intensity, and outcome of the work stoppage, considerable bitterness may be evidenced by the strikers against those who crossed the picket line to work. Under the best of circumstances, a strained relationship will exist until wounds are healed and emotions cooled.

Volunteers can make an important contribution toward the return to normal employee relationships by:

- Participating in a post-strike orientation program attended by the hospital administrator, the labor relations counsel, and the director of volunteer services. At this time, volunteers should be advised of the outcome of the strike, the resentment they may encounter from employees, and possible response to any employee ill will that may be directed at them or at others.
- Serving as ambassadors of good will to alleviate any employee bitterness.
- Refusing to take sides or become involved in employee arguments concerning the work stoppage, its conduct, or its outcome.

Although health care institutions do not wish to anticipate employee work stoppages, contingency plans for the continuity of patient care and for the possible use of in-service volunteers during such occurrences are needed.

# Index

## A

Accommodations for staff, 298, 299
Accounts payable department, 273
Additional time worked, 266
Administration of strike plan, 262, 264-265
Administrative personnel, 294
 nursing, 304
Administrative support services, 305
 central nursing, 304
Admitting, 314-316
Advance planning, 332-333
Advisory Committee on Labor-Management Policy, 145
Agreements
 hot cargo, 40, 212-213, 228
 no-strike-without-notice, 17
 nursing service administration, 304-305
Ahmuty, Alice Lynn, 34
*Allis-Chalmers Manufacturing Co.*
 case, 65, 66, 84, 85
Allocation of manpower, 329
Ally Doctrine, 17-18
Alternatives to strikes, 144-150, 158

Ambulatory accounts, 273
American Federation of Teachers-United Federation of Teachers, 99
American Hospital Association guidelines, 332-336
*American Journal of Nursing*, 93, 96, 99
American Nurses Association (ANA), 43, 44, 92, 93, 94
 Economic and General Welfare Program of, 43
 history of, 93, 94
 no-strike policy of, 93, 94, 95, 96-97
Amnesty, 45
ANA. *See* American Nurses Association
Analysis of Variance (ANOVA), 104, 105
Ancillary services, 318-330
 schedule of, 320-326
Anderson, Arvid, 150
Anderson, John C., 164
ANOVA. *See* Analysis of Variance
Arbitration
 *See also* Mediation-arbitration, 144
 binding, 144, 154
 "chilling" or "narcotic" effect of on collective bargaining, 151, 164, 167

compulsory. *See* Compulsory
  arbitration
  conventional, 144, 146-147, 152
  final-offer. *See* Final-offer arbitration
  interest, 144, 146-147, 152, 163-171
  last-offer. *See* Final-offer arbitration
Arbitration Act, 29
Arbitration clauses, 28, 30-31, 144
*Arlan's Department Stores, Inc.* case, 24
Ashtabula General Hospital in Ohio, 33, 39, 90
  nurse strike at, 53-58
Assignments, 27, 282
  departmental manpower, 270
  emergency, 297-298
  timesheet for, 270
Assistant director of plant, 293
Associate director of engineering, 293
Authority of NLRB, 229-233
Auxiliary services, 301
Available personnel inventory, 276, 278, 279
*Avco Wyoming Division* case, 46

## B

Back pay, 24
Baderschneider, Jean 167
Bars to election, 197-199
Beamer, John E., 144
Bed space survey, 306
Binding arbitration, 144, 154
Biomedical electronics engineer, 293
Board of inquiry (BOI), 6, 7, 9, 10, 11, 12, 13, 14
Boards for fact-finding, 10, 11
BOI. *See* Board of inquiry
*Booster Lodge* case, 49, 65, 76, 80, 84
Boycotts, 28, 40
  prohibited, 41, 180, 220-225
*Boys Market, Inc. v. Retail Clerks Local 770*, 29
*Buffalo Forge Co. v. United Steelworkers*, 25, 29

Building service, 331
Bureau of Labor Statistics, 34
Bureau of National Affairs *Grievance Guide*, 47
Butler, Richard J., 167
Bylaws of National Union of Hospital and Health Care Employees, 59-62

## C

California Nurses Association (CNA), 94, 95, 97, 149, 160, 161
Carpentry shop, 295
Causes of strikes, 33
*Cedar Coal Co. v. UMW Local 1759*, 31
Central listing, 305
Central nursing administrative support, 304
*Charles Dowd Box Co. v. Courtney*, 29
Chemical safety department, 296
"Chilling" or "narcotic" effect of arbitration on collective bargaining, 151, 164, 167
Choice-of-procedure systems, 169
*Chromalloy American Corp.* case, 48
Clerical staff, 301
Clinical resource division, 304
Clinic schedule, 327
Closing of units, 305
CNA. *See* California Nurses Association
Coercion of employees, 214-216
Collective bargaining, 150, 155, 158, 177-178, 191-202
  "chilling" or "narcotic" effect of arbitration on, 151, 164, 167
  defined, 33
  with nurses, 99, 104-114
  purpose of, 33
Command post, 303
Committees
  financial operations, 268
  Interns and Residents, 90
  manpower planning, 266
  personnel policies, 267

staffing of, 262
strike plan, 262, 264-265
Communication network, 263
Compensation. *See* Pay
Compensatory time, 266-267
Compulsory arbitration, 159-160, 163
　effectiveness of, 164-170
　impact of on wages, 168
Conciliation, 161-162
Consumers and strikes, 142-143
Continuous negotiation, 159
Contract negotiations, 5
Contract notice, 4
Contract renewal, 5
"Contract zone," 151
Conventional arbitration, 144, 146-147, 152
Convergence of positions, 165
Coordination of emergency deliveries, 301
Costs of strikes, 38, 39
　extraordinary, 267
Costs, 299
Council on Ethical Practice, New York State Nurses Association, 115-139
Council of Nurse Practitioners, Mount Sinai Hospital, 43
Court enforcement of NLRB orders, 238
Crossing of picket lines, 299
Cullen, 169
"Cultural necessity," 142

**D**

Damage suits for unlawful strikes, 40-42
Darwin, Charles, 143
Data processing services, 318-328
Deliveries, 301
Demographics of nurses, 104
Departmental manpower assignment timesheet, 270
Department of medicine, 311-317
Depatment of nursing strike contingency plan, 303-304
Director of engineering, planning & real estate, 293

Director of fire safety, 293
Director of volunteers, 333, 334
Directory of NLRB, 241-243
Disability benefits during strike, 267
Discharge, 46
Discipline for activity during strike, 45
Discrimination
　against employees, 205-207
　membership fee, 225-226
　for NLRB activity, 207-210
*District 1199E, National Union of Hospital and Health Care Employees (CHC Corporation)* case, 24

**E**

Economic and General Welfare Program, ANA, 43
Economic strikes, 23-24
　defined, 189
　notice in, 23
Effectiveness of compulsory arbitration, 164-170
Ehrenberg, Ronald G., 167
Election
　bars to, 197-199
　representation, 199-202
Electrical shop, 295
Electronics engineer, 293
Elements of in-progress strikes, 39-50
Elevator shop, 295
Emergency assignments and patrols, 297-298
Emergency deliveries, 301
Emergency room, 314
Employees
　*See also* Manpower; Staff
　discrimination against, 205-207
　nonstriking, 261, 263, 266, 299
　representatives of, 192-194
　restraint and coercion of, 214-216
　rights of, 186-191
ENA. *See* Experimental Negotiating Agreement

Enforcement
   of NLRA, 181-182, 228-238
   of NLRB, 238
Engineering, 293-298, 300
Ethics Code, New York State Nurses
   Association, 94
Exceptions to requirements for
   section 8 (g) notices, 21
Excessive membership fee, 225-226
Expenses. *See* Costs
Experimental Negotiating Agreement
   (ENA), 158-159
Extraordinary strike expenses, 267

## F

Fact finding, 8, 144, 145-146, 160
   boards for, 10, 11
   reports from, 9, 12, 13, 14, 155
Faculty compensation during strike, 267
Featherbedding, 28, 180, 226
Federal Mediation and Conciliation
   Service (FMCS), 4, 6, 7, 23, 34, 155
   Office of Arbitration Services of, 6, 7
   reports of, 9, 10, 11, 12, 13, 14
*Federal Register*, 6
Federation of Nurses and Health
   Professions, 99
Final-offer arbitration, 144, 147-148,
   152, 154, 161
Final position arbitration. *See*
   Final-offer arbitration
Financial operations, 269-273
   committee on, 268
Fire and safety department, 296
Fire safety director, 293
FMCS. *See* Federal Mediation and
   Conciliation Service
Forced choice arbitration. *See*
   Final-offer arbitration
*Fortex Manufacturing Co., Inc. and
   Local 1065, Amalgamated Clothing
   and Textile Workers of America*, 42
*Foster Grading Co.* case, 42
Fund accounting, 273

## G

Gallagher, Daniel G., 163
*Gary Hobart-Water Corp. v. NLRB*, 25
General Counsel of NLRB, 19, 20
General stores, 331
Geographic factors, 38
Good faith bargaining, 180, 210-212,
   218-220
*Granite State* case, 49, 65, 68, 69, 76,
   80, 81, 84
*Grievance Guide*, Bureau of National
   Affairs, 47

## H

"Half-life" effect, 168
Health care amendments to NLRA,
   18-19
Health care institution defined by
   NLRA, 3
Helsby, Robert, 154
Hospital complex admission screening,
   301
"Hot cargo" agreements, 40, 212-213,
   228
House rebuilding after strike, 331
House staff compensation during strike,
   267
House staff physicians, 302
Housing accommodations for staff, 298,
   299

## I

Illegal strikes, 28, 45
Illinois Nursing Association, 95
Inflation, 38
Information and traffic, 331
Initial contract negotiations, 5
Inquiry board. *See* Board of inquiry
Interest arbitration, 7, 144, 146-147,
   163-171
   conventional, 144, 146-147
   last-offer-by-issue system of, 152

Inventory of available personnel, 276, 278, 279
Investigations, 301
Issue reduction, 166

## J

Job satisfaction of nurses, 104, 105-107
Johnson, Lyndon, 161
Jurisdictional strikes, 27, 28, 40

## K

Karsh, Bernard, 141
Keewanee Hospital, 95
Kennedy, John F., 145
Kochan, Thomas A., 165, 167, 168

## L

Labor Department, 34
Labor legislation, 3-22
    *See also* specific laws
Labor organizations. *See* Unions
Last-offer arbitration. *See* Final-offer arbitration
Last-offer-by-issue system of interest arbitration, 152
Laundry, 331
Laws. *See* Specific laws
Lawsuits for damage, 40-42
Leaders in nursing, 158-162
League of Voluntary Hospitals and Homes of New York, 28-29
Legal costs, 39
Legal office role, 263
Legislation. *See also* specific laws
    labor, 3-22
*Local 174, Teamsters v. Lucas Flour Co.*, 29
Locksmithing, 301

## M

Machine shop, 294
Maintenance engineering, 293, 294-296
Management
    preparation for strike by, 39-40
    unit, 305-311
Management Science Associates, Inc., 91, 92
Manpower
    *See also* Employees; Staff
    administrative, 294
    allocation of, 329
    assignment of, 270, 282
    available, 276, 278, 279, 328
    command post for, 303
    departmental, 270
    inventory of, 276, 278, 279
    needs survey on, 275-276
Manpower planning, 274-282
    committee on, 266
Manpower policies
    committee on, 267
    during strike, 266-268
Mass nurse resignations, 95
Meal policy during strike, 268
Med-arb. *See* Mediation-arbitration
Media, 44, 263
Mediation, 4-15, 161-162
    to "finality," 161
Mediation-arbitration (med-arb), 144, 148-150, 160-161
*Mediation and the Dynamics of Collective Bargaining*, 33
Medical records department operational strike plan, 328-330
Medical services, 302-317
Medical student compensation during strike, 267
Medicine department, 311-317
Membership fees, 225-226
*Metropolitan Edison Company v. NLRB*, 45
Metzger, Norman, 3
Miller, Michael H., 93, 95
Mills, D. Quinn, 144
*Montana-Dakota Utilities v. NLRB*, 25

*Montefiore Hospital and Medical Center v. NLRB*, 16
Moratorium on vacations, 267
Mount Sinai Medical Center, 26, 27
  Council of Nurse Practitioners of, 43

## N

"Narcotic" or "chilling" effect of arbitration on collective bargaining, 151, 164, 167
National Alliance for Fair Licensure of Foreign Nursing Graduates, 91
National Association of Nurse Recruiters, 91
National Labor Relations Act (NLRA), 3, 18, 23, 27, 28, 29, 40, 45, 97, 99, 173, 332, 333
  defined, 3
  enforcement of, 181-182, 228-238
  health care amendments to, 18-19
National Labor Relations Board (NLRB), 15, 24, 25, 27, 28, 49, 233-235
  authority of, 229-233
  and discrimination, 207-210
  enforcement of orders of, 238
  General Council of, 19, 20
  organization of, 228-229
  powers of, 235-237
  regional directory of, 241-243
*National Labor Relations Board (NLRB) v. Rockaway News Supply Company*, 25
National nurse turnover rate, 91
National Union of Hospital and Health Care Employees, 24, 42, 89
  bylaws of, 59-62
National War Labor Board, 94
Needs survey on personnel, 275-276
Negotiation
  continuous, 159
  contract renewal, 5
  initial contract, 5
Network of communication, 263
Neutral hospitals, 17, 18

News media, 44, 263
*News Union of Baltimore v. NLRB*, 25
New York State Health Advisory Council, 91
New York State Nurses Association, 43, 90
  Council on Ethical Practice of, 115-139
  ethics code of, 94
New York State Taylor Law, 166-167
Nightingale, Florence, 90
"Nightingalism," 90
Nixon, Richard M., 3
NLRA. *See* National Labor Relations Act
NLRB. *See* National Labor Relations Board
Noncertified untions, 226-228
Nonstriking employees, 261, 263, 266, 299
Norris-LaGuardia Act of 1932, 25, 29
No-strike clause, 25, 26, 30-31
  strikes in violation of, 28-31
No-strike policy of ANA, 93, 94, 95, 96-97
No-sympathy-strike clause, 262
Notice, 15-17
  contract, 4
  contractual agreement not to strike without, 17
  for economic strikes, 23
  section 8 (g), 19-21
  for sympathy strikes, 25
  for unfair labor practice strikes, 24
Nurses
  collective bargaining with, 99, 104-114
  demographics of, 104
  job satisfaction of, 104, 105-107
  mass resignations of, 95
  private duty, 304
  salaries of, 92
  turnover rate for, 91
Nursing administrative staff, 304
Nursing department, 274, 302
Nursing home strikes, 34, 38
Nursing leaders, 158-162

Nursing service administration
  agreements, 304-305
Nursing strikes, 89-139
  at Ashtabula General Hospital, 53-58

## O

Office of Arbitration Services,
  FMCS, 6, 7
Office of Collective Bargaining,
  New York City, 150
Office of the General Council, NLRB,
  19, 20
Ohio Nurses Association, 33
Opening of units, 305
Operations, 318
  engineering, 293-298, 300
  financial committee, 268
  financial division, 269-273
  plant, 293-298, 300
Operations base for union, 44
Orders of NLRB, 238
Organization of NLRB, 228-229
Owley, Candice, 99

## P

Paint shop, 295-296
Patient accounts, 273
Patient transfer/relocation, 310,
  312
Patrols and emergency assignments,
  297-298
Pay
  for additional time worked, 266
  back, 24
  during strike, 266-267
  sick, 267
*Payne & Keller, Inc.* case, 47
Payroll department, 269-273
PERB. *See* Public Relations
  Employment Board of New York
Personnel. *See* Employees; Manpower;
  Staff

Physicians
  activities of, 308
  house staff, 302
  poststrike coverage of, 316
  salaries of, 92
  strike change of, 315
  triage functions of, 314
Picketing, 16
  by noncertified unions, 226-228
  publicity, 227
  right of, 191
  sympathy, 16
Picket line crossing, 299
Plan of action, 333-336
Planning
  advance, 332-333
  director of, 293
  manpower, 274-282
Plant assistant director, 293
Plant engineering, 296-297
Plant operations, 293-298, 300
Plumbing shop, 294
Pointer, Dennis D., 3
Policemen's and Firemen's Act of
  1972, Michigan, 148
Ponak, Allen, 169
Position convergence, 165
Post-strike coverage of physicians, 316
Post-strike house rebuilding, 331
Powers of NLRB, 235-237
Preparation for strikes, 39-40
*Price Brothers Co.* case, 45
Private duty nursing officer, 304
Professional Practice Committee, 96
Programming and systems, 319
Prohibited boycotts, 41, 180, 220-225
Prohibited strikes, 180, 220-225
Proof-of-illness requirement, 267
Public Employment Relations Act of
  1974, Iowa, 148
Publicity picketing, 227
Public Law 93-360. *See* National
  Labor Relations Act
Public Relations Employment Board
  of New York (PERB), 154
Purchasing, 331

## R

RCIU. *See* Retail Clerks International Union
Real estate director, 293
Reasons for strikes, 33
Rebuilding after strikes, 331
Recognition strikes, 27-28
Records of time, 266
Reduction of issues, 166
Refusal to bargain in good faith, 180, 210-212, 218-220
Regional directory of NLRB, 241-243
Relocation of patients, 310, 312
Renewal of contract, 5
Representation election, 199-202
Resignation
 of nurses, 95
 from union, 48
Resources
 clinical, 304
 manpower, 328
Restraint of employees, 214-216
Retail Clerks International Union (RCIU), 43, 44
Rights of employees, 186-191
Rural areas, 38

## S

Sabotage, 39
Safety, 296
Salaries of physicians and nurses, 92
Schedule
 ancillary service, 320-326
 clinic, 327
*Scofield* case, 68, 69, 75, 80, 81, 84, 85
Screening of admission to hospital complex, 301
Secondary strikes, 28, 40
Section 8 (g) notices, 19-21
Security department, 300-301
SEIU. *See* Service Employees International Union
Selective discharge, 46

Senior Biomedical Electronics Engineer, 293
Senior Maintenance Engineer, 293
Service Employees International Union (SEIU), 43, 44
Shared governance, 99
Shutt, Barbara G., 93, 96
Sick pay during strike, 267
Simkin, William E., 33
Simons, Jesse, 152, 154
Sit-down strikes, 28, 40
Sleeping accommodations for staff, 298, 299
Staff
 *See also* Employees; Manpower
 accomodations for, 298, 299
 house, 267
 nursing administrative, 304
 security clerical, 301
Staffing, 266
 of committee for strike contingency plan, 262
Staff physicians, 302
Staten Island Hospital, New York, 90
Statistical techniques, 104, 105, 106
"Stock effect," 142
Strategy for strikes, 44-45
Strike funds, 43-44
Strike notice. *See* Notice
Strike plan, 261-263
 administration of, 262, 264-265
 committees for, 262, 264-265
 medical record department operational, 328-330
 nursing department, 303-304
 outline of, 274-282
 overview of, 274
Strike resident, 316
Strike strategy, 44-45
Strike volunteers. *See* Volunteers
Student compensation during strike, 267
Subcommand post for engineering, 293-294
Suits for damage, 40-42
*Superior Switchboard and Service Division* case, 46
Supplies and services, 283-292

Surveys
   bed space, 306
   personnel needs, 275-276
Sympathy picketing, 16
Sympathy strikes, 16, 25-27, 262
   notice in, 25
Systems and programming, 319

## T

Taft-Hartley Act. *See* National Labor Relations Act
Taft, Senator, 16
Tanner, Lucretia Dewey, 34
Taylor-Higgins-Reedy Board, 145
Taylor Law, New York State, 166-167
*Textile Workers v. Lincoln Mills*, 29
Time records, 266
Timesheet for departmental manpower assignment, 270
Title Two, Conciliation of Labor Disputes in Industries Affecting Commerce, National Emergencies, 4
Traffic and information, 331
Training of volunteers, 304
Transfer of patients, 312
Transition period following strike, 268
Triage functions of physician, 314
T-Test statistical technique, 104, 105, 106
Turnover rate for nurses, 91

## U

Unemployment, 38, 142
Unfair labor practices, 208
   of employers, 178-179, 203-213
   of unions, 179-180, 213-228
Unfair labor practice strikes, 24-25
   notification for, 24
Unfair labor practice strikers, defined, 189

Unions
   actions of during strikes, 42-45
   disciplinary action against members by, 45
   membership fees of, 225-226
   noncertified, 226-228
   operations base for, 44
   resignation from, 48
   unfair labor practices of, 179-180, 213-228
Unit closings and openings, 305
United States Arbitration Act, 29
Unit management, 305-311
Unlawful boycotts, 41, 180, 220-225
Unlawful strikes, 41, 188, 189-190
   damage suits for, 40-42

## V

Vacations during strikes, 267-268
Violations of no-strike clauses, 28-31
Violence, 28, 40, 45
Volunteers, 263, 333, 335, 336
   activities of during strike, 332-336
   director of, 333, 334
   training of, 304

## W

Wages and compulsory arbitration, 168
Washington State Nurses' Association (WSNA), 98
Weinstein, Harriet Goldberg, 34
West Shoshone General Hospital, Kellogg, Idaho, 90
Wheeler, Hoyt N., 169
Wildcat strikes, 28, 40
Work assignment. *See* Assignments
Workers. *See* Employees; Manpower; Staff
Workers' Compensation, 267
WSNA. *See* Washington State Nurses' Association

# About the Authors

NORMAN METZGER is vice president of The Mount Sinai Medical Center in New York City. He is responsible for labor relations. He was a director of the League of Voluntary Hospitals and Homes of New York City, and was president of the League from 1967 until 1972 and from 1980 until 1982. He is a professor with tenure in the Department of Health Care Management, Mount Sinai School of Medicine, and a professor in the Graduate Program in Health Care Administration, Bernard M. Baruch College, City University of New York, as well as an adjunct professor in the Graduate Program in Health Services Administration at the New School for Social Research. In 1969 he served as president of the Association for Hospital Personnel Administrators of Greater New York.

Mr. Metzger's experience in labor relations and personnel administration spans 35 years in both the health services sector and industry. He is the author or coauthor of 10 books, as well as of nearly 100 articles in health care journals. He is a five-time recipient of the American Society for Hospital Personnel Administration's Literature Award. He has twice received the Association of Hospital Personnel Administrators of Greater New York's citation for outstanding contribution to the field of Human Resources Management.

JOSEPH M. FERENTINO is director of labor relations at The Mount Sinai Medical Center, where he is responsible for multiunion contract negotiation and employee relations. He is regional board member for the American Society for Hospital Personnel Administration, representing the professional interests of member personnel/labor relations administrators in New York, New Jersey, and Pennsylvania. He is past president (1980–1981) of the Association of Hospital Personnel Administrators of Greater New York, and he served as the association's program coordinator from 1978 to 1980. He received the 1983 Literature Award from the American Society for Hospital Personnel Administration.

Mr. Ferentino, a practitioner in the field of health care labor relations for more than ten years, has lectured at various New York City colleges and at hospitals throughout the state, in addition to conducting educational programs for the Association of Hospital Personnel Administrators of Greater New York and the United Hospital Fund. He is responsible for the development of a comprehensive labor relations seminar that is part of The Mount Sinai Medical Center supervisory educational program.

**KENNETH F. KRUGER** is employee relations manager at The Mount Sinai Medical Center, and is responsible for grievance and arbitration administration servicing nonunion employees and employee members of District 1199-National Union of Hospital and Health Care Employees, the New York State Nurses Association, Local Union #3, Mount Sinai Hospital Pharmacy Association, American Physical Therapy Association, Local 32B–32J, and the International Brotherhood of Security Personnel, Officers and Guards. In addition, he assists in contract negotiations with these unions, and administers National Labor Relations Board, Equal Employment Opportunities Commission, human rights, and civil claims against the Medical Center.

Mr. Kruger is a member of the American Society for Hospital Personnel Administration. He has served at various times as vice president, secretary, chairperson of the program committee, and chairperson of the compensation committee of the Association of Hospital Personnel Administrators of Greater New York. He has lectured at the New School for Social Research, as well as at Bernard M. Baruch College. He is a member of the League of Voluntary Hospitals and Homes of New York's Education Committee, which schedules seminars on the development and presentation of labor relations.